The Great War in
the Middle East

The Great War in the Middle East

Allenby's Final Triumph

W. T. Massey

LEONAUR

The Great War in the Middle East: Allenby's Final Triumph
by W. T. Massey

Leonaur is an imprint of Oakpast Ltd

ISBN: 978-1-84677-684-7 (hardcover)
ISBN: 978-1-84677-683-0 (softcover)

http://www.leonaur.com

Publisher's Notes

Contents

Preface

This narrative, it is hoped, will serve to remove the impression which prevails among a not inconsiderable section of the British public that the Army commanded and handled with such consummate skill by Lord Allenby in Palestine had a comparatively simple task. I have endeavoured to set out several matters in order to prove the contention of every superior officer who served two years or more with the Egyptian Expeditionary Force that General Allenby gave the Allies a victory at least as great as any Commander, and that when the historian can view the world-war as a whole, and has the full facts on which to base a calm and dispassionate judgment, he will bracket Allenby's name with any he selects as being responsible for the strategy which ended the struggle.

The public in Britain and America still talks of the capture of Jerusalem as being the military event f which will make Lord Allenby's name remembered for all time. Sentiment, of course, is responsible for it, and the deep veneration for the Holy City which is felt by people professing three of the great religions of the world, will make it easy for Jerusalem to be recalled when the names of much sterner battles are forgotten. But the conquest of Jerusalem, important though it was, will not, as a military triumph, compare with the stupendous victory obtained in the last six weeks of the campaign in Palestine and Syria.

In 1918 General Allenby had to contend with enormous difficulties. He was faced with the problem of having to arrange his operations so as to fit in. with the calls made upon him to reinforce the Western Front. At a time when the Turkish moral was still good, he had to send to France the bulk of his veteran British infantry when they were in the highest state of efficiency, and, with new Indian troops in their place, he had to build up another army. In these pages I have tried to show how, while increasing the power of his fresh troops, he forced down the fighting capacity of his enemy, and then, when by a most ably worked out scheme of camouflage he had concealed scores of thousands of men and horses at the place of attack, he launched his host against an army whose moral he had reduced to a low level. By employing a magnificent body of cavalry he gave another lesson to the armies of the world in the employment of the mounted arm, and, uninfluenced by the desires of London and Paris that this or that should be his aim, his own plans, worked out in his own way, secured far more than War Councils or War Cabinets had any right to expect. The Army's appreciation of Lord Allenby is correct.

W. T. M.

CHAPTER 1
Cross Currents

Begun at the right moment, conceived on bold lines, executed with magnificent energy and skill on every section of the front, General Allenby's final attack in Palestine will go down in history as one of the most successful operations in the war. It marked the beginning of the war's last stage, and by destroying the Turkish armies and capturing practically all their war equipment the Palestine force precipitated collapse of the Allies' enemies on all fronts, and brought hostilities to an end much earlier than any one had anticipated at the beginning of the summer. If it would be over-stating the facts to say the world-war was won in Palestine, it is beyond dispute that General Allenby's absolute triumph made the Allied victory certain, and when the historian is able to marshal his military facts alongside the political questions which swayed the councils of the Allies, he will appraise Allenby's work as highly as that of any commander-in-chief. His strategy was based on a masterly appreciation of the situation, not merely in his own theatre of operations but on the whole of the European fronts, and by postponing the delivery of his mighty blow till its effect would turn the balance in favour of all the Allied armies, his victory exerted a power that directly influenced every nation fighting against us. It came at the psychological hour. Bulgaria saw her days were numbered when Turkey's flank was smashed, and Austria recognised the inevitable. The Palestine triumph, as much as anything else, made them sue for peace, and Germany, left alone on a line where America was soon to pull her full weight, could not continue through another winter. The Palestine Army's efforts have won a permanent place in history, and Lord Allenby of Megiddo will go down to posterity as one of the greatest soldiers who saved the world from German *kultur*.

This book, I believe, is the first full record of the final phase of the

Palestine campaign. I do not claim to put forward a complete story of the political side, though I refer to one or two matters which have not been given to the public hitherto. But in the delicate condition of international affairs, when disclosures of facts are considered unfriendly to some of the peoples who conquered a common foe, it will probably be several years before the world knows how military strategy in Palestine had to fit in with the desires and claims and ambitions of our Allies, and how policy decided upon in Paris affected the trend of events. The public did not understand the conditions on the Palestine front, and there was every excuse for the public, for even after explanations by generals who had the conduct of operations, certain politicians visiting the front could not appreciate the difficulties of attack in the wild hills of Judea and in the mountains east of the Jordan. They expressed themselves too hurriedly, but a curb was put on their premature desires by the generals who had to study the problems of water supply, transport, communications, and, above all, the cost in lives. In Palestine no operation was started without counting the cost, and there was always a doubt whether Britain could adequately fill gaps created by the wastage of war. When General Allenby's Army had won the world-resounding victory of Jerusalem, arm-chair strategists at home studied the map and asked for the Haifa-Nazareth-Nablus line. Central Palestine had then been secured at the cost of tens of thousands of casualties after months of bitter fighting. Divisions had been depleted by fierce contact with a stubborn foe who never gave battle except in country which suited his tactics. They had not been fully made up in numbers, and in the then condition of the Turkish army, holding as it did positions of great natural strength, the Egyptian Expeditionary Force would have had to be increased by several new divisions before there was any hope of gaining by the early summer the more northerly line that was suggested. The requirements of the British Army on the Western Front prevented fresh divisions being sent to Palestine, and the struggle on the Somme in March fully justified the military advisers of the War Cabinet in refusing to sanction any weakening of our force in France. Yet when the Supreme War Council came to consider the situation in 1918, the Palestine Army was regarded as the force which should achieve victory without any increase of its strength.

That august body was not optimistic of victory on the Western Front in 1918. America could not be at the high-water mark of numbers and efficiency in that year, and calculations had to be based on a defensive along the whole line in France. The people of the Allied nations and neutrals had to be considered, and if there was the appearance of stalemate, with nothing to show that the tide was flowing towards victory, might not some regard favourably suggestions Germany would assuredly throw out for peace? In short, it was necessary to obtain victories in order to keep the people as staunch and confident as the troops. Could Italy be ready to regain her prestige which was unfortunately damaged at Caporetto? She had a great deal of reorganising to do, and she must wait till later in the year. Was the Salonika force in a position to make certain of success in the Balkans? That, too, was quickly ruled out, and Palestine was the only field that remained.

But the Supreme War Council expected too much. They wanted an immediate advance in March, the early occupation of Nablus, and, I think, of Haifa and Nazareth by June, with nothing but the old, tried, war-worn divisions to do it. It may not have been an impossible task. General Allenby and his Army had done wonderful things, of which the Supreme War Council had ample knowledge, and they might have succeeded. But that hypothesis is extremely doubtful. General Smuts came to Palestine in March, and there was great activity among the staffs of G.H.Q. and Corps. They set about preparing plans for an offensive to conform to the wishes expressed in Paris. On the 20th Corps front the attack had to be made over a series of mountains athwart the Nablus road. The ridges were high, there was practically no flat, many boulder-strewn water courses had to be crossed, roads had to be constructed every yard of the way, and guns could only be moved forward by a long and tedious process.

The 20th Corps had just made an advance, and after three days of very hard fighting by troops who had no superiors in the world they had managed to wrest a few thousand yards of country from the enemy. The tactics of the Turks were to employ an exceptionally large number of machine guns and, with rocky hills affording them the best of cover, it was hard to dislodge them, and until they were dealt with an advance was bound to be slow. The result of the operations in the first fortnight of March proved conclusively that the enemy would hold tenaciously to the hills, and though General Allenby would probably have got to Nablus his army would have suffered heavy losses, and the casualties might have crippled his force and prevented the execution of the bolder, wiser, and infinitely more effective scheme which the Commander-in-Chief had in view. And what would Nablus have meant to the world? Nablus without Haifa and Nazareth would have had no moral effect, and the world would have regarded it as a trifling incident of the war. Nablus alone was not worth the price we should have paid for it, and except for being compelled to give up a few miles of country, the Turks would have remained in a good position, nearer to their main railway line, and with better communications with their base than they had on their old entrenched system. If General Allenby had been given the divisions required to take Haifa and Nazareth when London suggested those places as the aim of the force, there is not the slightest doubt that the line would have been secured in the early summer, but the plan of the Supreme War Council put an enormous burden on the Commander-in-Chief and his Army, and some of those who were on the spot thought they were being asked to do more than could be reasonably expected of them. Perhaps those responsible for putting forward the plan imagined the Turks' moral was broken, and despised the fighting qualities of the soldier of the Crescent. At this time the Turk was still a gallant man in attack and defence. He failed in attack because his attack always lacked depth, but he was a stout enemy until late in the summer, when his moral failed under the relentless tactics of General Allenby. The German thrust on the Somme created an entirely new situation, and instead of the Supreme War Council relying on the Palestine Army to bring the world to support their view that victory was coming to the Allies, General Allenby was called upon to reduce his strength by sending a considerable proportion of his best troops to reinforce the Western Front. Accordingly before the end of March all preparations for an offensive were abandoned. Operations on a big scale could not possibly have been carried through with the same far-reaching results as the autumn offensive, even if the work in the coastal sector had had the most favourable turn, but the withdrawal of many of his veteran troops also compelled General Allenby to hold up a scheme for summer operations against the Turks. If these could have been carried through the war might have been over before November. After the Somme General Allenby was left alone to proceed with his campaign on his own lines. He had to reorganise his force in face of the enemy and to train comparatively raw troops. If there were anxious days there was no pessimism. While making ready for the grand effort the Commander-in-Chief, by a system of continuous raids by large and small forces, wore down the enemy's moral until, at the moment he launched his famous divisions of cavalry and infantry to the attack, he was faced by an army depressed in spirit and haunted with the fear at meeting better men. Doubtless it was wiser that the end should be worked out in this way. The lives of thousands of gallant men were saved by the abandonment of the earlier operations of 1918, and those lives were more important than the money Britain poured into the battle for the Holy Land. Moreover, the Turk was more completely finished when he reeled and fell before the hammer blow in September than he would have been by a series of battles fought during a slower progress northwards.

There was one other suggestion from home which, if acted upon, might have made the autumn victory less crushing. I will refer to it in detail later on. Briefly the idea was that when the Turkish defensive line north of Jaffa to the Jordan was broken, General Allenby should make a cavalry raid on Aleppo, more than 300 miles as the crow flies. The proposal came from the War Cabinet, but it was merely a suggestion and was in no sense intended as an interference with General Allenby's plans. Indeed when the Commander-in-Chief showed that the wiser plan was to proceed to his goal by stages, his opinion was at once accepted, and the War Cabinet made no attempt to argue or dictate. There was good sense in that attitude. General Allenby working out his own scheme at what he judged to be the proper time, without any outside interference except the observance of certain regulations which were to be put in force when particular areas of enemy territory were occupied, won for Britain and her Allies a victory as complete as any in the war. His triumph was gained at an astonishingly small cost. Preparations were made for 30,000 casualties; the battle casualties were a sixth of this number. There was genius in the General's strategy. He took the only route by which his cavalry could get into position to close the Turks' avenues of retreat, yet his operations for the preceding six months had so mystified the Turks that the enemy High Command made all their calculations to resist him on the other flank. He concentrated a mass of cavalry and infantry in comparatively open country within a few miles of the line, but so cleverly were the troops concealed that the enemy was completely surprised, and in a few minutes, certainly in less than half an hour, the infantry had secured their first object, that of breaking through the defences and opening a way for the cavalry to pass on. General Allenby was an ideal Commander-in-Chief. He set a fine example by never leaving the front unless his presence in Egypt was necessary to attend an official function or to inspect the base, and he was never absent longer than a day or two. A Spartan life was the rule at G.H.Q. Work was the order of the day every day. Continually with his troops, it can be said with absolute truth that no commander-in-chief was better known by his soldiers, and none possessed in a higher degree the affection and confidence of his men. They knew his deep sympathy for them; they knew that if his enterprise was characterised by boldness it was never rash. Over and over again he decided against operations which would incur substantial losses, and the high value he placed on the comfort and well-being of his command was reflected in the remarkably low sick rate of the Army while it was in the country he controlled.

CHAPTER 2

Cavalry's Opportunity

The last part of the campaign in Palestine was unlike anything else in the war. It afforded the opportunity all cavalrymen hoped for of proving that a large force of mounted troops was as necessary in an army today as in the past. Indeed, the operations firmly established the fact that cavalry were more than ever required in the British Army, which has to protect every link of a far-flung Imperial line, and may at any time be called upon to operate in country where mobility is most essential, and though the big following of the school trained in the trenches of the Western Front will probably continue to maintain that the day of mounted troops is past, there is little fear that the lesson of the Palestine campaign will be ignored. Tanks, aeroplanes, and the best of the new mechanism of war are, we know, indispensable parts of an army in the field, but they cannot take the place of cavalry. No engine has yet been devised which could capture more than 400 miles of country in six weeks—the feat which General Allenby's cavalry accomplished. Only a cavalry force could have done it, and though infantry, after smashing the whole of the Turkish line, could have kept the enemy on the move, they could not have captured the three Turkish armies, even if they had had the support of many squadrons of armoured cars and tanks. It was General Allenby's cavalry that was responsible for the complete overthrow of the Turk. The infantry was able at any time to break through any line of defences the Turks might occupy after the entrenched line from the sea to the Jordan had been carried, but alone they could not prevent a more or less methodical retirement.

Nothing but the splendid mobility of the cavalry could have closed all the roads by which the enemy might have escaped, and, while it is equally true that without the infantry and artillery the cavalry could not have gained a passage through the entrenched line, the big results of the last months of the campaign were obtained by mounted troops.

They accomplished in six weeks what the infantry would have taken at least a year, and perhaps two years, to do. Without a great preponderance in cavalry the advance through Northern Palestine and Syria would have been slow. Experience had shown us that in the rude hills of Judea a progress of five miles in three days' stern fighting, when our attack was pushed home by a much larger body of troops than was available for the defenders, was the best that could be hoped for, and for many miles in their rear the enemy had equally good positions. This sort of fighting could have gone on for months, and while no one doubts the ultimate success of the infantry, it would have been at the cost of great sacrifice, and the majority of the enemy would almost certainly have got away to hold new lines right up the country. If this went on the Turks could have replaced many of their losses by fresh troops from Anatolia and the Caucasus. But the Turks were faced with a very different problem when the cavalry had dealt with them. Three Turkish armies were wholly destroyed by the cavalry passing round the flank to their rear and sitting astride every road the enemy could take to the north. No reinforcements could replace them; no new armies, if they had been available, could, in the existing state the Turkish communications, have prevented our cavalry getting to Damascus and Aleppo, and holding the ground they won. The two hours' work of the infantry on the morning of the attack was all that was required to enable the mounted men to finish the war with Turkey. The infantry for three days continued to perform a hard task with grand skill and determination. They were all-conquering and irresistible, and were continually pressing forward, but if they had been held up in the hills the result would have been the same, for the cavalry cordon was unbreakable, and the Turks were between upper and nether millstones.

A man of strong will and rare energy, General Allenby had the gift of imparting to others his own enthusiasm for work. The heads of his various departments at G.H.Q. were as untiring as himself, and they well served the Commander-in-Chief. Major-General Sir L. J. Bols came to Egypt as the Chief Of the General Staff when the attack on the Gaza-Beersheba line was being prepared. He brought with him a ripe experience of latter-day warfare gathered in the strenuous fields in France, and he applied the lessons learned there with consummate skill and judgment. His appreciations of the situation were masterpieces of sound reasoning and judgment, and a more hard-working, conscientious, and capable C.G.S. never served an army. The Brigadier-General in charge of the earlier operations was General Dawnay, who remained in Palestine until Jerusalem had three lines of defences

WATER EXPRESS ON DESERT RAILWAY DRAWN BY LONDON AND SOUTH-WESTERN RAILWAY ENGINES

which no force that the Turks could put into the field could break. The enemy had not given up hope of retaking the Holy City, and documents secured at Nazareth told us how the Germans and Enver Pasha were looking for a victory which they rightly judged would have a great political effect. But their intention to make an attack from the Jordan Valley was never prosecuted, and had it been attempted it would have been a hopeless failure. General Dawnay was called to France to take up a high position on Field-Marshal Haig's staff, and his place at G.H.Q. was filled by Brigadier-General W. H. Bartholomew, who had been B.G.G.S. of the 20th Corps. General Bartholomew had earned his higher post by the work he did as General Chetwode's chief staff officer. The plans for the attack on the Beersheba flank were worked out by him in most elaborate detail, and in that complicated movement which had to be hidden from the enemy's eyes till the battle burst upon him there was not the slightest hitch, every part of the intricate machinery of a big Army Corps assembled for battle running as true as a well-tested engine. The scheme for the capture of Jerusalem was also passed on by him to divisional commanders, and in the gaining of successive lines in the Judean hills his soldierly hand arranged the details. But before this, when the 20th Corps took over the right of the line after the 21st Corps had failed to thrust the Turks back from Jerusalem by striking at the Nablus road north of the Holy City, General Bartholomew, under Sir Philip Chetwode's direction, was largely responsible for the heavy reverse sustained by the enemy who tried to force through the positions we held about the Beth-horons. If that enemy counter-attack had got home, the capture of Jerusalem would have been postponed. The line at this part was held by troops who had been fighting hard in the hills for days, and the situation was saved from becoming critical only by the fortuitous circumstance, of which the 20th Corps?

Made the most, that the 52nd Division, which had been relieved at Nebi Samwil by the Londoners, was marching to rest by the Beth-horon road. That counter-attack was boldly dealt with, and the defeat took the heart out of the Turks that their resistance in the defences outside Jerusalem was not so strong as we expected. General Bartholomew was chief of the operations staff at G.H.Q. when the scheme for the final overthrow of the Turkish armies was settled, and in its preparation he took a leading part. To point to the result is to pay the finest tribute to 'Operations,' for everything had been provided for, and not at any one point did anything miscarry.

The Quartermaster-General's department was another ably-managed branch of G.H.Q. Major-General Sir Walter Campbell was assisted by Brigadier-General Evans, who, like General Bartholomew, was attached to the 20th Corps in the first stage of the campaign. General Campbell had seen the Egyptian Expeditionary Force grow from a comparatively small army sitting on the Suez Canal to defend that waterway. Being responsible for transport he had a great deal to do with the building of the Desert Military railway, and with the establishment of an enormous supply base at Kantara. From 1916 onwards he saved an immense amount of tonnage and a vast sum of money by organising local resources boards in Egypt and in getting wheat and potatoes grown in place of other crops. When supplies could only be obtained with difficulty from home, General Campbell procured them in nearer markets, and even at the period when submarine activity was at its height in the Mediterranean the Force was never short. On his shoulders, too, rested the burden of assisting the civil population of Jerusalem, who were found with little food when the Turks were forced out of the city. But of all the many problems that faced the Quartermaster-General during the war, none was so serious as that of. supplying the Army in the great advance of September and October 1918. For an advance of this magnitude General Campbell was inadequately supplied with motor transport, butt all his men loyally responded to the call for a sustained effort, and 'Q' made a meritorious record. I have devoted a chapter to this work, and the one; fact that the lorries had a mileage of 720,000 miles in three weeks, or a daily average of 70 miles per lorry, is sufficient to show with what untiring energy the supply branch laboured to keep the fighting men fit for their stupendous task. Haifa was a long way short of 100 miles from the big supply depôts formed at Ludd, but the country was so bad for wheeled traffic that it was found easier to send stores back to the Suez Canal, 200 miles by railway, and to ship them to Haifa, than to forward them by road.

In Major-General Smith, the senior artillery officer, General Allenby had one of the most scientific gunners in the service. Some of the batteries on joining the Force saw action for the first time. They were opposed by skilful Austrian and Turkish gunners, but we obtained a marked superiority in artillery, and the accuracy of our gun fire well maintained the traditions of the Royal Regiment. On September 19 the artillery absolutely drowned the enemy's fire, but magnificent as was their work that day, I doubt if the artillery did any finer service during the campaign than that which helped on several occasions to win positions in the Judean hills. The drivers and gunners got their guns over almost inaccessible ridges, man-handling them for long distances, and sometimes coming into action as far forward as the infantry, and it was only their close support in keeping down machine-gun fire which enabled the infantry to carry the heights. The Royal Engineers can likewise look back with satisfaction at their part in the campaign. Major-General Wright, the C.R.E., had to make new roads and repair existing highways, arrange a water supply for a quarter of a million men and more than a hundred thousand thirsty animals, build bridges, and keep an eye on every yard of communications. On the main roads the engineers were able to call into service a large number of the civil population, who received pay above the market rate for labour, and when the Army went forward there was far more money in the hands of the poor than within living memory. Signals under General Sir M. G. E. Bowman-Manifolds direction, and the Remount and Veterinary departments under General Bates and General Butler, were highly efficient and contributed to the attainment of final victory.

All these departments and some others, such as Intelligence, were housed at Bir Salem, a mile and a half from Ramleh. General Headquarters in Palestine was of modest dimensions, and if we could credit a statement in an enemy reconnaissance report captured by us when the war was nearly over, the Turks regarded our G.H.Q. as an infantry camp. In the Yilderim flying and air photograph report for the period 1st to 16th September 1918, it is stated 'the permanent infantry camps at Bir Salem and El Kubeibe remained unchanged with two battalions each.' It is hard to believe that the enemy thought Our G.H.Q. was an infantry camp. A friend of mine, wandering through Liman von Sanders' headquarters at Nazareth just after we occupied the place, came across a mosaic of photographs of Bir Salem taken from the air. There was not a detail in the camp missing. I could even see my tent that was pitched amid some young eucalyptus trees. The wooden-frame mat houses and square tents that were the offices of the different branches, the wireless sets, the motor depôt, and the wire roads all suggested that Bir Salem was far more important than an infantry camp, and the Turks' spy system, if it was worth anything at all, must have told them that the place was our G.H.Q. That they never bombed it was from fear of reprisals, and unquestionably they would have got a great deal more than they gave.

In his Corps Commanders General Allenby was fortunate to have three generals of great distinction. Both the 20th and 21st Corps Commanders had come to the East after experience of heavy days in! France. Lieut.-General Sir Philip W. Chetwode, D.S.O., reached Egypt a year before Sir Archibald, Murray handed over the command of the Egyptian] Expeditionary Force to General Allenby, and, as commander of the Desert Column, Sir Philip was responsible for driving the Turk out of the Sinai Peninsula. His progress across the barren desert: from Bir el Abd to Rafa, his occupation of El Arish, and the brilliant dash on Rafa and capture of the Turkish garrison there, gave us the line from which: in October 1917 the advance was made on Jerusalem. It was General Chetwode's plan, suggested in the appreciation of the situation which he handed to General Allenby when the latter landed in Egypt, that was adopted for the attack on the Gaza-Beersheba, line, and his consistent success throughout the whole campaign, whether in the desert, on the plain, in the hills, or in the Jordan Valley, marked him as one of the most capable of the younger British generals. Most of the important work of the Force up to the taking of Jericho fell on the 20th Corps, and the handling of the Corps in situations which were generally difficult was always done with consummate skill. In the autumn operations the 20th Corps' part was subsidiary to that allotted to the 21st Corps, but the task was performed with a minimum number of troops in a manner which added to the already high reputation of General Chetwode and confirmed the opinion of his divisional commanders that they were serving under a general of great capacity.

Lieut.-General Sir Edward Bulfin had his 21st Corps reinforced by a division from the 20th Corps, and he began the action of September 19 with five infantry divisions. In speaking of his conduct of the operations it is impossible not to use superlatives. The care and forethought with which he arranged the preparations were only equalled by the enthusiasm he threw into the anxious work of concealing from the enemy everything that would give an indication of imminent operations. The element of surprise was a potent factor, and a careless man might have betrayed a sign for which the Turks were looking, but General Bulfin's instructions were so admirable and concise that the camouflage was perfect. The tactical work of the Corps on the day of attack was a remarkable effort; along the whole of the twenty-five miles of the Corps front there was not one incident that had not been arranged for. The staff work was a splendid tribute to the good leadership of the Corps Commander. In the description of the opening of the battle it will be seen that General Bulfin had given a time-table to each of his divisions on the left. He asked his divisional commanders to do a great deal, but he knew how capable the divisions were,

TOWER OF THE CHURCH OF FORTY MARTYRS
NEAR GENERAL ALLENBY'S G.H.Q

and his extraordinarily accurate estimate of when he should open a path for the cavalry and when three-fifths of his corps would wheel east wards to get to the hills showed the soundness his judgment. No corps commander ever had more loyal divisional generals and brigadiers. The secret was that they had supreme confidence in General Bulfin, and he gave them that whole-hearted support and sympathetic encouragement which gets the best work done. There was little fear of failure, but a general had taken a risk he knew that his corps commander would stand by him.

Desert Mounted Corps was commanded by Australian of the finest type, Lieut.-General Sir Harry Chauvel, one of the officers on the permanent military staff of the Commonwealth. The selection of an Australian officer for so high a command should be a source of deep gratification to our brethren under the Southern Cross. Rarely have four cavalry divisions been placed under one general in the field, and in this age when results count more than any thing else, Australia can point with pride to the part taken by a son of hers in one of the greatest cavalry exploits in history. A modest, retiring man, Genera Chauvel combined firmness with tact, and he always took a big view of his responsibilities. He was in charge of the Australian Imperial Force in Egypt a large body of troops who were as stout in the defence of Egypt in the early days of the war as they were in Palestine and Syria, but he never favoured his men at the expense of others. The Empire stood first, though, naturally, he was proud of the achievements of the Light Horsemen he had taken a large share in bringing to a high state of efficiency, and he was jealous in protecting the honours they had won. An article was printed in an official paper circulated among the troops that the Arab army was first in Damascus. The credit of winning Damascus and being the first in the city belongs to the Australian Light Horse, and General Chauvel was quick to have the error rectified, but while anxious that his own countrymen should get their due, he was just in apportioning praise, and in his official narratives of Operations the good work of British and Indian cavalry regiments received the reward of his ample commendation. Like that exemplar of the soldier's .Virtues, Lord Roberts, General Chauvel 'did not advertise,' and the British public knows little of his triumphs in the war, but if his name will stand out boldly in Australia's story of her contribution to the Empire's Army, it must also figure largely in our official history of the war as the leader of the mighty force of cavalry which finished the Turks.

CHAPTER 3

Troops of the Empire

The campaign in Palestine and Syria should always arouse feelings of pride among the peoples of the British Empire. In a war where circumstances compelled British troops to take their part in the French, Italian, and Balkan theatres alongside the soldiers of other nations, it was only on the fronts against Turkey that Imperial troops were exclusively employed. There was a French detachment with General Allenby, but it took only a minor part, and entire credit for the victory was Britain's. The glory was shared by no other nation. We incurred the responsibilities and paid the hundreds of millions the campaign cost us, and France went to Syria as the result of our broad outlook and enterprise. The work from the start to the finish was ours. The strategy was a British general's, and his plan was carried out to complete success by the courage and endurance of the British Empire's soldiers.[1] There may be some among our Allies who fail to recognise the full value of Britain's efforts in France, Italy, and the Balkans, but no honest man can deny to us the glory of delivering the Holy Land and Syria from the corrupting, blighting influence of the Turk. Every Briton should know the story of what the Empire's men did for him. We are not a people given to boasting over things accomplished, and I must say after having recently spent four months in Canada and the United States that I found more genuine interest on the other side of the Atlantic than at home in the triumphs of General Allenby's Army. Neither the Dominion of Canada nor the United States had a single representative in the Palestine Army, but the conduct of the campaign, its share in bringing the world-war to an end, and the historic cavalry advance through 400 miles of enemy country in six weeks, made a great appeal to the American public. They made no mistake in

---

1 See Appendix A.

awarding praise, and they seemed to appreciate the important bearing General Allenby's victory had on the struggle in Europe.

While recognising his military genius and the meticulous care with which he prepared his final, stunning blow, the average man at home appeared to regard General Allenby as having had a 'walk over,' and though all rejoiced at the Turks' defeat and saw in it a welcome sign that the end of the war was a matter of a few weeks, they failed to realise how hard-won the victory was. In measuring the value of the work the public should always keep in mind the material fact that General Allenby's command underwent a substantial alteration in 1918. The Army which broke through the formidable Gaza-Beersheba line, beat back the Turks from the Maritime Plain and relieved Jerusalem from Ottoman dominion, was changed very considerably by the demand for veteran troops for the Western Front. The reinforcements being sent from England to France in 1918 mostly consisted of young men recently called to the colours, or men of an age which it had been hoped eighteen months earlier would have exempted them from front-line service. Their courage was superb, but it was impossible that they could stand the wear and tear of war as well as men of sound fighting age. There had to be a stiffening of seasoned troops, mature, highly efficient, and fresh from scenes of victory. No other front than Palestine could give Field-Marshal Haig any substantial number of troops of this classification. Therefore some of the best of General Allenby's men recrossed the Mediterranean to take a heroic part in the final overthrow of German military power on the Western Front. Two complete infantry divisions and twenty-five battalions of British infantry from other divisions left the Egyptian Expeditionary Force. It was a sad parting for those left behind. I had then been with the Force for more than two years. We had had our trials and set-backs, and had tasted defeats as well as victories. But we had seen battalions, brigades, and divisions grow in fighting power until they were unrivalled in any of the world's armies. The men were in hard condition. Their marching powers had been tested in the desert and on the firmer soil of the Maritime Plain and in the Judean Hills, and they had proved their efficiency in many a battle. They were at the top of their form, hardened in the crucible of attack, full of the cunning which comes of frequent ventures by small parties in enemy lines, emboldened by the consciousness that they were superior to the enemy in all points of warfare, and possessing to the full the spirit of conquerors. But just at the moment when the moral of General Allenby's command was at its highest, when the health of the troops was magnificent, and when they had been brought to the finest pitch of military efficiency, the Army had to be reorganised.

The 52nd Division and the 74th Division were ordered to France, and three-fourths of the British, battalions serving with the other infantry divisions were sent back over the Desert railway to embark for the same destination. The 52nd Lowland Scots could not stay to finish a job they began on the Suez Canal. They were the oldest of the infantry veterans in this theatre, and those who survived the fearful losses sustained by the division in France can tell the story, as no other troops can, of digging and entrenching all the way across the hundred miles of desert from Kantara. The men of the 74th Division had been under the scorching suns of Egypt as long as the Scots, but in the early days they were first-line yeomanry, and had campaigned as horsemen in the Libyan Desert and in the torrid sandy wastes four hundred miles south of Cairo, in search of the elusive Senussi. Then when the Egyptian Expeditionary Force was in need of infantry which Britain could not supply, the yeomanry were dismounted and formed into the 74th Division. The men were mostly yeomen who had served with their regiments before German ambitions forced war on the world, and when the division was ordered to France it was, man for man, the finest in the Army. The men were the pick of the shires, whose love of soldiering and an open-air life had not worn off. Their value was recognised in France. The bloom was still on them; it had indeed been increased by their fighting experiences in Palestine. They were the equal of any two German divisions, and for a month, when a fresh German offensive was anticipated, they were held in reserve ready to be thrown in at any sorely-pressed spot to stop an enemy thrust. Then these dismounted yeomen went into the line and fought with that grand courage and skill which all their friends expected of them. Their record in the final stage was as fine as any division in Haig's Army, and their casualties were as great. The division came out of the line at one time only 700 strong. The 60th (London) Division gave up nine of its famous battalions for France, and they, too, added to the fame of the Cockney as a fighting man on the Western Front. The 10th (Irish) Division and the 53rd (Welsh) Division also sent liberal contributions, and the 54th (East Anglian) Division was the only division exclusively composed of white troops remaining with General Allenby's Army. Though it was obvious that if an offensive was begun in Palestine cavalry could be used to the best advantage, some of the yeomanry regiments which had served in the Yeomanry Mounted Division were also sent to France. They were broken up and trained as sections of the Machine-Gun Corps, for which yeomanry personnel were admirably suited.

In place of the troops sent away General Allenby was given the 3rd (Lahore) and the 7th (Meerut) Divisions which had done excellent service in Mesopotamia. They were valuable. Each division had three regular battalions of the British Army and nine battalions of Indian infantry, and nobody had the slightest doubts about their quality. But to fill the vacancies caused by taking British battalions from other divisions, General Allenby received second-line Indian infantry, men drawn from martial races with good traditions, though with a new and louder and stronger mechanism of war no one could prophesy how they would develop. They had to be trained in a stern field with great patience and watchfulness, and by a steady process brought up to a state which rendered them fit to stand and fight by the side of our seasoned troops. The training of these young Indian soldiers was one of the finest things done by devoted officers who deserve well of their country. In each brigade was a battalion of British infantry and the Indians were taught to live up to their example, and were proud to do it. In many minor operations arranged so that the Indian infantry could prove themselves, the white troops were also employed, and when they did well, as they invariably did not only were they suitably thanked by their battalion commanders and brigadiers, but by the divisional generals; and Corps Commanders always paid visits to Indian troops after a successful raid. The Corps Commanders could speak some Hindustani, and there was many a senior native non-commissioned officer willing to repeat to the ranks the words of congratulation which had come from distinguished generals. The Indians grew in efficiency, and by August had passed through their tests with such consistently sound results that their fighting qualities were rated high, and the new Punjabi Mussulmans, Dogras, Deolis, Kumoan Rifles, and Baluchis stood the trials as stoutly as Sikhs and Gurkhas and other warriors of the older Indian regiments. There were forty-nine Indian battalions of infantry in General Allenby's Army, thirty-four battalions of British Infantry, and two battalions of the British West India Regiment. Of these only twenty-four British and nine Indian battalions had taken part in the first portion of the campaign which ended in the capture of Jerusalem and Jericho. In short, so far as infantry were concerned the final operations began with what was largely a new army.

There were some alterations in the cavalry too, but the change was not nearly so marked, and the troops which came to Egypt to replace yeomanry regiments sent to France as machine-gunners and to increase the mounted force were regular Indian cavalry. Desert Mounted Corps consisted of four cavalry divisions, and constituted one of the largest bodies of mounted troops ever manœuvred under one command. In it was the Anzac Mounted Division, made up of regiments of Australian Light Horse and New Zealand Mounted Rifles, which, except for their dismounted service on Gallipoli for a few months, had served with the Egyptian Expeditionary Force throughout the war. These regiments were kept up to strength by the Dominions, and the story of the work done by them has made a proud page in the history of the young nations of the Empire. There were nine other regiments of Light Horse in the Australian Mounted Division, which was exclusively Australian except for a regiment of French Chasseurs d'Afrique attached to them for the last operations. In the 4th and 5th Cavalry Divisions were five regiments of British yeomanry and thirteen regiments of Indian cavalry, three of them Imperial Service Lancers, and the remainder regiments which had served with regular Indian troops in France.

General Allenby was stronger than the enemy in troops of all branches. In cavalry he had an immeasurably superior force, not merely in numbers, but in quality. One regiment of our cavalry was stronger than an enemy brigade. His infantry also far outnumbered the Turkish divisions, and he had a great preponderance of guns.[1] In the air the superiority was even more marked, and the Germans, though they had a fair supply of good aeroplanes, were hopelessly outclassed. But the Army was not too large for the task it had to tackle. The Turk was in a strong defensive position, and if it had not been possible to take him by surprise or if we had not lowered his moral, the battle must have been longer and more costly. But the enemy's moral was steadily declining; nothing proved that more eloquently than the desertions. In three months 12 Turkish officers and 458 other ranks deserted to our lines. This is how the desertions grew:

Desertions during June—3 officers, 85 other ranks.

Desertions during July—6 officers, 164 other ranks.

Desertions during August—3 officers, 209 other ranks.

In the first week of September 1 officer and 34 Other ranks deserted to us, in the second week 2 officers and 68 other ranks, and in the third week 4 officers and 93 other ranks came into our lines.

1 See Appendix B

The Turks were at their wits' end to stop this leakage. They repeatedly changed the positions of their regiments so that the men might not have time to study the country with a view to desertion. The fact that officers were deserting showed the poor condition of the enemy. Not only were they leaving the front but many got away on the journey south. An officer of an attack battalion taken prisoner on September 6 said he left the Haidar Pasha station, Constantinople, with 150 other officers but 50 of them deserted before they reached Aleppo. In the enemy's 26th divisional orders on July 6 was the following statement:

As new troops sent to the front are partly composed of deserters it is probable that in case of attack they will cause panic. To prevent this machine guns should be posted behind the line in order to fire at deserters.

A regiment of the 37th Division arrived at Messudieh the day before the attack composed of young and discontented soldiers, and 70 of them deserted. Another regiment of the same division which came to the front from the Caucasus had lost 700 men by desertion on the journey. A German officer wrote in his diary:

One can hardly wonder that so many Turks desert. Their pay amounts to two marks a month, and their clothing and rationing are miserable. They live in rags and tatters, and one hardly ever sees a soldier decently dressed, for the Government spends precious little on their upkeep. Everywhere money and all sense of cleanliness are lacking. Were the soldiers fitted out as we are they would make fine troops.

The German officer might have pointed to another reason for the Turks wishing to leave the front. The Germans were advocates of flogging. Many of the German officers were overbearing and brutal, and as far back as June 1917, von Falkenhayn issued this order to all German personnel:

Reports have come to my ears, not only of unfriendly behaviour but also of rough handling of their Turkish comrades by the Germans. Moreover there have been cases of insubordination to Turkish superior ranks. I can hardly think there can be a German in the Army Group who does not realise the great danger of such behaviour to our Holy Cause, or who is so foolish as not to realise it when pointed out by his comrades or officers. These incidents can, therefore, only be explained by deliberate hatred or malevolence. He who shows himself unworthy of representing the German name and the German Army here upon the front deserves no compassion. I hereby request the senior ranks to look into this matter and expect with confidence that comrades will not permit of any such behaviour, so detrimental to our cause.

No doubt it was in consequence of this brutal conduct of the Germans that the Kaiser's officers could not go about unarmed. All were warned:

Recent events necessitate my pointing out that all German officers, even when on short walks, should have a weapon on them, so as not to be in a defenceless position in case of attack.

And it is interesting to note that in the courts-martial at which Germans were charged with brutal conduct towards the Turks, the Turkish War Office insisted that Ottoman officers should participate. But British propaganda also had its effect in lowering the enemy's moral. Fevzi Pasha, the commander of the Turkish 7th Army, told von Falkenhayn that the widely distributed English propaganda stated that the British were simply and solely carrying on the war against the Turks in order to drive the Germans from the soil of Islam. Fevzi held that the employment of officers and men in German uniform in the neighbourhood of the Hedjaz railway would strengthen that belief among the fanatical inhabitants, and he requested that all Germans should be withdrawn or given Turkish uniforms. Another commander spoke of the devilish action of the British in getting Turks to desert.

Just before the operations began the strength of the Turkish forces on this front were computed by their Quartermaster-General—for the purpose of drawing rations—at a higher figure than in the belief of our G.H.Q. represented the fact. A captured document gave these figures as follows:

Units.	Ration Strength.		Daily Supply.		
	Men.	Animals.	Food.	Forage.	Total.
			tons.	tons.	tons.
8th Army	39,783	17,817	28	53·5	81·5
7th Army	28,575	10,815	20	32·5	52·5
Jordan Group . . .	5,223	2,324	3·5	7	10·5
Palestine Menzil (L. of C.) .	4,958	1,877	3·5	5·5	9
4th Army	21,899	6,601	15·5	20	35·5
	100,438	39,434	70·5	118·5	189

The numbers were exaggerated. It was the practice of supply officers to over-estimate, as otherwise they received insufficient rations to feed the troops. German officers attached to the 8th Army gave the strength to the German staff as 28,672 men and 10,890 animals, and probably the over-estimate in the other armies was in the same proportion

CHAPTER 4

Crossing the Jordan

Jerusalem had been made safe by the extension of our line north of Ramallah and Bireh and by the; capture of Jericho, and if the whole of Falkenhayn's Yilderim troops had come south from Aleppo they would not have regained the Holy City for the tottering Turkish Empire. The enemy's lines of communications were insufficient to support adequately the troops already in the field of active-operations, and though there were new arrivals, and among them some German battalions sent to infuse more spirit into the Army of the Crescent, the enemy was never in strength or condition to warrant any fear that the security of Jerusalem was jeopardised by the despatch of large numbers of our men to France. What we had we held, and if General Allenby was not able till the autumn to make his further big effort, he continued throughout the spring and summer to bite into the main front from the sea to the Jordan, weakening the Turks by frequent severe losses, lowering their moral by constant successful raids, and always keeping them in anxious suspense. The Commander-in-Chief did more than this. He made two big dashes across the Jordan-and over the Moab Plateau into the region through which the Hedjaz railway runs. These two raids served a very useful object, though neither entirely fulfilled the hopes of the General Staff. They were daring in conception, and were carried out with such speed and courage under exceedingly difficult conditions that the enemy must have become fearful of his approaching doom. We did not obtain a secure hold on the Hedjaz railway in either attempt—to occupy Amman in the first instance was not contemplated, nor was it intended our troops should stay In Es Salt—but because we got so far as to destroy bridges and culverts on the railway line the enemy was obliged to draw to the northward a large part of his troops defending Maan and to keep them about Amman, and matters were thereby made more easy for the Emir Feisal's Arab army. We paid a price in men and material to gain this object, but the result justified the cost.

The over-Jordan venture was being prepared before the battle of the Somme told us the war was still a long way from its close. The first raid would have been the prelude to an attempt to roll back the whole Turkish line to beyond Nablus and across the Plain of Armageddon, and if the situation on the Western Front had not been anxious a summer Campaign in Palestine might have taken us to Damascus. Would the position have become better for us than it was in the late autumn? It is a matter of speculation and I have not the ability to give an answer, but it seems to me that the intervening months of waiting, of preparation for a mighty whirlwind sweep by a magnificently directed powerful Army did more service to the whole Allied cause than a slower progress of a conquering host would have done. There is no doubt that General Allenby would have made very substantial progress during the summer of 1918 if the cream of his infantry and some of his mounted troops had not gone to swell Field-Marshal Haig's command in France, and Allenby's strategy makes it certain that what he did with less seasoned troops he could certainly have accomplished, even against greater opposition, with his grim veteran Crusaders who bore the brunt of the stern fighting which rescued Jerusalem from the rule of the Crescent. But it was worth waiting through the long summer months to bring about a complete loss of moral in the enemy, and possibly when we galloped through Syria in September and October 1918, the Commander-in-Chief saved thousands of precious lives because he had delayed to effect the utter collapse of his enemy.

One must read of the Army's work during the summer in the light of the superbly executed last phase of the campaign. It was hard work and there was very little of it that was spectacular. It was consistently good, although, as I have said, the results did not always come up to expectations, and each attack and each stubborn resistance to an attack was wearing down a foe who fought stoutly, so that when the psychological moment arrived for the beginning of the knock-out blow the Turkish Army was winded and bruised, and also, though it did not know it, off its guard.

The first raid east of the Jordan must be regarded as one of the many elements to be reckoned in the Turks' downfall. When it was over the Palestine Army did not estimate it as fully successful, and the Army was right. The same may be said of the second raid, but

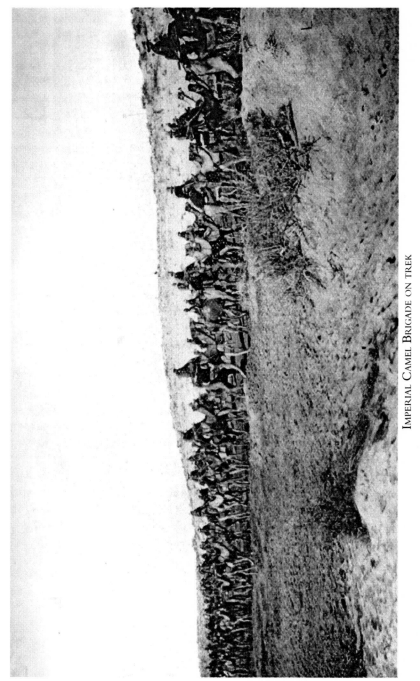

IMPERIAL CAMEL BRIGADE ON TREK

it was not until months after that; the Army was able to appreciate these operations in proper proportions. We crossed the Jordan under the greatest disadvantages when the river was in full flood, we had thousands of horsemen and camelry across the mountains of Moab before the enemy understood that craggy hills could be negotiated by the intrepid Anzac and British cavalry, and London infantry penetrated far into the plateau close on the heels of mounted men. In consequence the Turks had to bring thousands of troops who had been cramping the tactics of the Hedjaz Arab Army to hold a line east of the Jordan, and the enemy was made to feel that if he was not to have a flank enveloped he must let his left rest on the Hedjaz railway. It meant a large extension of his line when he could only call on insufficient troops to hold it. We know of recriminations among the Turkish staffs at this time, and captured documents tell of the deep concern occasioned to the Germans by the raids. They gave the German advisers of the Turkish High Command furiously to think, and coming as the raids did just at the moment when the enemy must have known that troops would depart for France, they must have marvelled at the strength and power of Allenby's arm. The crossing of the Jordan was a feat of the Palestine Army which was typical of its work throughout the campaign. The weather was against us, as almost invariably it was. The obstacles were tremendous. Violent storms had made the valley of the Jordan very soft and sticky, and the movement of supplies round about Jericho, as well as down the steep road from Jerusalem, called for a repetition of the devoted work which the Army Service Corps had given since the great movement in front of the Gaza-Beersheba line in the previous October. The horse-transport teams faced an even harder task than the motor columns, for they had to haul loads of material and supplies over ground which probably never before was used by wheels, and adhesive mud on an uneven surface made the conditions terribly difficult. When the rain ceased we knew the heat in the Jordan valley in the early spring would soon bring the ground into a better state, but the anxiety of the Staff would still be heavy until they discovered whether the storms had been general along the whole length of the river to its source. The rise in height of the Jordan would show that; nothing else would, because the valley, excepting for a few miles at the Dead Sea end, was in enemy hands. A date was given to the engineers and infantry by which to make bridges for the crossing, and it was adhered although it became obvious that a deluge had fallen right up to the country of Dan. The river, which even in the torrid heat of summer is a rapid stream rose higher and higher. It came down in full spate a muddy, tearing volume which left a big brown stain where it emptied itself in the grey-blue salt laden waters of the Dead Sea. But the crossing was fixed for the night of the 21st-22nd of March, and the effort was made. The attempt was worthy of the: gallant Londoners. Two places had been decided upon for the bridging of the river. One was at Ghoraniyeh, where there were remnants of a bridge, destroyed a month earlier by the Turks. It connected the tracks between Jericho and the road up the Moab mountains to Es Salt, and as these tracks were more or less passable for infantry and wheels it was a natural place to select.

The other spot chosen was Makhadet Hajlah, some three miles nearer the Dead Sea. Here stood the only building within a radius of several miles. It is a white monastery with a blue dome, and in this solitude lived three Greek monks willing to dispense hospitality to any traveller, whatever his religion. This is said to be the spot where Christ was baptized. The state of the river at Ghoraniyeh was wild in the extreme. The water roared along, overflowing the banks, tearing up scrub by the roots and making the surface black with driftwood. Men who left a dry spot on the bank to fetch a plank or a rope came back to see water covering it, and in a few hours the river had risen eight feet. Nevertheless an effort was made to get to the left bank. The 2/17th Londons selected some of their strongest swimmers to breast the stream. They made heroic attempts, but not one of the stout-hearted men had the slightest prospect of success. They were carried far down the river and were fortunate to make the western bank again. Two punts and a raft were put on the face of the waters in the hope that men could embark in them and paddle over, but the craft were immediately caught in the current and torn from strong men's hands. The moon had gone down and the bridging parties tried to work in silence, but some unavoidable noise was heard on the opposite bank and the enemy opened fire. Though it had become apparent to the officers engaged at Ghoraniyeh that they would not bridge the Jordan that night they strove might and main to achieve the impossible, until at half-past one on the morning of the 22nd they were ordered to abandon the attempt and to send men to concentrate on Hajlah where our troops had met with more success.

There an officer and six men of the 2/19th Londons had succeeded in swimming across the river, taking with them a rope. The enemy did not detect them, and at a little after one o'clock they hauled across the first raft bearing twenty-seven men. It was not until that load had been safely deposited on the east bank that the Ghoraniyeh attempt was temporarily given up, and the 2/19th Londons marched to Hajlah with the 180th Brigade Headquarters to help with the good work there. The 2/17th Londons with a machine-gun company and the 180th Trench Mortar Battery were kept at Ghoraniyeh to watch the crossing until relieved by the 179th Brigade, and the 303rd Brigade R.F.A. were directed to open fire at dawn to keep the enemy occupied there and so assist the operations at Hajlah. At five o'clock on the morning of the 22nd March the 180th Brigade were in a concealed position west of Hajlah, where the country was full of mounds and shallow watercourses, and in getting into their position they disturbed not a few gazelle and many a snake. The 181st Brigade had moved to Tel es Sultan before daybreak. These movements in the dark hours had been performed almost without noise, but, although the silence of night had not been broken by marching columns, the enemy had discovered that troops were getting across the river before a pink flush over the Moab Plateau told of approaching dawn.

Facing the crossing place at Hajlah was a mass of scrub so thick in places that our infantry could not penetrate it without hacking it down. In this strong undergrowth were many Turkish snipers who were good enough riflemen to hold up our progress, and the enemy posted a number of machine guns on a hillock about a thousand yards north-west of the crossing from which they could bring to bear a heavy enfilade fire on the rafts. In the turbulent state of the river it was not thought prudent to put more than eight fully equipped men into a raft, and these had to lie at full length in the bottom of the craft. The machine-gun fire was so accurate that of one raft-load seven out of the eight men were hit. The position of the enemy machine-gunners was however soon located by two sections of the 180th Machine Gun Company, who delivered a magnificent covering fire. One cannot speak too highly of the 60th Division staff and the Brigade staffs who directed the crossing, or of the sterling, highly disciplined infantry and engineers straining every nerve to win complete control of the river. Not a man hesitated to accept the risks of flood and fire. Many had doubts, but all were ready to test them, and so it came about that while a cyclone of bullets from our machine-gunners kept down the heads of Turkish marksmen, there was a continuous passage of troops from the right to the left bank of the Jordan on rafts tossed about by a rushing stream and buffeted by tree trunks borne on the heaving bosom of the waters. It was a great performance, and by a quarter to eight in the morning the whole of the 2/19th battalion of the London Regiment was digging itself in on the east bank of the Sacred River, whilst the 2/18th Londons, who had been waiting since half-past four, were preparing to follow them.

Arrangements were already in progress for improving the crossing facilities. The Bridging Train of the Anzac Mounted Division had moved across the valley in the early hours with their steel pontoons carried on light waggons. This bridging train was a highly efficient section of the pick of Australian mounted troops. They had not had many opportunities during the campaign of showing their smartness, though whatever they had been called upon to do had been carried out with the enthusiasm of strong-backed, patriotic fighting men. They made the most of the opportunity given them at Hajlah. It has been officially recorded that they completed their bridge very rapidly 'despite very trying circumstances.' These official reports are written by gallant men who rarely do more than state bald facts, as if ashamed to suggest anything pointing to exceptional gallantry in the performance of duty. All honour to them. But to throw a pontoon bridge over the river in the rage of flood with snags continually coming down, and to complete it ready for the passage of troops within, two hours, is not an, ordinary feat of war. And the bridging engineers had not merely to face the perils of rushing waters. Their work was done in daylight under the observation of the Turks. Enemy gunners and riflemen were busy, but the Australians toiled on heedless of bursting shells and the rush of bullets, and got a fine, strong, comparatively steady bridge ready for infantry by ten minutes past eight in the morning. General Shea told them it was a 'good and rapid performance.' There was not a Londoner who watched the bridge builders during that exciting and momentous morning but thought the praise well deserved, and the Australians, than whom none appreciated better the merit of the Cockney soldier, would sooner take a compliment from him than from anybody.

But the forcing of the passage of the Jordan was not yet complete. By midday the 2/18th Londons as well as the 2/19th Londons were across the river, but the remainder of General Watson's 180th Brigade and General Humphrey's 179th Brigade were concentrated in the wadi Kelt near Hajlah. There was a mountain battery firing the vicious 20-pounder shells from a spot 500 yards west of the bridge, and at this time there was not much hostile fire. About an hour later the 180th Brigade endeavoured to enlarge the bridgehead under cover of artillery fire, and in places the line was carried forward another hundred yards. It was desperately hard work. The scrub was tough

CAMELRY PASSING NATIVE VILLAGE

as well as thick, and no advance could be made until paths were cut. Enemy machine-gun fire was deadly and the attempt to widen out our front was not successful. In the afternoon it was decided that there should be no further advance till night, and orders were issued that the 180th Brigade should press forward at midnight and try to gain the flat ground beyond the clayhills which enclose the banks of the Jordan. The Turkish resistance had been very stubborn, and it was not advisable to risk heavy losses in a daylight attack the success of which was problematical. The 180th Brigade, however, found that the enemy had suffered greatly during the previous day's fighting and could not offer much opposition, and by three o'clock in the morning it won and held hillocks covering the crossing at places a little more than a mile north-east of Hajlah, at a mile due east of it, and was also strongly posted at a spot roughly a mile south-east of the pontoon bridge. This substantial enlargement of the bridgehead made it possible to bring cavalry over, and at 4 a.m. the Auckland Mounted Rifles were saddling up to be in readiness to achieve the honour of being the first of General Allenby's horsemen to cross the Jordan. The regiment certainly distinguished itself that morning of the 23rd of March. It was over the river by half-past seven, with orders to push out east and north-east towards Ghoraniyeh. These capable and cheerful New Zealanders had a great day. I have it on the highest authority that the regiment as a whole was very well handled and that the squadron and troop leading alike were excellent. When they had passed through the infantry lines the horsemen, moving fanwise, were continually charging Turkish detachments, accepting surrenders when offered, and killing and dispersing the remainder. By noon they had sent in as prisoners six officers and sixty-two other ranks with four captured machine guns, and had secured the ground covering Ghoraniyeh.

This success came at an opportune moment, for though the 181st Brigade had been held up in a renewed attempt to effect the crossing at Ghoraniyeh, the height of the flood water in the river was now beginning to lower, and swimmers of General da Costa's Brigade at once entered the cold brown water to take lines to the other side. Though Ghoraniyeh was an extremely important point for bridging the stream, far more important than Hajlah, General Shea was unwilling to risk any delay in getting more-troops and stores over to the east bank of the Jordan, and long before it was known that bridges would be thrown across at Ghoraniyeh that day, preparations were in hand for building a second pontoon bridge at Hajlah. By half-past one this second bridge was in position 600 yards north of

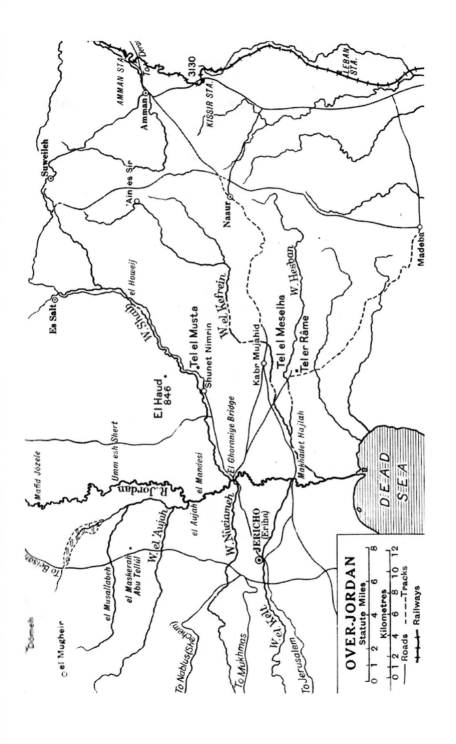

the Anzacs' first pontoon bridge, but the banks of the river were too sodden to allow of any wheels approaching it, and it had to be allotted to infantry and cavalry. The 23rd March was indeed a busy day for the bridging parties. Time was the essence of the business, for the Intelligence department had received information that the enemy was getting heavy reinforcements, some coming up from the Hedjaz railway, others by march route from the country around Kerak to the south of the Dead Sea, and yet others going over Jordan from the direction of Nablus (Shechem). The Moab hills were peculiarly suitable for defence, and a few brave, well-posted men in the hills holding the Es Salt road in their folds, would have made the march to that hill town a hazardous and a slow undertaking. So the bridge builders were called upon for a supreme effort. Bombing from the air did not stop them. By half-past four in the afternoon a light infantry bridge was in use by the men of the 181st Brigade. When I crossed over it I did not think it as strong as it really was, and I marvelled at the resource of the men who could keep this narrow bridge in safe order with a stream which fell several feet in a few hours and then rose again as rapidly. A barrel pier bridge and a pontoon bridge were also completed at Ghoraniyeh before ten o'clock at night, so that by midnight five military bridges spanned the Jordan, and all were being used to their utmost capacity.

Not even when Joshua made his camp at Gilgal did the Jordan Plain hold such a mighty host. In General Shea's group, to which was entrusted the passage of the Jordan, the capture of Es Salt, and the raid on the Hedjaz railway, were the Anzac Mounted Division, the 60th London Division, the Imperial Camel Brigade, the 9th British Mountain Artillery Brigade, the Light Armoured Car Brigade, the Army Bridging Train, Desert Mounted Corps Bridging Train, and the 10th Heavy Battery Royal Garrison Artillery. In addition the 160th Brigade of the 53rd (Welsh) Division were in the valley to make feints at various fords north of Ghoraniyeh, thus holding the enemy while the real attempts were being made nearer the Dead Sea. There were many more than 20,000 British and Australian troops on the Plain with almost as many horses and camels. Piles of stores had been collected and a vast number pack animals were equipped for the task of carrying food and ammunition into the hills, while lorries and light cars were standing by to hurry up stores soon as the Es Salt road was made good by infantry. The completion of the bridges was the the signal for movement everywhere, and by dawn of March 24 the flat ground east of the Jordan was covered with advancing troops, the mounted men working into the hills between the Dead Sea and the Es Salt road, while the infantry proceeded to attack the enemy at Shunet Nimrin, the village at the mouth of the pass through which the road runs.

Before describing the fighting on this eve of Lady Day I will refer to the enterprise of a small party of two officers and forty-two men who volunteered to embark on three motor boats at Rujm el Bahr, which had been the enemy's grain depôt on the northern end of the Dead Sea, to gain the other side of the Jordan's mouth and, by working up the eastern bank of the river, to endeavour to assist the crossing at Hajlah by taking the enemy in the rear. The party belonged to the 2/24th Londons and they were given the title of 'Societé Anonyme Maritime.' For a time their enterprise promised a favourable issue. They landed safely and, following an Arab guide who was supposed to know every inch of the valley, they made some progress up the eastern bank. The distance, taking into consideration the bends of the river, was a trifle over five miles, but in this area there are pockets of exceedingly soft soil which are almost as treacherous as quicksands, and the party had to make many detours to avoid them. Somehow the guide was lost. This was disconcerting, but the little band of adventurers pressed on, and a young officer made his own way to the Hajlah ford. A small Turkish post was rushed and two men captured, but the others running away must have given news of the approach of the party. On getting nearer the ford the Londoners found they were opposed by a superior body of Turks, and they had to creep down to near the water's edge and hide in the scrub. The Turks were searching for them all day and came quite close to them, but during the night these Dead Sea marines managed to come up with their friends and opened communication with the 180th Brigade at dawn on the 23rd. The adventure served a useful purpose, for the enemy knew some troops were on their flank which they had to watch carefully.

CHAPTER 5

First Attack on Amman

The infantry attack on Shunet Nimrin was supported by cavalry moving a long way out on their northern and southern flanks. General Cox's 1st Australian Light Horse Brigade was well away to the northward, and it was arranged that when the infantry, having driven the enemy out of Nimrin, was working up the Es Salt road, this brigade was to march to Es Salt by (what for want of a better name was called) 'No. 7 Road,' in other words a goat track from Umm esh Shert, across the mountains. The 2nd Australian Light Horse Brigade and the New Zealand Mounted Rifles Brigade were, with General Chaytor's Anzac Mounted Division Headquarters, getting in the hills to the south with a view to making a dash on the Hedjaz railway. The 181st Brigade made the attack on Nimrin supported by the 303rd Brigade R.F.A. which, with two howitzer batteries and two mountain batteries attached, had crossed the river at Ghoraniyeh during the night, and the 179th Brigade pushed forward to El Haud, a hill 2000 feet above the level the Jordan, which gave us great trouble during the second expedition against Amman. The attacks began between eight and nine in the morning. Shunet Nimrin is some six miles from the spot where the river had been bridged at Ghoraniyeh. A rough rudely metalled road runs to the village, but many of the troops were taken along the protecting banks of the wadi Nimrin. The howitzer and mountain batteries also advanced up this wadi. The 181st Brigade were shelled and came under machine-gun fire from a house just to the north of the village, which is a remarkable landmark as one stands on the edge of the craggy hills of Judea fifteen miles away. The enemy's opposition was soon broken down and Nimrin was ours at three in the afternoon, but just beyond the village where the road sweeps to the right and a wooden bridge spans a wadi there was a keen fight for the possession of the road. A high hill to the right dominates the highway, and three German field guns were in action just behind the crest, plastering the road and holding up the advance. Some men of the 2/22nd Londons were despatched round by the right of the hill to stalk the gunners. They moved with the stealth of chamois hunters, and a handful of men with Lewis guns got within effective range and shot down all the teams and captured the guns. This was a typical example of the alertness and resource of the men composing Shea's group operating over Jordan.

The 179th Brigade's capture of El Haud was a notable feat. The hill is a bold feature. It does not absolutely dominate Shunet Nimrin, but until it was in our possession movement in the Jordan valley was difficult, and without it being in our hands progress up the Es Salt road was precarious, if not impossible. It was the enemy's right flank, by the turning of which he was forced to retire. The infantry stormed the heights, supported by the fire of two batteries under Major Price and Major Barry, who brought their guns into action under heavy fire. In doing so Major Price was severely wounded, and Major Barry was hit in the shoulder but persisted in carrying on. I may remark parenthetically that Major Price's share in the action cost him dear. He held the acting rank of major for many months and had fought his battery with exceptional skill in many operations, but now, being severely wounded in the execution of gallant work; he was reduced to the rank and pay of a subaltern. This is one of the injustices which give rise to much comment among combatant officers, who are subject to the rulings of gentlemen sitting comfortably at home. The 181st Brigade lost no time in pursuing the retreating Turk up the road, and he was hurried along by a squadron of Wellington Mounted Rifles who went forward close on his heels to prevent his blowing up a bridge at Howeij, at a left-hand bend in the mountain road some five miles south of Es Salt. The road passes through a short cutting in the mountain side and comes out to a narrow shelf cut into a cliff face, and probably several valuable hours were saved by compelling the enemy to leave it intact. The 179th Brigade left a battalion on El Haud and had another battalion on the high ground north of the wadi Arseniyet. The 181st Brigade pressed on with two mountain batteries close behind them, which were followed in turn by two howitzer batteries, their guns hauled by eight-horse teams. During these operations excellent work was done by the Australian Air Line section. These signallers moved rapidly behind the infantry, and they put up their air-line to Nimrin under fire and operated it with splendid efficiency.

The cavalry were facing extraordinary difficulties with their customary determination. The 1st Australian Light Horse Brigade, a long way out on the northern flank watching for Turkish reinforcements which might pass over the Jordan by the Jisr ed Damie ford, was not opposed, but the horsemen on the south encountered tremendous natural obstacles. Though for a rapid movement across the Moab Plateau in the direction of the Hedjaz railway the employment of mounted men was a necessity, the country was quite unsuitable for cavalry, and the clay ridges were very slippery after the rain. But the 2nd Australian Light Horse Brigade and the New Zealand Mounted Rifles Brigade surmounted them and were well in the hill country by the afternoon In working up the wadi Kefrein the advance of th 2nd Light Horse was delayed by the deplorable condition of the track. It was quite impossible to get guns and vehicles along it and they were sent back to Shunet Nimrin. The explosives to be used railway demolition were taken from vehicles and placed on pack animals, but so bad was the state of the track that horses and mules had to be dragged and pushed for long distances over a path so narrow that there was no room for them to move except in single file. Just before dusk the brigade found body of 500 enemy cavalry between them and the New Zealanders, but these retired in an easterly direction when the Australians tried to close with them. At the end of the day the 181st Brigade was south of Howeij, clearing the enemy off the hills on both sides of the road, their enthusiasm for the job being heightened by the capture of fifty German including an officer, belonging to the 703rd Infantry. Bad as were the conditions on the 25th they were infinitely worse on the next two days, and the troops had to labour against elements which were forbidding in the extreme. Allenby rarely had the luck of the weather; indeed falls of rain during operations this roadless country were so remarkably consistent that the Commander-in-Chief had always to take them into account in his calculations. From 8 a.m. till noon on the 28th rain was particularly heavy. The soil on the mountains was soft and greasy, and the watercourses carried away a big volume of water. The air was bitterly cold, and the mounted men whose cloaks were sodden had to endure much personal discomfort while incessantly coaxing and urging their tired animals to make another effort to climb the slippery mountain paths. Nor were the infantry in a more favoured state, although most of them were operating on the road. As with everything the Turk touches, the road he had made was only half done, and when rains came the surface was quite a foot deep in clay and crushed limestone, a mixture which gave a hopelessly slippery top to the road. The highway was narrow and the gradients were steep, and so bad was the surface that no vehicles were sent up except those absolutely necessary to carry supplies to victual men and horses. I wished to get to Es Salt and was permitted to go some distance beyond Nimrin, but as every extra person on the road meant inconvenience to the fighting man I was asked to go no farther. Of course I stopped, and while I was eating an 'iron ' meal I saw the Commander-in-Chief go up the road and return a few minutes later. Much as General Allenby wished to see how things were progressing at the front—he was ubiquitous and whenever possible obtained his information at first hand—he would never allow his motor car to stand in the way of a supply waggon. During the day the 2nd tight Horse Brigade did marvellously well under these pressing circumstances, and by midnight they had ached Naaur, about fourteen miles as the crow flies from the Jordan, but fully twenty as they had travelled in the mass of broken country. They were ordered to raid the railway next day. The 181st Brigade had made good progress towards Es Salt, considering the mud and precipitous country they had to clear, and when darkness set in they halted about a mile from the town. The 179th Brigade, toiling up the Arseniyet track, had met with no opposition to speak of, and the 3rd regiment of the 1st Australian Light Horse Brigade which was with them went on and entered Es Salt at six o'clock, the 179th Brigade following at midnight. The picturesque old town had been evacuated by the enemy, and the inhabitants, many of whom were Christians, extended to General Shea, when he rode in next day, a characteristic welcome, the male population running beside him and blazing off antiquated firearms as a kind of fantasia.

On the 26th March the Anzacs continued the march from Naaur, and early in the morning the 2nd Light Horse Brigade joined up with the Ne Zealand Mounted Rifles Brigade one mile beyond Es Sir. It was still raining heavily and the whole country was a sea of mud. The 2nd Light Horse went ahead, and crossing to the north of the Amman-Es Salt road took 170 prisoners near Sweileh. At two o'clock the further advance of the Anzac Mounted Division became impracticable owing to both men and horses requiring rest, but arrangements we made for raids on the railway during the night. The party which set out to damage the line north of Amman did not succeed, but the men who went to the south destroyed a section about seven miles from Amman. The 179th Brigade took over the defence of Es Salt, and two battalions of the 181st Brigade with two howitzer batteries prepared to proceed to Amman next morning. A field gun and 145 prisoners had been taken in Es Salt. The road to Amman was broken up and water-logged and

47

quite unfit for wheeled guns, so two mountain batteries were substituted for the howitzers, and another mountain battery was detached from the 179th Brigade. Three battalions of the latter brigade and 'B' section of the 303rd Battery were sent back to Howeij to ease the supply situation, which was giving the Quartermaster-General's branch no little anxiety. The column of the 181st Brigade left Es Salt before daylight, but the advance was considerably delayed by the necessity of having to settle a local feud between the Circassian village of Sweileh and the Christians of El Fuheis. These Circassians had been 'planted' in the country by the Turks to bolster up and support the bad régime. The Circassians were wholly favourable to the Turk, who gave them concessions which were rigidly refused to Christians and Arabs, and they were guilty of several acts of treachery to us. When I was hereabouts at the time General Chaytor captured Amman in September, I was warned to be on the alert in passing through or near Circassian villages, but though I believe some long-range pot shots were directed at my car, the Circassians had learned a lesson, and they had become less aggressive than they were in the spring.

The 181st Brigade had to halt for the night two miles east of Sweileh, but the mounted troops had advanced. The hills in this undulating country were covered with rocks, and bushes and piles of stones gave good cover for machine guns and riflemen. Off the roads, in the boggy state of the land, it was difficult to move, and the wadis were troublesome obstacles. The banks were very steep, and the wadi Amman could only be crossed in one or two places in single file. During the day the Anzac Mounted Division and the Imperial Camel Brigade made an attack on Amman and the railway station, which kept the enemy busily engaged while demolition parties were moving towards the railway both north and south of the town. The camelry began a direct advance on Amman at eleven o'clock, but were held up by shell and machine-gun fire. The New Zealanders, after a lot of delay in getting over the wadi Amman, reached the railway south of the town in the afternoon, but the 2nd Light Horse Brigade were prevented from getting to the line north of the town though a counter-attack by the Turks was quickly beaten off. News came in that the demolition parties were blowing up the line and culverts towards Libban and the 181st Brigade were ordered forward at dawn next day to co-operate with the cavalry. It was a hard day, and with any luck at all the raid would have been a far greater success than it proved to be. In the early hours of the morning an Australian squadron carried out a dash to the railway several miles north of Amman with admirable swiftness, and blew up a two-arch bridge, making a gap of twenty-five feet. To prepare for the attack on Amman there was considerable movement at Es Salt, where constant vigilance was necessary in view of the ease with which reinforcements could be moved from the neighbourhood of Nablus to the town in the hills. The two battalions of the 181st Brigade who were picketing the hills on the north of Es Salt were released to rejoin their brigade by battalions of the 179th Brigade, and a further battalion was brought up from Howeij. The wisdom of this movement was seen later in the day when the 1st Light Horse Brigade reported that 1000 enemy infantry with two guns were moving east of the Jordan along the Jisr ed Damie-Es Salt road, and that another 500 infantry were holding a position south-east of and covering the Damie ford. Two Royal Horse Artillery batteries were moved up in support of the Light Horse.

The attack on Amman was timed to begin early in the afternoon. The 181st Brigade was to operate with its right on the Sweileh-Amman road with the 2nd Australian Light Horse on both its flanks, while the Imperial Camel Brigade moved farther south. The task of the New Zealand Mounted Rifles Brigade was to assault from the south the bold hill known to us as 3039, a big feature overlooking the town. The 2/23rd Londons and the 2/21st Londons began their advance over exposed ground. Despite heavy shell fire they went forward 1000 yards, but were then held up by intense machine-gun fire and rifle fire from the lower slopes of a convex hill. The 2nd Light Horse Brigade on the left and the camelry on the right were pinned down by strong opposition, and the infantry could not get on without co-operation on the flanks. The New Zealanders, after gaining some ground on Hill 3039, were held up by machine-gun fire, and at this time the enemy heavily counter-attacked on the northern flank and caused the Light Horse to yield some ground. Our right was also heavily shelled and twice counter-attacked. General Chaytor at dusk decided to go on with the attack next morning, but later on postponed a renewal of the attack till the following night.

Not merely were the heavy rains a source of trouble and difficulty to the troops on the Moab Plateau. They were giving a lot of anxiety to the engineers by the banks of the Jordan. The flood water which was beginning to subside when Nimrin was taken, again came down with tremendous force, showing that the head waters of the Jordan had been heavily reinforced by the numerous wadis carrying to it the rains from the hills. To get away a despatch I had occasion to cross the river on the 28th. The stream had swollen to big dimensions. It overflowed the banks, and a causeway had to be made of scrub and trees covered with soil to enable supply vehicles get from a bridge through the flood. This causeway was 900 feet long, and in making it and keeping it from being washed away engineers and infantry had to work most arduously. Twice while I was waiting to cross I was told my Ford car might have to halt till the following day, but well-applied energy set matters right, and I not only got over myself but saw a heavy armoured Rolls-Royce battery go across the river. There was only one bridge open at this; period, and, the river having risen nine feet in a few hours, so much driftwood and timber was coming down that men had to be stationed in each pontoon to divert the logs and rubbish beneath the bridge and prevent a jam. The steel pontoon bridge at Hajlah had had to be dismantled as it could not be used in the existing state of the Jordan. There was another anxiety arising from the threat of more reinforcements from the direction of Nablus, and while every additional mouth to feed on the east of the Jordan meant more difficulties to the supply branch, a battalion of infantry—the 2/20th Londons—and a light armoured-car battery were sent north from Nimrin to strengthen the force of Light Horse under General Cox. As if knowing this the enemy air force despatched thirteen aeroplanes to drop bombs on Nimrin just as the sun was going down, and these caused 130 casualties among animals and killed two officers of the 301st Field Artillery Brigade, including Major Beck, who was one of the two officers present when the Mayor of Jerusalem went out on the high road near Lifta to surrender the city on December 9.

During the morning of March 29 enemy reinforcements were seen arriving at Amman station. At this time there was a gap between the 181st Brigade's left and the 2nd Light Horse Brigade and, the enemy discovering it, tried to get round the infantry's left flank, but though the situation was acute all our positions were retained throughout the day. Information from what was regarded as a reliable source led to the belief that the enemy would evacuate Amman during the night of March 29-30, and orders were issued for a general attack at 2 a.m. In the meantime there was continuous sniping against our positions covering Es Salt, and a strong attack on one post was driven off. A battalion from the 53rd Division at Kakun was sent over the Jordan to relieve the 2/20th Londons with the 1st Light Horse Brigade. The night attack on Amman began at 2 a.m. on March 30 in a pitiless downpour of rain. We ascertained afterwards that it was quite unexpected, but the enemy proved very stubborn and fought with grim determination. By half-past four the New Zealand Mounted Rifles brigade had taken part of

Hill 3039, capturing six machine guns, but they could not drive the enemy off the eastern and northern ends of the hill. On the left of the New Zealanders the Imperial Camel Brigade took two lines of trenches and some prisoners, and the 181st Brigade made a substantial advance during which the 2/22nd Londons captured 135 prisoners and four machine guns before the break of day, but they had not reached their objective, which was the wadi Amman, north of the citadel. The 2/18th Londons between the 2/22nd and the Camelry got within half a mile of the Citadel but were then stopped by heavy frontal fire. Again and again the enemy endeavoured to break round the left of the brigade. There were frequent attacks against the 2/21st Londons, and both sides met repeatedly with the bayonet, but the Turks were always driven off, and they must have suffered heavy losses here. Some New Zealanders succeeded in getting into Amman at nine o'clock, but they found troops in the houses and had to come out again. The camelry could not move because of enfilade machine-gun fire from both flanks, though they were assisted by the Royal Horse Artillery battery which had left Nimrin the previous day and had made a meritorious march. Before midday the Turks tried to drive the New Zealanders off Hill 3039, but their counter-attack, though vigorously launched, was caught by our artillery, and shell fire dispersed it. At three o'clock there was a fresh attempt to take the Citadel. After a bombardment the 2/18th Londons rushed forward to within four hundred yards of the ancient square walled building, but once more the Turkish machine-gunners were so placed as to enfilade the advance and it was stopped. At sundown the New Zealanders on 3039 were heavily shelled, and prisoners telling of strong enemy reinforcements, a general withdrawal during the night was decided on, the 2nd Light Horse Brigade, the Royal Horse Artillery battery, and the 2/13th Londons taking the road through Es Salt, and the remainder travelling over a track which had been put into some sort of order by infantry of the 179th Brigade. To make the supply situation somewhat easier, the Imperial Camel Brigade retired on Nimrin the same night.

It had not been all clear sailing at Es Salt. The Turks were rushing forward strong reinforcements. We discovered later from captured documents that the Turkish High Command were furious at the evacuation of the place, for they had the idea—and once that idea was rooted in their minds General Allenby worked on it with consummate skill—that if and when we attempted to march on Damascus we would take the route of the Hedjaz line, and not the route chosen in the early autumn. The Turks wanted Es Salt at all costs, and prisoners told us they had 2000 reinforcements in the neighbourhood of Kefr Hudr. A battalion of the 180th Brigade was sent to be at the disposal of the Brigadier of the 179th, but beyond a midnight attempt to rush a post near the town the enemy did not attempt any hostile action. Nevertheless there was considerable anxiety at Es Salt, and if the Turks had attacked boldly they could have done a good deal of damage, and the retirement across the Jordan would not have been accomplished without severe losses. The 181st Brigade was diverted to the track through Sweileh to Es Sir because the Fuheis road proved so bad as to be unfit for infantry. Es Sir was reached at midnight on the 31st, and the infantry tramped on all through the night under most unpleasant conditions of weather and country. The track was almost impassable for animals in the darkness and rain, and the 2nd Light Horse Brigade which covered the withdrawal had a very trying time. When the New Zealand rearguard was passing through Ain es Sir the Circassians in the village made a treacherous attack upon them. Some people in a stone house had waited till the main body was out of sight and then fired into the backs of the rearguard, killing a popular officer and inflicting a dozen casualties. The New Zealanders exacted a speedy retribution. They wheeled about and galloping up to the house, surrounding it, compelled every armed man to come out. They were not soldiers at all. There were thirty-six of them and they died on the spot.

The 179th Brigade withdrew from Es Salt without incident after blowing up all the Turkish ammunition, and destroying nearly thirty German lorries and many transport waggons which the enemy had been obliged to leave behind. The brigade left Es Salt at night, and it had concentrated in the Jordan valley at dawn. The 180th Brigade was on El Haud and Tel el Musta to deal with any possible interference by the enemy, but the Turks did not face them and throughout the 2nd April there was a wonderfully orderly procession of troops over the river to the west bank of the Jordan, the only troops remaining on the east side of the river at midnight being the 180th Brigade, which formed the bridgehead at Ghoraniyeh until the 1st Australian Light Horse relieved them. As an illustration not merely of the stability of the bridges but of the good traffic order at the crossings, it may be stated that 30,000 animals, two brigades of infantry and two brigades of cavalry, many guns, limbers, lorries, and cars passed over the bridges during daylight without trouble or accident. Colonel Thompson, the officer of the Royal Engineers in charge of the bridges (I think he was formerly our military attaché at Bucharest), had pointed out to me the strength of his men's work when the river was in high flood, and there could have been no prouder man in the Army than he when he saw the bridges withstand an altogether exceptional strain on that arduous day in April. Swelling the column were a number of the Christian inhabitants of Es Salt. They had welcomed our men with heartfelt enthusiasm, but at the moment of the withdrawal certain Mahomedan elements in the town had indicated that revenge was in store,so to prevent massacre a large party was brought away with our troops and for months all were well cared for in the neighbourhood of Bethany and Jerusalem. On the way down the pass from Es Salt enemy airmen bombed them, and a woman gave premature birth to a child. Some humane Anzacs gave the contents of their water bottles (which they could ill spare) to wash the infant, and the mother and her offspring had a softer bed in a limber with soldiers' coats to cover them than in the rude dwelling left behind at the top of the pass.

During these operations 1886 wounded and sick cases were evacuated from the east of the Jordan. The proportion of sick was unusually high, but the wet weather and the intense cold of the nights accounted for it. The Army medical branch can point with satisfaction to the fact that within forty-eight hours of the order to withdraw from Amman all the sick and wounded had left Nimrin for Jerusalem. Our casualties during the twelve days from the forcing of the passage of the Jordan till the withdrawal to the west bank were: 60th Division, 40 officers and 584 other ranks, and Anzac Mounted Division and Imperial Camel Brigade, 53 officers and 671 other ranks killed, wounded, and missing. A conservative estimate of the enemy's casualties was 400 killed and 1000 wounded. In addition we took 986 prisoners, of whom 61 were Germans. Four guns, 13 machine guns, 5 automatic rifles, 269 rifles, 24,800 rounds of small-arms ammunition, 2316 rounds of gun ammunition were taken, and 5 motor cars, 25 motor lorries, and 1 aeroplane destroyed.

As I have said, the full object of the raid was not achieved. The force set out to destroy a tunnel and viaduct south of Amman and the railway for some distance north and south of that town. All these things were not attained, but considerable destruction was effected. North of Amman two arches of a bridge were blown up and the central pier shattered. The demolition party south of Amman destroyed four and a half miles of railway track, and three large and three small culverts. The crossing and points at Alanda station were also put out of action. The Turks had had a great deal of experience in repairing their line, and with the material available the railway should have been reopened for traffic in a few days. But there were many stoppages in the work caused by the bombs of our airmen. The raid unquestionably assisted the Emir Feisal's arm about Maan, because the Turks, realising that we could cross the Jordan whenever General Allenby chose, were forced to maintain a larger army about Es Salt, and they could only do this by withdrawing some of their troops who were operating against the Arabs. In this Amman enterprise some assistance was expected from the army of the King of the Hedjaz. As a matter of fact there was no sign of Sherefian troops north of Kerak. We seemed to have more trouble in reconciling the differences of various Arab tribes east of the Jordan than in obtaining their promises of support. For instance the Belga Arabs were quite willing to co-operate with us, but not so ready to help the Sherif. The Christians of Madeba were entirely in sympathy with us, but they had an old feud with the Belgas and were nervous of them. Some of the Beni Sakh tribe did come out, and had a time they had sighed for in sacking Ziza station while we were attacking Amman, but they then retired. They, too, had troubles of long standing with the Belga Arabs.

CHAPTER 6

Over Jordan Again

The situation east of the Jordan continued to demand more consideration than any other portion of the front. If it had not been for the German thrust on the Somme and the withdrawal of some of General Allenby's troops to France, there would have been an attack on the whole front. Preparations for a general advance to the Nablus line were in a forward state, but while General Smuts was still at General Allenby's headquarters the programme for an attack on the whole front was indefinitely postponed because of the Germans' Somme success. It could not be otherwise. The urgent call for reinforcements for France seriously weakened the Palestine Army. All our generals took a calm view of the situation created on the Western Front by the Germans breaking our Somme line and capturing immense quantities of guns and war material. Some of us who were not fully seized of the facts felt that the position was grave in the extreme, but I was reassured by the opinions expressed by some officers of the 20th Corps staff (who, I am proud to remember, were always right in their outlook on the world struggle) that it signified nothing more than the prolongation of the war for a few months. Think what it meant to the Commander-in-Chief and his staff, to the Corps Commanders, the generals of divisions, indeed to every officer and man in the force, to know that all their labour of preparation to knock the Turk out of the war in the early summer was rendered vain by what had happened on the Western Front. They were grievously disappointed They all felt confident of success, and they had reason to be, for upon the foundation of their sound solid work they had built up an army which it would have been impossible for the Turk to stop. Sound in discipline, of high moral, magnificent in physique; thanks to the splendid watchful care of the medical branch and sanitary sections, and wholly efficient the Palestine Army had grown into a mighty force which only awaited the signal to crush the strong barrier of the Turkish lines. No one who was spectator of the Army's work ever had a moment's doubt about its triumph, or if any onlooker had doubts the Army certainly had none. The men's hopes were significant of their enthusiasm. But the Somme changed the situation. It was necessary to send aid to France. If there were disappointments—and there certainly were—no grumbling was heard. Two complete divisions, the gallant, cheery 52nd Lowland Scots, and the sturdy dismounted yeomen of England of the 74th Division, and twenty-five other battalions of white troops, all of them veterans worthy to stand beside the cream of an army, left Palestine for the Western Front, and in their places General Allenby was to receive Indian troops who were only half trained. In these circumstances the Commander-in-Chief for the next few months could only arrange operations on a minor scale compared with the programme he had drawn up in the last months of the winter. It is remarkable he could do as much as he did in the spring. His British effectives sent away were the bulwarks of his force, and until the new arrivals had become efficient there was a doubt whether he could hold the entire line he had won in face of a Turkish army which was being steadily reinforced. As an example of how anxiously G.H.Q. viewed the outlook I will merely refer to the decision to remove the big railway depôt which had been established at Ludd, through which the main line to Jerusalem ran, and to make Junction Station, seven or eight miles farther back, the central depôt.

However, it was important that General Allenby, while temporarily abandoning his general offensive, should give support to our Arab allies. They had to be kept in a proper humour. I should be the last person to minimise the importance of the Emir Feisal's work. Without question the raids of the Arabs on the Hedjaz railway, their constant attention to the Medina Turkish garrison, and the trouble they gave the Turks about Maan, were of assistance to the Palestine Army. For this we have good reason to be thankful to Colonel Lawrence. His is one of the most remarkable and romantic careers in the whole war, and by his steadfastness to the Arab deals, and by his staunch advocacy of British friendship for the Arabs, he kept our allies in Arabia actively championing our cause. But, as I have said, we had to give them support, and we gave it ungrudgingly, even at a time when shortness of men made it important that the Commander-in-Chief should not unnecessarily risk a single life. General Allenby gave help at the moment when many of his white troops were being sent to Alexandria for transport to France. Emir Feisal intended to make an extensive raid on the railway near Maan during April, and to prevent the Turks sending troops to interrupt that enterprise further operations east of the Jordan were arranged. Before going into the details of this important dash over the river I will refer to the shock received by the enemy when he essayed to test our strength at the Ghoraniyeh bridgehead. The bridgehead was held by the 1st Australian Light Horse Brigade whose men had for more than a week been busy wiring themselves in and digging defensive posts within the wire ring. There was plenty of broken ground with low sandhills and scrub to aid the defenders, and the Australians made the fullest use of them. Though much had been done the work of putting the place into a state of defence was not complete when, on the night of April 10, a large body of Turks stole out of Shunet Nimrin to try to break through the bridgehead, to destroy our pontoon bridge, and to wreck the permanent bridge our engineers were building over the river. They had not counted upon the alertness of the Australians or the cost of the attack. In the brigade were many men who had come to Egypt with the first of the Commonwealth's contingents. They had formed the cavalry screen during the long advance across the Sinai Desert into Palestine, and none knew better the need for vigilance against a Turkish night attack. On this night they were wholly ready for the enemy, and they inflicted upon him such terrible losses that he never tried to come near this spot again. The instant the Turks were found outside our wire they were received with a tremendous volume of rifle and machine-gun fire. The night was very dark and favourable for an attack, but all round the bridgehead, which had been well thrown out and formed a wide semicircle, the posts were rapidly reinforced. The Turks did not accept defeat as soon as it was obvious that they had no chance of success. They persisted in their attack in the most stubborn manner with the result that their losses were piled up till out of a force of less than 3000 attacking, quite 2000 were casualties. Once they had got up to our wire it was very difficult for them to retire, as our guns on the west bank of the Jordan put a heavy fire into them and behind them. The Light Horse at daybreak chased the remnant back to Nimrin where they hastily entrenched themselves. A measure of the enemy's losses during the attack may be taken from the fact that 367 dead bodies were found about our wire and there were many bodies in newly-dug graves. The Australians also took 83 prisoners. A good morning's work. The Turks also tried to break through our line at Musallabeh, across the wadi Aujah, a few miles north of Jericho. They attacked under cover of artillery fire, but

SAND SLEDGE USED BY SIGNAL SECTION, ROYAL ENGINEERS

the Imperial Camel Brigade beat them off. Seventy dead lay in front of our trenches and another 120 dead were afterwards seen by our patrols. Our losses at the two places were 23 killed and 73 wounded. The same night the enemy made an effort against the 21st Corps front, but here again they were caught by a fierce artillery fire, and they left 60 dead on one battalion front alone.

Feisal in one raid had destroyed sixty miles of railway south of Maan and nearly captured the town. If the raids over Jordan had done nothing else they,would have achieved a very important object, but they accomplished far more than the dislocation of the Hedjaz railway system. Before we made our first advance on to the Moab Plateau the Turkish forces in Nimrin, Es Salt, and Amman comprised 4000 rifles and sabres; at the time we made our second threat against the railway they had increased to 8500, an edition so substantial as to ease the situation in the Area in which the Arabs were operating. Another reason why we should harass the Turk in this district, even if we did not entirely wrest it from him, was that he drew a considerable portion of his grain supplies from the fertile fields on the uplands. He would have been in a parlous state if this source were denied him. General Allenby wished to start on his second raid about the 20th May, when he would have had a new mounted division organised and ready for the field, but the Beni Sakha tribe sent in a deputation to report that they had concentrated 7000 men at Kabr Abdullah, five miles north of Madeba and about sixteen miles south-east of Nimrin, and if the operations began before the 4th of May they would co-operate, but if the operations were postponed their supplies would be exhausted. General Allenby therefore put forward his date, and used a brigade of the 60th Division instead of the new mounted division. Unfortunately the promise of help from the Beni Sakhas was not forthcoming and they never attempted to do what they promised—close the Ain es Sir-Nimrin track. The right flank of the Army was taken over by Desert Mounted Corps The Corps, which was responsible for the front west of the Jordan from the right of the 20th Corps and for the whole of the front east of the Jordan and Dead: Sea, was made up of the Anzac Mounted Division, the Australian Mounted Division, the Imperial Service Cavalry Brigade, a brigade of the 60th Division, the 20th Indian Infantry Brigade, the Imperial Camel Brigade, the Dead Sea flotilla, the 10th Heavy Battery R.G.A., and the 383rd Siege Battery R.G.A. As a preliminary operation to securing a wide stretch of country included in the parallelogram, Jisr ed Damie-Es Salt-Amman-Kisser station and the Dead Sea, it was proposed to make a start at the end April with clearing the district between Nimrin and Es Salt, the harvest about Es Salt being ready early in May, and if the operations had been fully successful there is little doubt a further advance would have been attempted to Deraa, an important junction on the main line to Damascus. It was a month since our troops had been on the mountains of Moab. Summer comes rapidly in these climes, and in place of low temperatures and rain Desert Mounted Corps troops found a heat that was pleasant. In the Jordan valley the days were very hot, and we had a foretaste of what men would have to endure during the summer in that terrible region from 1000 feet to 1300 feet below sea-level. But at this time the sun had not lifted all the moisture from the ground and there were still some fine flowers and green grasses to please the eye.

The attack began at four o'clock on the morning of April 30, when the Anzac Mounted Division engaged the enemy holding a position on the foothills about Kebr Said, some miles down the valley from Nimrin, while a brigade of the 60th Division attacked El Haud, which was now in a much stronger state of defence than it had been a month earlier. The Anzacs got a good line south of Nimrin, but the Londons, though they soon reached the western slopes of El Haud, found progress very difficult. There were stone sangars and machine-gun nests everywhere, and as fast as the gunners got on to one team another bobbed up in as secure a spot. he Australian Mounted Division moved up the road from Ghoraniyeh to the Damie crossing, and by eleven o'clock had reached the wadi Sidr, where they left the 4th Australian Light Horse Brigade to watch the crossing and to endeavour to prevent reinforcements reaching the enemy from the west of the Jordan. The 1st, 2nd, and 3rd Australian Light Horse Brigades And the 5th Mounted Brigade then turned eastwards and proceeded along the tracks from Umm esh Shert and Damie towards Es Salt. Their rôle was to form a barrier to prevent the enemy retreating, and threaten Nimrin from the north by sending troops down the Es Salt road to beyond Howeij. By night the Australians had men within two miles of Es Salt and they entered the town at four o'clock next morning, capturing 350 prisoners, including 33 Germans. Two brigades were left to hold Es Salt and the 5th Mounted Brigade and the 2nd Light Horse Brigade moved south-west to attack Nimrin from the east and north-east.

So far matters were going well with this portion of the force, but down in the valley there was a situation of considerable difficulty. During the night about 4000 enemy of their 3rd Cavalry Division and part of the 24th Infantry Division had got across the river at the Jisr ed Damie crossing and had forced back the 4th Light Horse Brigade holding our left flank. There was very hard fighting all the morning, and while the mounted men yielded ground slowly they were compelled by the weight of opposition to retire a considerable distance. The left of the brigade was driven in, and the enemy got on to the north and south road leading to Ghoraniyeh, but the Light Horse came back through the foothills of the mountains to a position covering the Umm esh Shert road. The country was terribly broken, and the three batteries of Royal Horse Artillery with the brigade were in such bad ground that they lost nine out of their twelve guns; and a light armoured car, a general service waggon, and four ambulance waggons were also lost. The retirement was well conducted against overwhelming odds, but the flank had been left too weak. An inquiry was subsequently held into the loss of the guns and the failure to render them unserviceable. It is but justice to the gunners to say they were completely exonerated. The batteries concerned were 'A' and 'B' batteries of the H.A.C. and the Notts battery R.H.A. Major Allen, the officer commanding the artillery brigade, reported that there never was a question of the permanent destruction of the guns as there was always the possibility of a counter-attack by the Corps reserve whose dust could be seen moving north. The gunners had been practically without sleep for forty-eight hours. On the morning of the retirement they had fired over 200 rounds per gun, and for nearly five hours they had fought a running fight in full view of the enemy, always under shell fire and mostly under rifle fire. They came into action for the last time under decisive rifle and machine-gun fire, and at this point so many horses had been killed and wounded that they proceeded to help the fallen drivers and to assist to extricate the teams. Three officers were wounded, one of them mortally. In these circumstances Major Allen submitted that the value of the services of the 19th Brigade R.H.A. should be considered to outweigh by far their oversight in not completing the removal of the breech fittings.

> I even venture to claim that had it not been for the action of the artillery the 4th Australian Light Horse Brigade might have been forced to withdraw to Es Salt, and the enemy might quite possibly have closed all exits from the hills to the Jordan valley.

General Chauvel expressed the opinion that all ranks behaved with the greatest gallantry and were of the highest assistance in the withdrawal of the 4th Australian Light Horse Brigade. Needless to say the gunners were very gratified to receive the following high opinion of their work from General Allenby:

> After making full inquiry into the operation of May 1, the Commander-in-Chief wishes to congratulate the 19th Brigade R.H.A.—'A' battery H.A.C., 'B' battery H.A.C., and Notts battery R.H.A.—on their conspicuous gallantry and devotion to duty. The Commander-in-Chief is convinced that the R.H.A. were not to blame for the loss of the guns or for the failure in part to destroy them.

Reinforcements were quickly forthcoming to relieve an anxious situation. By noon the Turks must have known they could not get farther south, and that their hopes of reaching the Umm esh Shert road and, of closing an exit which our force in Es Salt would have to take if Nimrin and El Haud were not captured, could not be realised. I was in the western valley of the Jordan at the time, and looking across the river there was abundant evidence that we were checking the advance. By several tracks columns of General Chaytor's horsemen were raising high pillars of dust as they hurried to assist their comrades, and early in the afternoon the long lines of camel transport, which had halted pending the clearing up of the situation, were on the way to supply the troops fighting about Es Salt. Emboldened by their partial success in the valley, the Turks on El Haud and at Nimrin put up a strong resistance. The infantry could do little against El Haud. The 180th Brigade had been depleted in numbers by several months' hard fighting, and it was as much as they could do to hold the enemy to his position. They were magnificently supported by the artillery of the 302nd R.F.A. brigade. At one point a company gave ground, and Lieut. Geoffrey Bridgeman, a youth of nineteen who had received a decoration for gallantry during a strenuous time which ended in the capture of Jerusalem, called on them for a rally. This young officer had been shelled and shot at for two days and was left with a signaller in a sangar, but he crawled down a steep hill and rallied forty men, and with shouts of 'Follow the artillery!' led the men back to reoccupy the trenches. All the batteries were registered and shelled by enemy guns, but although the gunners were for days bombarding the Turkish trenches, the infantry were not strong enough to storm the heights, which were manned by a superior number of the enemy and protected by machine guns.

The mounted troops which had marched down the Es Salt road

were held up about Howeij. The six regiments holding Es Salt had to withstand attacks from the direction of Damie, and on the east by two battalions which had detrained at Amman, whilst other cavalry and infantry were seen moving on the town from the direction of Amman. During the night and early on the morning of May 3 the attacks about Es Salt were renewed several times, but the Australians were as sound in defence as they were alert and determined in attack, and not only did they repulse the enemy with heavy losses, but the 2nd regiment of Light Horse captured 314 prisoners including nine officers. At ten o'clock the enemy had an element of success, for during the fighting around the north and east of Es Salt he managed to take the village of Kefr Huda, about two miles to the north-east of the town. Strive as they might the brigade of the 60th Division could not open the Nimrin-Es Salt road, and it became obvious that the enemy had a road available through Ain es Sir which should have been closed by the Beni Sakha tribe. The enemy forces had been considerably increased during the day by reinforcements coming down this road from Amman. A division was also known to have left the neighbourhood of Nablus, and other troops were moving from farther north into the Es Salt area.

The Commander-in-Chief therefore ordered Es Salt to be evacuated. We had not held the town itself but had established ourselves in the outskirts, so that when we withdrew the Turks should have no ground for wreaking their vengeance on the few Christian inhabitants remaining there. Es Salt was evacuated on the night of May 3. The retirement was an able piece of work. Throughout the dark hours the available track, a narrow, precipitous path, was full of troops and animals, but nothing was left behind, and on the following day the whole force was again on the west of the Jordan excepting the men holding the bridgeheads at Ghoraniyeh and Aujah fords. We were constructing a new bridge at the latter place. Our casualties in these operations were less than 1300 all told. The Turks undoubtedly lost heavily in killed and wounded, and in addition we took from them 46 officers and 885 other ranks prisoners, among them 47 Germans.

As neither of the raids over the Jordan had been completely successful, it was important to consider what effect they had had on the Arabs. They were; regarded by them merely as raids with the primary object of drawing off enemy troops from the Maan area. In this they unquestionably succeeded, and as the Arab likes to have ocular demonstration to support what he is told, there is no doubt he was satisfied with the result of the operations. But after the second raid General

Allenby told the Emir Feisal that for the present he should undertake n operations on a large scale east of the Jordan, though he would be prepared to assist him by further raids if he brought his force up to Madeba. The Turkish High Command held the view that General Allenby would not advance west of the Jordan until he had secured his flank by the capture of Amman. They therefore kept a whole army facing our troops in the Jordan valley, leaving the extreme right of their line comparatively weakly held.

There was a good deal of hard and successful fighting in the sector of the 20th Corps astride the Nablus road, and in the line held by the 21st Corps from the western fringe of the Judean hills to the Mediterranean, but instead of taking this battling for positions in chronological order I will complete the story of the summer work in the Jordan valley. Here in a country where few white men have lived during the summer, a large number of white troops endured the agonies of awful heat and blinding sun, with the air so hot and dry at night that a shirt washed at midnight was bone-dry at daybreak. There were scorpions, tarantulas, centipedes, and snakes. The horned viper bit some men and I heard we had deaths from snake bites. The heat was so frightful that it killed the flies. During August the Turks, who never believed it possible that white soldiers of the King could occupy the Jordan valley in the hot months, sent over an aeroplane to drop a message: 'This month flies die; next month men die.' That would have been true had we not taken sanitary precautions. All through the summer troops who were not in the line had little rest. They searched for pools of stagnant water, drained them, and oiled them to suffocate in their breeding places all malaria-carrying insects. They travelled far to rout out the pests, and a comparatively low sick rate was the reward. The heat was responsible for most of the sick cases, and it was absolutely necessary to make frequent changes in the troops holding the Jordan valley line. As a rule three weeks was considered the limit beyond which men could not remain in the torrid heat without serious risk to their health, and they were then brought up to the sweeter atmosphere of the south of Bethlehem, where good water and an invigorating breeze again made them fit. During July and August I did not spend a night in the valley but I was there several times in the heat of the day. It was dreadfully oppressive and I never came out of it without a violent headache. The Dead Sea flotilla of motor boats, the transport drivers who suffered from choking dust as well as from the heat and whose work was much harassed by enemy bombs from the air, had a bad time, but so did everybody whose duty pinned him to the Jordan.

SUPPLY TRAIN RUNNING FROM NILE TO KHARGA OASIS

It was somewhat of a relief from the trials of the climate when the enemy decided to take action There were numbers of small nibblings at our line| and probably we should have had to resist several big attempts if the one major effort made by the enemy had not ended in absolute disaster. He did not get over the severe thrashing he received, and nothing would make the Turk try again. During the second and third weeks in June the Turks largely reinforced their lines on both sides of the Jordan valley, and we ascertained their numbers rose in a week from 10,600 to 14,125 rifles, and that their cavalry and machine guns had also increased considerably. This indicated a pending operation, and we heard from prisoners and deserters that the. enemy proposed to attack us on the Nablus road and in the Jordan valley during the period of the Feast of Bairam. The Anzac Mounted Division held our northern line in the valley on the 13th of July, and they sent in reports of an unusual movement of the; enemy equipped with pack transport throughout the day, whilst their artillery was active about Musallabeh, our northernmost position 4000 yards from the wadi Aujah. Musallabeh was a very important point of defence. It was on the ancient road built by the Romans from Jericho up the valley to the Jordan fords, and was quite close to the branch road made by the same famous road engineers for traffic up the Steep hills into the heart of Judea. We knew that the Turks were thirsty and that their water situation was getting desperate. The wadi Aujah would have satisfied them, and their attack of July 14 was really a fight for water in the Aujah, though Jericho was their objective. Little did they know what was in store for them.

To appreciate what occurred during the attack one must understand the nature of the ground and the position and character of our defences. North of the Aujah was a series of mounds in the form of a triangle. The apex, Musallabeh, was 4000 yards from the wadi, and Abu Tellul left and Abu Tellul right formed the base, about 1000 yards from the stream. Some 1000 yards south-east of Musallabeh was the knob of Maskerah, a little east of the road, while on the western side of the triangle were hillocks named by us Vyse, Vale, and View, the latter nearly 1000 yards north-west of the left Abu Tellul. Five hundred yards due west of View post was a defended position on Vaux, and inside the triangle about half a mile south-south-east of Mussalabeh stood a bold mound called the Bluff. The tiny garrison of twelve men on the Bluff played an important part in the operations of that day. These were the positions the enemy set out to take. It was to be a first-class show, And the plan of attack suggested that there was a good deal of window-dressing in the scheme. The Turks and Germans were not getting on very well together. The Turks had not seen any large proportion of the available Germans in the front line, but now the dictators were going to show how the soldiers of the Fatherland could do things. Three battalions of German infantry were to carry out the attack, the 702nd and 703rd Infantry and the 11th Jagers; the 53rd Turkish Division was to operate in the Mellehah district nearer the Jordan, and the 24th Turkish Division was to support the main attack. The Turks had been told by the Germans that the Australians and New Zealanders were all sick in hospital in Jerusalem, and that they would not find any of them in the trenches, but when the show was over the few Turkish prisoners in our hands cursed the Germans as lying dogs. They had learned their cost that the Australians and New Zealanders were sitting very tight and were the hardest men in the world to move when they decided to stay where they were. During the night a long-range gun which Desert Mounted Corps christened Jericho Jane fired from a distance of 20,000 yards into Jericho but did little damage. The first news of the approaching attack was given at half-past one by the 3rd Light Horse regiment, which discovered an enemy movement in a wadi between View and Vale posts All the posts had wire round them, but no attempt had been made to connect the posts by wire, and the work of the morning was a complete justification of the system of leaving gaps, where posts were adequately wired in.

At half-past two the posts and back areas were heavily shelled, and enemy who had been massing in the wadi broke through between Vale and View having many casualties on the way. The troops on Vale post were obliged to fall back after the enemy had passed, and they occupied Abu Tellul left. View was entirely surrounded and Vaux post was attacked with vigour from the west. Vyse, Musallabeh, and Maskerah were entirely cut off and for the time being were out of communication. General Cox immediately ordered a counter-attack, but before this was organised the Germans had gained Abu Tellul and had secured a footing on the Bluff. As already mentioned, a troop of one young officer and twelve men belonging to Colonel Bourne's Light Horse regiment was stationed on the Bluff. Six of them were hit, but the remainder held out very finely against great odds. They fought with magnificent determination and severely defeated several determined attacks, a Hotchkiss rifle accounting for many Germans. The counter-attack on Tellul began at half-past four by squadrons of the 1st and 2nd regiments of Light Horse, and in half an hour the hill was regained. At daybreak the Germans found the Turks had not supported them and that, unable to establish themselves in any post, they were being attacked in front, while machine guns in posts behind them threatened their retirement. A few surrendered, but it was not until the Australians, supported by the Notts battery and 'B' battery H.A.C., had cleared the slopes of the Bluff and relieved the garrison, taking over a hundred prisoners, that the Germans gave a general signal to submit. The pressure on Vaux post was continued till nine o'clock, when a squadron of the Wellington Mounted Rifles galloped the enemy and the whole position was restored. Our casualties were 2 officers and 33 other ranks killed, and 10 officers and 95 other ranks wounded. We captured 285 German prisoners, of whom 9 were officers, and 67 Turks. The best of evidence of the severe nature of the German casualties was that of a letter written by a prisoner of the 702nd battalion, who said: 'We had very heavy losses and I should imagine that the Asia Corps has practically ceased to exist.'

The enemy had had another bad time of it east of the Jordan. A feint was made to try to deceive us that the Turks were attempting to seize our crossing at Hajlah ford, and so turn our position in Jericho. It was realised at the outset that this was a demonstration, but effective measures were taken to deal it. Between 400 and 500 Turkish cavalry took up a position 1500 yards east of the Jordan with their left about 2000 yards north of the Dead Sea. We held the river at this point with Imperial Service Cavalry, and farther north were more Imperial Service Cavalry and a mixed mounted brigade of yeomanry and regular Indian cavalry. General Barrow ordered one regiment of Imperial Service Cavalry to charge the Turks from the south, and a yeomanry regiment to charge them from the north. The Sherwood Rangers had the latter duty, but it was unfortunate for them that a deep wadi quite impassable for cavalry separated them from the enemy, and they had to halt within a hundred yards of the Turks' flank without reaching them. The Jodhpur Lancers made a splendid charge from the south and, getting well in with the lance, speared sixty and took thirty-five prisoners, including the commanding officer. The Turks cleared off into the foothills and did nothing that day to prevent the Corps reserve moving to resist the more serious attack on the other side of the wadi Aujah. One good result of the day's operations was to increase the ill-feeling existing between Germans and Turks. The German prisoners expressed great contempt for the Turks because they had not supported them, and their wrath was particularly directed against the 53rd Turkish Division which had done practically nothing against Mellehah. On the other hand the Turks made no secret of their view. This, they said was a German plan of attack. They never believed in it, and never gave it approval. So the good work went on. The Commander-in-Chief marked his gratification at the fine defence of Musallabeh and the charge at Hajlah by sending the troops the following message:

> The Commander-in-Chief heartily congratulates the Australians and New Zealanders who took part in yesterday's successful operations. He also sends congratulations to Sir Pertab Singh and the Jodhpur Lancers on their exploit.

Sir Pertab Singh happened to be in Palestine on a visit to Indian troops at the time of his regiment's charge, and the gallant old warrior was pleased indeed that his men had had an opportunity of adding to the glory of their race and their regiment.

,

CHAPTER 7

Fighting in the Judean Hills

We must now move to the front held by the 20th Corps in the jumble of rugged, rocky hills through which the road from Jerusalem passes north to Nablus Long before events on the Western Front compelled General Allenby to give up part of the force he had brought to such a high state of efficiency, the 20th Corps was preparing to force the enemy out of successive lines of mountains which barred our progress northwards. The country immediately in front of the Corps was the most difficult in Judea. Right and left of the road there was a succession of high hills with precipitous sides and deep sinuous valleys. The slopes of the hills were sometimes clothed with olive-trees, others were terraced where natives could scrape together some earth to yield a crop, but many of the hills, especially on the eastern side of the road, had faces of bare rock relieved only at wide intervals by vegetable growth. Flat open spaces were extremely rare, and it was clear that, unless for some unaccountable reason the Turk abandoned his stubbornness in defence, progress was bound to be slow. The enemy had an enormous number of machine guns. There were boulders everywhere to shelter a machine-gun crew, and nothing but a direct hit could dislodge them. One gun properly handled could do fearful execution among troops descending a slope and excepting where there was a lot of cover it was found more economical of life to take positions at night than to attempt them in daylight. If the infantry had difficulty in moving it was harder still for artillery, and the problem of getting supplies to the advancing line was a never-ending one, although engineers and every infantryman in reserve were occupied in making roads and tracks whenever an advance of a few hundred yards was achieved. The 10th (Irish) Division proved themselves wonderful pioneers. They had harder work than any other infantry, not only because they had longer distances of track to prepare, but because they were in an area without the semblance of a track to work on, and they had to select the sites of their roads before starting on construction. When they were not levelling or using crowbars to lever away boulders they were helping pack transport to find its way to the line, and they fed their front so well that the fighting men frequently had hot tea carried to them in tanks on the backs of donkeys. And it is an eloquent testimony to the work of these road-makers that when after the operations it was arranged to improve the roads, there was very little deviation from the tracks they had cut in the hurry and bustle of battle. Many of these roads were given Irish names; perhaps the names will remain as a record of the sterling efforts made during a period of strenuous fighting.

In the operations which commenced on the night of March 8, Lieut.-General Sir Philip Chetwode, the 20th Corps Commander, aimed at advancing his line from the positions it had won in February to the hill of Mugheir east of the Nablus road, through Sinjil, a lofty village on the road itself, to Jiljilia and Abwein, native villages on high hills to the west of tile road. The advance was on a front of roughly 20,000 yards with a maximum depth of 10,000 yards, and considering the nature of the country and character of the opposition it was a heavy tag Three divisions of infantry were to attack in a northerly direction, and in the Jordan valley the 181st Brigade of the 60th Division, assisted by th Auckland Mounted Rifles, was to occupy a line from Beryudat in the hills to Abu Tellul in the valley north of the wadi Aujah, keeping in touch with the infantry of the main attack by means of mounted patrols. The 1st Australian Light Horse Brigade protected the right flank of the 53rd Division whose objectives were the big obstacles to the east of the Nablus road. The 74th Division were in the centre, and the 10th Division, who were to swing in a north-easterly direction, had the 3rd County of London Yeomanry to watch their left rear. The operations began under unfavourable   conditions. Banks of fog drifted across the front and rendered communication difficult, and from the start there was strong opposition at almost every point. The 231st Brigade got to Selwad just as day was dawning, but the 230th Brigade on their left rear found the enemy full of fight and hanging on to the village of Yebrud with great tenacity. The ground in front of the village was swept by machine-gun fire, and though two strong attacks were launched against it the village was still held fast at daybreak. It fell however, at eight o'clock, and its capture was the signal for resuming the advance.

The Irish Division attacked in two columns. Fog prevented their advancing till daybreak, but by bold and rapid movements they reached their day's objectives, beating down stubborn opposition in many places. The 181st Brigade had a hot time of it in the Jordan valley and did not get Abu Tellul till they assaulted it at three in the afternoon. The 53rd Division was held up for a long time till it won the rocky summit of a hill about a thousand yards from Kefr Malik. Then there was a lot of trouble from 300 to 400 Turks on a hill a couple of miles farther to the eastward, but under cover of an excellent artillery barrage riflemen rushed up the hill and after a few minutes' work with the bayonet the enemy withdrew. Tel Asur, one of the most prominent features in this part of the Judean hills, was very important to us. Its possession would give us a wide field of observation as well as a position of great natural strength. It fell to the 53rd Division. The enemy resisted with the determination of desperate men, and only yielded after the Middlesex battalion, which had distinguished itself on the isolated hill of Obeid on Boxing Day, had given them an example of excellent bombing practice. Then the Turks fled down the reverse slope of the hill, but they did not accept defeat as final till much later in the day, by which time they were reduced in numbers by three futile counter-attacks. In the meantime the Australian Light Horse had crossed the wadi near Deir Jerir, and combined attacks by the 158th and 159th Brigades carried some formidable ridges. But enemy counter-attacks prevented any advance from that position. After taking Yebrud the 74th Division captured Burj Bardiwil, a hill of 2600 feet close to the Nablus road, but the advance was held up because the flanks of the 231st Brigade were left exposed owing to the brigades on the left and right being unable to push ahead. It was found impossible to cross the wadi Nimr which bends round Selwad till darkness had fallen. The dip from the village to the wadi was almost like a cliff face, and the only paths down it were commanded by machine guns, lo the advance was postponed till night. The 31st and 30th Brigades of the 10th Division got Attara and Ajul by noon, but they had much difficulty in bringing their guns up the Bir es Zeit road owing to the enemy's shell fire. The 29th Brigade did not have much opposition and secured Neby Saleh and a number of other villages. On the following day there was very severe fighting, and the Turk maintained his reputation as a sound fighter behind sangars. However, he met his match and there was substantial progress everywhere.

The dismounted yeomanry of the 74th Division especially distinguished themselves. On the 10th of March their endurance and condition were put to severe test. To gain any ground meant stout fighting, but beyond that they had to negotiate hills the descent from which was as difficult as the ascent and all the time the enemy rained shells and machine gun bullets on them. The 74th gave more than they received, and they forged ahead faster than position of the troops on their right flank really warranted. But by biting into the enemy's centre they helped their comrades on the right and made the Turks very watchful of their rear. During the night the dismounted yeomen took the ridge Lisaneh after a hard climb and some hand-to-hand fighting, and at once established themselves firmly. Between 3 a.m. and daybreak the enemy mad three counter-attacks, but the yeomen always had the winning hand and the Turks left a bloody trail behind them. It was the 230th Brigade that took the ridge. They could only move slowly on its northern slope, but once on lower ground they made a dash across the Nablus road where it takes a right hand turn between a fork in the wadi Jib, and advanced rapidly towards two hills south of Salhat. The farthest of the hills was a desperate nut crack. It had steep high terraces, in climbing which each man had to help another. For a long time this mountaineering was carried out under the fire of machine guns, but the brigade persisted in the attack, and, after guns had been brought up to shell the crest, the boys from English shires carried the top in a triumphant rush and made the hill theirs. Without staying to rest they cheerfully obeyed the order to press on to attack Salhat, which was soon taken. Not satisfied with this success the same brigade turned their attentions to two hills 1500 yards or more to the eastward and both covering the road. They had to fight hard for the more northern of these heights, but on occupying it they found the gunners who were supporting them had made such excellent shooting on the other hill that the Turks had fled. The right of the 10th Division had found the wadi Jib a big obstacle. The sides of the hills down to the edge of the wadi were terraced and there was no track, whilst opposite them the enemy were posted in strong positions. The left brigade, however, crossed the wadi about a mile east of Deir es Sudan in the morning and the 31st Brigade got close to Jiljilia before midday, but the enemy made it plain he intended to make a stand north of the wadi, and every movement on our side was received with a torrent of machine-gun fire, the weapons being placed in posts from which an enfilade fire could be poured on to both flanks. A concerted attack was arranged for 3 p.m., when a hot barrage put down by the gunners enabled the 31st Brigade to advance past Jiljilia in a line due east of Abwein. At 7 p.m. the Turks delivered a fierce attack on the left wing of the 30th Brigade at Neby Saleh, and for four hours the steadiness of the Irish troops was submitted to a supreme test. The enemy came to within one hundred yards of the line, but a terrific fire from Lewis guns prevented any further advance and the Turks were driven off at 11 o'clock. They continued very active and being reinforced, delivered another attack on Neby Saleh at 9 p.m. which was broken up with the assistance of the 74th divisional artillery.

If the 53rd Division had not been able to go far forward they had made some progress, and a particularly good piece of work was done by the 159th Brigade in capturing a rugged ridge east of Kefr Malik, which permitted patrols to enter that village at two o'clock. During the next night the 53rd Division made a substantial advance, and by 9 o'clock on the morning of March 11 had crossed the wadi Kola and had established themselves 3000 yards north of it. The 231st Brigade still advancing on the eastern side of the Nablus road had to face desperately bad country in the darkness of the night, and their trials were increased by heavy rain and sticky ground. Nevertheless they managed to get to the tomb of Sheikh Salim, not far from the 53rd Division's advanced post, by 11 o'clock. It was not possible for the 230th Brigade to move, and only after extraordinary exertions were they able to send rations to the men in the line. The 231st Brigade could not drive its attack right home to its objective because the position of the 53rd Division left the right flank open, but about midday the brigade gained touch with the 230th Brigade and began an advance on Turmus Aya, a little village almost abreast of Sinjil. On the flat surrounding Turmus Aya there was no cover and our line had to be withdrawn slightly. When the 230th Brigade got on the move it made a rapid advance, and, though under continuous shell fire, won the ridge overlooking Sinjil from the west, compelling the Turks to abandon that place. The 10th and 74th Divisions were ordered to consolidate the positions gained, the 53rd Division pushing forward again during the night and reaching all their objectives by the morning of the 12th with the exception of Amurieh. We held these positions for months afterwards and there never was a fear that the enemy could break through them. When the operations began the Turks were in as good a situation to resist as they could possibly be, for they intended to take the offensive against us in this sector on the very night after we began. An officer prisoner of the 53rd Turkish Division stated that his division crossed the Jordan on the 8th and was fighting against our right flank. Once more the 20th Corps Commander had forestalled the enemy.

Lieut.-General Sir Edward Bulfin, the 21st Corps Commander,

also made the Turk feel his strong arm. In the second week of April, between the two over-Jordan enterprises, Major-General Palin's 75th Division, which occupied the low stony foot-hills running from the mountains of Judea, carried on operations lasting three days, and secured some positions which the enemy was very unwilling to vacate. General Palin attacked through the wadi Ballut, a watercourse with a deep boulder-strewn bed. His troops were British and Indian, and they acquitted themselves well, especially in beating off many counter-attacks. The whole of the places they set out to obtain were not taken, but they won sufficient to form a strong jumping-off ground for the major operations of September.

Brilliant work was also done in the coastal sector by Major-General Sir V. B. Fane's 7th Indian Division, who won some high ground which gave us splendid observation over the Turkish lines. At the end of May General Fane advanced his line three miles on a five-mile front, but the enemy still held two knolls known as the Twin Sisters. It was decided to eject the Turks from these, and on the 8th June battalions of Seaforth Highlanders and Black Watch crept stealthily up the coast, while Indian troops advancing behind a barrage rushed into the high ground and accounted for all the Turks holding it, capturing 100 prisoners. It was a perfect little operation. From their works at Tabsor the enemy poured a heavy artillery fire into the northern sister, and it became untenable, but as the enemy could not occupy it, it was left as No Man's Land.

The biggest and most complete of all the summer raids was unquestionably that organised by the 20th Corps on the night of August 12-13 against the El Burj-Ghorabeh ridge. This ridge, lying a little to the west of the Nablus road and north-west of Sinjil, was a tremendously strong position, not only because of the difficulty in climbing it and the protection its received from the wadi Gharib which ran immediately in front of it, but because the Turks had built strong sangars throughout its length and had used what was for them a prodigal amount of wire to hold us up. The ridge was 5000 yards long and 2000 yards from our front. The 20th Corps always did things thoroughly, but this operation was as complete as anything done in the campaign, and it was particularly satisfactory because it illustrated how fully the Commander-in-Chief, could rely on his Indian troops. Indeed their fine fighting spirit and perfect discipline afforded as much gratification the Corps Commander and their white comrades the successful accomplishment of a daring venture. In forwarding his report to General Allenby, General Chetwode said:

I wish to point out that the success of the raid was mainly due to Major-General Shea, who drew up the plan for the operation and supervised the training for it. Great credit is also due to Brigadier-General Morris, who was in temporary command of the 10th Division and made the detailed arrangements for carrying out the raid, and to Lieut. -Colonel Wildblood who was in temporary command of the 29th Brigade, for the most efficient manner in which he trained his brigade and conducted the operation.

The work was hall-marked by this commendation of the Commander-in-Chief: 'A first-rate piece of work in preparation and execution,' and there were proud men in the 29th Brigade when this high approval was circulated among them. The 29th Brigade were drawn out of the line on July 20 to train for the operation. Not far from Ramallah an exact replica of the trenches on the ridge had been prepared, photographs taken from the air giving the necessary material for the design, and great pains were taken to keep the men up to a time-table. The scheme provided that the ridge should be attacked by two columns, one assaulting each end of the position. Behind each column other troops were to march, and when the columns had attacked and gained the positions on the flanks of the ridge the rearmost troops were to pass through the columns and, turning inwards, were to advance along the ridge and clear all the trenches on it. The operation was to be carried out under a heavy artillery fire by the guns of two divisions, supplemented by the 20th Corps' heavy artillery and one brigade of mountain artillery. On the night of August 12 the moon set at a quarter to ten, and as it was quite light by 5 o'clock, and as the whole raid had to be performed in the dark and the troops brought back to camp before daylight, very little time was available. Special boots with felt soles were issued to the troops who carried electric torches, materials for marking out roads, and the essential wire-cutters. The columns were to move ten minutes after the moon had gone down, but slightly before that they had moved out to their positions of deployment, any sound they might make being drowned by a gun on either flank which fired a round every fifteen seconds prior to the minute fixed for the start.

At five minutes to ten there began a bombardment of great intensity, and some of us at G.H.Q. that night, who were not aware of the nature of the operation—it was kept very secret—watched the flashes behind the black line of hills with interest and, wonder.

It was a remarkable spectacle. The artillery programme was carried out without a hitch, as the artillery work generally was in the Palestine Army. They were very efficient gunners, and remembering that some of them had only learned the art of gunnery in face of the enemy, one formed the impression that the field of battle was the best ground for instruction. The artillery's task was to bombard the ridge and beyond it so as to cover the enemy's lines of retreat, as well as to put up a creeping barrage in front of the columns. When the columns had achieved their object by capturing the flanks, the gunners were to move their fire inwards from both ends of the ridge, timing it to be just ahead of the detachments working towards the centre of the enemy's position. This was done to a time-table, and if the guns had been fired by synchronised clocks their work could not have been more perfect. The column on the right was composed of three companies of the 1/54th Sikhs in front and one in reserve. Everybody agrees that the Sikhs advanced with fine determination and dash. They crossed the wire through gaps made by the artillery before the bombardment was lifted and before the enemy machine guns opened fire. On the extreme right the artillery fire had been less effective in wire-cutting than elsewhere, and the leading platoon had fifteen casualties including its leader from machine-gun fire. A havildar who was also wounded led the remainder of the platoon supported by the rest of the company right into the barrage, which caused a slight pause, after which the position was assaulted and a number of prisoners taken. A feeble counter-attack was speedily beaten off. Elsewhere on the right column's front the opposition was not strong, and only a few men and machine-gunners were bayoneted. A subadar with two platoons of the centre company dashed right through into our forward barrage on the reverse side of the position and brought in six prisoners who were trying to escape, and ten animals. A number of other prisoners and ten machine guns were captured by the column. The troops who had to work along the right centre of the ridge were two companies of the 1st Battalion of the Leinster regiment. One cannot give them higher praise than to say they fought like loyal Irishmen. They had followed very rapidly behind the 1/54th Sikhs, and, meeting little fire, they passed through the wire at the same spot as the left company of the Sikhs and rushed the first of the enemy's works, taking a machine gun and some prisoners. The leading company then advanced to the next works where the enemy had been kept more in hand and resisted stoutly, but the position was stormed and prisoners secured. Some

Turkish officers were in dug-outs from which they had to be driven by bombs, and it was not possible to collect their papers. The second company passed, as arranged, through the leading company while the latter was clearing up the captured works and speedily captured the next position, with prisoners and machine guns, and proceeded to their final objective. Everything was taken that could be found and probably nothing of any value was left behind, but as time was short it was not possible to be certain that the whole position completely cleared up.

The left attacking column had a long stiff climb and the ground was so bad that the deployment of the 1/101st Grenadiers was not fully completed when, the guns commenced the bombardment. The Grenadiers hurried on and began the assault with two and a half companies in front and one and a half companies in reserve before the last two platoons arrived. Like the Sikhs they advanced and assaulted with great determination. They dealt with an enemy post of five men on the way and went on so close to our barrage that they often got into it. On their right the Grenadiers found the Turks were unwilling to yield. The wire and the trenches had been badly damaged by our gun fire, but the men holding the trenches did not appear to have suffered much, and as the Indians dashed through the wire they were hotly received by the fire from machine guns. There were casualties, but undaunted by them the Grenadiers went on and took the position after hand-to hand fighting. On the left the high-explosive shells had not done a great deal of damage to the wire which had to be cut before the infantry could pass through it. Two platoons crossed the entanglements at first and rushed into a trench from the flank. The other platoons were soon on their heels and between them the remainder of the position was carried, some prisoners were rounded up, and with one of the captured guns some snipers were suitably dealt with.

The two companies of the Leinsters who were to follow through the Grenadiers, were delayed at the outset by the unavoidable loss of time in deploying the last two platoons of the Grenadiers. The Irishmen had no intention of being late for the show, so they saved time by not waiting for a steady deployment. They passed through the splendid Grenadiers when the latter had taken their works, and were right up to the barrage when they wheeled to the right to advance on the line of sangars. The Leinsters went over the breastworks in a hurry and took prisoners and a machine gun, but the enemy were still very strong and the Irishmen had to yield the position for a little while. Then they retook it with an impetuous dash, and, overrunning the Turks, pressed on to another series of works. As enemy parties were seen approaching, a partial withdrawal became necessary, and after a short wait it was found time would not permit a further advance before the hour arranged for the final withdrawal. This commenced at midnight and was done very rapidly without incident. The troops marched back to their camps clear of all artillery fire, and they arrived at their bivouacs at half-past two contented with a good night's work. Our captures amounted to 239 prisoners, and 80 dead Turks were seen in the positions. The enemy's casualties were estimated at 450 exclusive of those caught in the forward barrage while trying to escape. Thirteen machine guns, one automatic rifle and ten animals were brought back, and after the troops had left the ridge there were two explosions in the centre of the position, due either to the blowing up of ammunition or to the explosion of land mines. Our total casualties were 6 officers and 101 other ranks killed and wounded. Information given by a spy had led the enemy to expect an attack on the ridge between July 22 and 28 and the Turks were on the alert between those dates. Some of their best troops were holding the position. They were part of the enemy's 11th Division which had fought in Gallipoli and the Caucasus before coming to the Palestine front, and their moral known to be relatively high, as, since the division's transfer, there had been very few deserters from it The Turks were completely surprised by the nature of the attack. Their artillery fire was poor—unusually poor—and a certain amount of it was wasted by firing over the centre of the position down to the wadi Gharib. The enemy anticipated that the attack was coming from his front and not from the flanks and when our artillery fire was lifted he made efforts to cover his front with machine guns which were fought well. There were very few attempts to defend the flanks, and our men coming inwards from the flank found the Turks firing to their front which was never threatened. The deployment of the Sikhs and the advance were carried on at the double, and throughout there was no confusion. The Leinsters were always rapid in their movements, and the prisoners said they were on the top of them before they knew what was happening. Of the work of the Indian troops I cannot do better than quote the words of the report:

> They were new to the Division, and the operation afforded a
> good illustration of their value. They showed they could carry

out movements in complete silence, and that they could carry out a complicated operation in the dark with great speed and without confusion. They showed the greatest determination and initiative.

This brilliant little operation was materially assisted by demonstrations on the left and right. The 30th Brigade arranged a small raid and sent out a number of strong patrols which, under cover of an artillery bombardment, approached enemy works and drew fire. On the right the 60th Division made a lot of raids. The 2/19th Punjabis rushed one post on a hilltop and found it deserted. The 2/13th Londons sent parties up the slopes of Norfolk and Beacon hills and drew the enemy's fire. The 3/151st Native Infantry set out to raid Turmus Aya. They found several roads barricaded and defended by machine guns which at first stopped them, but ultimately they reached the southern end of the village. Here they bayoneted six men in a post, took six prisoners in the main street, killed the officer commanding the place, and finally worked on to the northern end of the village, accounting for several Turks in hand-to-hand fighting. There was a raid on Amurieh by the 2/127th Baluchis, supported by two 6-inch trench mortar batteries which inflicted heavy casualties. The batteries fired 311 rounds, the rate of fire averaging twelve rounds a minute, and were of the greatest assistance to the infantry. When the mortar barrage lifted the infantry rushed the trenches, bayoneting men at a machine gun which was captured. Three strong counterattacks from the east were defeated by rifle fire and bayonet, and the Turks sustained serious losses through bombs thrown at them while trying to move up the eastern slopes of the hill. A cadet officer taken prisoner said his regiment, the 78th, had from sixty to seventy killed in this engagement. On Fife and Forfar hills the enemy ran away when the 130th Baluchis approached, and the 2/22nd Londons saw the Turks leave Bidston Hill when they attacked, The 2/152nd Infantry found the enemy well prepared for them on Table Hill, but a detachment of the same regiment bombed the defenders on Keen's Knoll and took prisoners. The total casualties in the 60th Division's raids were 57, and a deserter afterwards gave the information that in the 78th and 59th Turkish regiments there were 120 casualties excluding prisoners.

There were, of course, other raids than those have described in detail. Some of them were quite small affairs, designed rather to agitate the enemy than to inflict on him substantial losses. They served a useful purpose. The Turks were never comfortable, and the feeling of insecurity largely brought about by raids and 'pinpricks,' and the hopeless failure of all their counter-raids, had a great deal to do with lowering their moral. As the summer advanced desertions became more frequent, and, while deserters' tales have always to be discounted, they all agreed the situation in their lines was not happy. Rations were none too plentiful, water was not abundant, and though the Germans saw to that there was an adequate, even generous, supply of ammunition, warlike stores did not compensate for the decline in the spirit of the troops. That had been secured by the repeated successful raids more than by anything else.

CHAPTER 8
Camouflaging an Army

Why Liman von Sanders held the view that General Allenby would make his northward advance by way of the over-Jordan route will puzzle military historians. But we know that it was his belief that there would be no general advance until Amman was captured, and it is certain nothing was done to disturb it in the preparations made by our General Staff for the destruction of the 7th and 8th Turkish Armies in the forward movement commencing in September. The enemy saw nothing of those preparations. They were done in secret and very quietly, and between 100,000 and 200,000 men were kept extremely busy for weeks and yet appeared to be comparatively idle. Staffs were working at high pressure, but you saw nothing of them except at their customary every-day tasks. Unless you were inquisitive and walked into places you had never entered before, you could go along the whole front and see nothing but what you had been accustomed to for months past. There was nothing more on the roads and tracks during the day than was seen in July and June, and there was every appearance of that inactivity and rest proper to the hot season. We might have been in the Doldrums. The beginning of September had passed before I knew that we were close upon one of the biggest movements of troops in the whole history of wars. Even then I did not ask questions, because I was satisfied I should be told in due time. Anyone who appreciates the urgent necessity of keeping the news of an impending offensive within a small circle does not seek information. In the third week of September I was dining with a major-general holding an important position at General Headquarters and he asked me if I had been let into the secret. I replied 'Not yet,' and although all at the table were aware that I knew approximately the date and direction of the attack, not another word was said about it. Indeed it was not until about nine hours before operations were to start that the plan was revealed to me, and I then had to make all arrangements for getting to the best spot from which to see the attack, for provisioning myself and for sending off my despatches. The scheme of operations was in fact known to very few. The enormous amount of movement it involved was observed by no one except the troops concerned, and certainly the civil population behind our lines was absolutely ignorant of it. It was one of the finest examples of camouflage in the whole war and was worthy of the work of the General Staff throughout the campaign.

About a fortnight before the offensive began I wanted to see an officer on the staff of the 60th Division and I went up the Nablus road to find him. There a friend told me in confidence that the Division had moved from the 20th Corps area and was on its way to the coast. I had come up from Ramleh to Jerusalem and was surprised to have met no sign of the division on the road. I suggested that probably the Londoners had gone by the new road via, Beir es Zeit and across the Vale of Ajalon, and my friend replied that if I returned that way and kept my eyes open I would see them. My eyes were wide open and I searched many likely places on my return journey, but I missed the division entirely. There was just the everyday traffic on the road; nothing more. If a division could hide itself on the road, I thought, there was little chance of the enemy discovering it.

The whole plan was built up on the basis of a sudden, swift, unexpected attack coming at a moment when everything in and behind our lines appeared normal, dull, and uninteresting. How very different the situation really was. One complete division had been changed over from the hill country to the plains, three cavalry divisions had come out of the Jordan valley to the coastal sector, and a mass of heavy and field artillery had been brought by road into a new area. In the Jordan valley a pretty piece of camouflage was arranged to deceive enemy aircraft. Just where cavalry had been encamped one saw dummy horse lines and camps looking, doubtless, from the air precisely as they had appeared for months. Four sticks with an army blanket slung between them must have resembled a horse when an observer looked down from an aeroplane skimming above the valley at a height of ten thousand feet, and tents and shelters were left untouched after men had ceased to occupy them. The dummy horse lines answered so well that an enemy air reconnaissance report dated September 17, found among Liman von Sanders' papers at Nazareth, said: 'Far from there being any diminution in the cavalry in the Jordan valley there were evidences of twenty-three more squadrons.' Squadrons of clothes-horses! A cavalry division had long been in Duran, behind G.H.Q., and near by the Imperial Camel Brigade had been encamped for some time undergoing transformation from Camelry into Light Horse. Enemy airmen had seen these camps, but they had not had the opportunity of watching them grow little by little prior to the offensive because we possessed the mastery of the air, and air patrols kept prying eyes away.

In the 21st Corps area the precautions to prevent observation of what was going on were extraordinarily complete. No movement of troops into the area was permitted between half-past four in morning and six o'clock in the afternoon. Upon every man was impressed the importance of absolute concealment so that the enemy should not detect him from the air or from their lines. Special police were mounted by all units to stop movements in concealed bivouacs during daylight. The police carried field glasses, and on the approach of a hostile or doubtful aeroplane blew four blasts on a whistle whereupon every man had to remain absolutely stationary. All ration dumps were kept in the bivouac areas and no fires were lighted, all cooking being done by solidified alcohol to prevent smoke issuing from field kitchens. Horses were generally watered by bucket, but where animals had to be taken from their hiding-places for this purpose strict rule prescribed that this should be done between noon and two o'clock, when the Royal Air Force arranged to have fighting patrols in the air to keep away enemy aircraft. Special roads were made into and out of each bivouac area and none other could be used. No enemy aeroplanes could be fired at from concealed bivouacs, no lights were to be shown at night, and the visits of staff officers and despatch riders were kept down to a minimum. For a fortnight preceding the offensive no new tents were pitched, and all tents then standing were kept up whether occupied or not. When outgoing troops took their bivouac shelters with them, incoming troops had to pitch theirs in the same places. There were open as well as concealed bivouacs. The former were camps which had been in existence for some time. The enemy was accustomed to see these and in them men were allowed to move about freely, except in the case where the size of the camps had been increased by the addition of more troops, when care had to be exercised to prevent the enemy discovering the increase. Concealed bivouacs were usually in orange groves. The greatest precautions had to be taken in the use of telegraphs and telephones, and nothing even remotely connected with operations or movement of troops was mentioned in any message sent by wire. To prevent water shortage there was strict water discipline. Any body of troops which had not completed its march by

CAMOUFLAGE: A DUMMY CAMP

half-past four had to halt under the nearest cover until the evening, and if any column heard a night-flying aeroplane it would halt and remain stationary until the plane had passed.

These regulations were adhered to in the spirit as well as the letter. The men took a sporting interest in them. They were told that the success of the operations depended largely on surprising the enemy, and that it was to their own advantage that the Turks should know nothing of their movements. Troops in the cool shades of the orange groves were encouraged to take rest during the day, and there was rarely an occasion for the police to admonish a man for breaking bounds. So the casual observer saw nothing which would lead him to believe an attack was about to materialise. Spies existed within our lines, no doubt. In a mixed population there were bound to be people who had sympathies for the Turk or who would work in his interest for money. But as far as we could tell they either knew nothing about what was going on or were entirely mystified by it, and civilian spies, if there were any, told the Turks nothing that was of any use at this period. In one portion of the Turkish line, however, they did know something of what was impending. I got the story from an officer on the staff of the 21st Corps who was in Tulkeram former headquarters of the Turkish 7th Army—soon after the 60th Division entered the place, this is the first time it has appeared in print. The officer told me that one of the first documents they had captured was a statement made by an Indian soldier, a religious fanatic, who had deserted to the Turks a few hours before we started to break through. The deserter had given the information that attack was about to take place, but it was received too late to be of any service to the Turkish General Headquarters, for at half-past one in the morning our only Handley-Page, piloted by Koss Smith, the Australian aviator who won the distinction of being the first flying man to navigate a machine through the air from London to the Antipodes, dropped bombs on the signal station at Afuleh and completely destroyed telegraphic and telephonic communication between Turkish Army Headquarters and the front. I was told that not only did we capture the document, but among the prisoners secured at Tulkeram we took the Indian soldier who made the statement. He was shot. Not merely did all the movements of troops towards the coast take place at night for a long time before the concentration was completed, but to deceive the enemy some movements in the opposite direction were carried out in daylight. To complete the camouflage there was an elaborate scheme for turning Fast's Hotel in Jerusalem into a sort of battle headquarters for

General Allenby. The rooms were ordered to be vacated by a certain date and a big signal staff set to work to install telephones In every room, one apartment being arranged as a signal   station. The G.H.Q. camp commandant allotted rooms to members of the staff, and everything was ready for their occupation when the blow fell on the coast. There was some humour in the schemes   devised to deceive all and sundry. A British officer who occupied an important post in the civil administration of Jaffa had secured a desirable residence there, and he proposed to bring his wife to winter in the town. A general, however, told him he should require his house for the winter months, and the officer pointed out how inconvenient it would be to move at the moment. But the reply was that military necessities came first, and the officer, forced to renew his house-hunting, no doubt discussed his difficulty with Jaffa people on his staff, who in turn would talk the matter over with their friends. The same general visited the house of a Jewish gentleman in Jaffa, and, admiring the premises, told the owner he would take them as his winter quarters. The owner vainly pleaded he could not find another place, and then refused to budge, threatening the general that he would have a question asked in the House of Commons about the matter. The general only smiled, and left the householder under the impression that the military would while away the winter under his roof. Here was more food for talk in Jaffa, and when the attack came and thousands of troops (whose presence meant wealth to the Jaffa traders) disappeared into the country a long way north, and among them the general himself, people were astonished at what they thought must be a complete change in the Commander-in-Chief's plans. Still further to encourage the belief that if there was to be an attack it would come on the east, a brigade of the 7th Indian Division left the coast early in September and marched for three days up the Jerusalem road as far as Enab. They marched eastwards by daylight and returned by night. The 3rd and 7th Divisions were converted from wheeled transport to pack transport, and consequently there was considerable movement to and from Ludd, the large depôt at our rail-head. These movements were carried out by day towards Ludd, and by night in the opposite direction. In order to prepare for the advance it was necessary to build four new bridges over the Auja, which empties itself into the Mediteranean four or five miles north of Jaffa. It was hard to build bridges without creating suspicion in the minds of the Turks that they were to be used in a forward movement, but a scheme was devised about six weeks before the attack to establish schools for bridging instruction. One of these operated at Ferekiyeh and the other near Sheikh Muannis, close to the coast, and at both these places it was intended to bridge the river. These schools were continually building bridges and then dismantling them, and finally when the bridges were required they were left in position. Desert Mounted Corps would require two bridges near the mill at Jerisheh, and these were made by the 21st Corps and swung back along the bank of the river where long grasses hid them from any but low-flying aeroplanes.

The 21st Corps held a front from Berukin in the foothills to two miles north of Arsuf, the ancient Apollonia, on the coast, a distance of $25^{1/4}$ miles This was normally held by three divisions. The right division of the corps had to be relieved partly by troops of the 20th Corps and partly by the Détachement Français de Palestine et Syrie, which was placed under the orders of the 21st Corps. General Bulfin, as gallant, chivalrous, and skilful leader of men as any in the British Army, had to solve the problem of concentrating four divisions on a front normally held by his 7th, or left, division, without permitting the enemy to gain knowledge of it. He also had to concentrate a large number of extra guns, make emplacements and store ammunition for all types of guns, as well as to allow of the gradual registration of points by these guns. The 21st Corps' signal branch was called upon to lay an elaborate system of cable communications for artillery and infantry formations, and over thirty miles of motor roads and many miles of roads for other wheeled traffic had to be made. After the roads were constructed they were covered with dried grass and stable refuse to hide them. This organisation was in hand for two months. Most of the work was done at night, but of necessity a great deal of it had to be delayed till the last moment, and the Corps staff had a very strenuous time of it in September. The artillery allotted to the 21st Corps for the operations showed a big increase over the number of guns on the front during the summer, and the fact that many more batteries were brought into the area greatly increased the difficulty of preventing the enemy appreciating the situation. But the measures taken for hiding the guns were successful.

In normal times the guns on the left of the 21st Corps area were: two 6-inch Mark 7., ten 6-inch howitzers, ten 60-pounders, thirty-six 18-pounders, and twelve 4.5 howitzers—total 70. For the operations this number was increased to one 6-inch Mark 7., thirty-eight 8-inch and 6-inch howitzers, sixteen 60-pounders, one hundred and sixty-eight 18-pounders, twenty-eight 13-pounders, forty-eight 4.5 howitzers, and two captured 5.9 guns—total 301. In the hill area there was also an increase, but this was not so marked. For at least six weeks the attack positions were made for these guns, but in order to prevent their detection emplacements were not dug, the positions being merely camouflaged by nets. For several weeks registration was done by single guns or by sections from each battery on days of activity for each division, and by arrangement with G.H.Q. there were periods of activity by the artillery of the whole army. This enabled registration by the guns of the 3rd, 7th, 54th, and 75th Divisions, the 21st Corps' heavy artillery, the mountain artillery brigade, and the Royal Horse Artillery batteries lent by Desert Mounted Corps. Thus only the guns of the 60th Division, the heavy artillery lent by the 20th Corps, and the 9th Mountain Brigade were left to be registered in the last few days. All gun emplacements were occupied on the night of September 17, and care was taken to avoid all movement about the positions in daylight. Machine-gun barrages were registered and arranged and positions constructed by the 7th Division for the divisions coming in, and their work proved of the utmost assistance. Quite a number of raids were carried out to compel the enemy to put down barrages, the positions of which were carefully noted, and maps were circulated to show ground to be avoided or to be traversed rapidly. Without question these maps very materially reduced casualties on the morning of the attack. From prolonged observation, and from statistics compiled from information collected through reliable sources, it was believed that the enemy in front of the 21st Corps was composed of a force of five infantry divisions, 500 cavalry, 284 machine guns, 140 automatic rifles, and 169 guns. Of the five divisions two were in the hills, two between Fir Hill and the sea, and one in Army reserve about Et Tireh.

The country through which General Bulfin's force had to pass once the Turkish lines were carried varied considerably from left to right. The coastal plain was from seven to ten miles wide. Near the sea it was rolling sandy country with many dunes covered with stiff rank grass. Then there were wide stretches of black soft cotton soil, baked hard by the summer sun, but easily churned into a dusty mass by traffic. The black earth yielded much rank growth and the heavy crop of thistles gave cover for infantry. The sand dunes round about the most important part of the line during the early stages of the operations—that is, near the mouth of the wadi Falik where a passage was to be made for cavalry— were some four thousand yards deep from the coast line. They ended abruptly on the sea side in steep cliffs which only left a beach twenty yards wide. To the eastward of the Plain were rough rocky foothills, over which progress was much easier from west to east than from north to south. The mountains and foothills were to the east of the enemy's railway which came down from Tulkeram towards Ludd, and the sys-

CRUSADER RUINS AT RAS EL AIN

tem was cut by deep, steep gorges running from east to west. On the Turkish side of the line there were very few roads, and nearly all of the tracks were so bad that troops in charge of pack transport had a good deal of trouble in moving their animals over them. But three main roads running from west to east were of great assistance during the advance. That from Kalkilieh through Kefr Kasim to Bidieh was made by the Turks after they had been forced back from the Jaffa-Jerusalem road in the previous November. The Kalkilieh-Azzun-Funduk road joined near Deir Sharaf quite a good metalled road running from Tulkeram to Messudieh and Nablus, and the 7th Division found this road, and an alternative route by the wadi Kanak to Funduk, of vast importance to them during their advance on Messudieh Station. There was also another fairly well made road, probably improved where it ran through the hills by German engineers, from Messudieh to the edge of the Plain of Esdraelon at Jenin, whence it ran across the plain through Afuleh to Nazareth, and past Tiberias and the western shores of the Sea of Galilee on to Damascus. That road, which had fallen in places into a deplorable condition, was to be the scene of a remarkable cavalry advance to the capture of the ancient Arab city.

General Allenby's plans were decided upon at the end of July, but the details were not, of course, worked out till considerably later. In July the Commander-in-Chief decided against an early advance on the 20th Corps front. The nature of the hilly country made it certain that progress up the Nablus road would be slow and costly, without promising any really effective blow against the enemy. General Chetwode's attacks in this region had been most admirably planned and were carried out with the full force of highly trained, bold troops, but the natural obstacles had prevented him from securing more than a few miles of hills. These were admirable points, and the enemy had been forced to realise that we could push him back whenever we made an effort. But he had quite as good positions in the rear, and after one big attack he would be able to make another stand. To force him back on the backbone of the hills of Judea would have meant a long wearing-down process, costly in men and entailing much fatigue. This plan therefore was put on one side in favour of an attack in the coastal sector, and in the light of what happened in September we can see how the master mind of the great soldier grasped the opportunities and possibilities open to him. Probably few anticipated that the operations would secure such tremendous and far-reaching results as were gained in September and October. The soldier who predicted that we should be in Aleppo at the beginning of November and have forced the Turks out of the war would have been voted an unbalanced optimist, but it was because the Commander-in-Chief, having obtained what he hoped to secure in the coastal sector and foothills, never hesitated to call upon his troops to make the utmost use of the situation, that he was able to carry through the much larger scheme. General Allenby was the greatest optimist in his Army. He predicted what would happen and he told his Staff that he would beat, crush, and capture the Turkish armies opposed to him. His strategy was faultless. It was bold, but not risky, and boldness was essential in the then state of Turkish moral. It aimed at a more modest achievement than Damascus in the first days of October and Aleppo at the beginning of November, but if General Allenby did not look to winning those cities quite so early they were always within his field of vision, and if his overwhelming victory in the third week of September had not crushed the fighting power of the Turk and so helped to end the war in November, Damascus and Aleppo would still have been ours in the winter. But, as I have said, he set out in September to gain immediately a smaller area than he actually got.

This is how the nature of the operations was arranged. In this world-war international considerations influenced the direction of campaigns, and, possibly in some theatres, cramped the work of commanders-in-chief. Down to July General Allenby was uncertain what were to be the future plans for his campaign, and he did not even know whether he would be asked to advance to or beyond the Haifa-Nazareth line or whether his Army would remain about its existing line. He could only plan operations with the object of inflicting severe losses on the enemy rather than gaining ground, though he had to consider the position of the Army from a defensive point of view. To strengthen our hold on Palestine it was necessary that our front should be advanced to a line running from the mouth of the river Iskanderunieh through Tulkeram and Samaria to Nablus This would give us command of the roads proceeding in a south-easterly direction from Nablus to the Jordan valley, and thus materially add to the time required in the transfer of enemy forces from the front between the sea and the Jordan to the Es Salt and Amman area—a weighty matter, as shown by the operations over the Jordan in the spring. If we obtained this line the enemy would be dependent on the railway between Afuleh and Deraa and Amman, and on three roads running south from the Beisan-Deraa road, and the control of the railway between Messudieh and Tulkeram would pass out of Turkish hands, thereby greatly adding to their supply difficulties. These alone might require the enemy to retire to a line within twenty miles of his railheads and there is no doubt it would make an offensive by him out of the question. That he would attack us as soon as he could concentrate sufficient troops we were bound to assume. While a rapid advance from the west or south-west to Messudieh would place in jeopardy the Turks south-east of a line drawn from Jiljilia to Samaria—that is, the troops on the hills west of the Nablus road—a slow, methodical advance such as alone was possible on the 20th Corps front would give the enemy time to move his material from the coastal plain by the railway, and his troops could retire north of the Iskanderunieh. Not less than four infantry divisions would be necessary for an advance on the front of the 20th Corps, and this would leave an insufficient force in the coastal sector for an effective attack. Even if a movement on this front were combined in the early stages of the battle with a 21st Corps advance in a north-easterly direction, the nature of the country would still render it very slow, and there would not be sufficient troops available to protect the left flank from attack by Turks from the direction of the coastal plain.

The other alternative was chosen of employing an overwhelming force to break through the Turkish lines on the Plain and to advance to Tulkeram, thirteen miles from our line, within twenty-four hours, and then to press on to Messudieh, another eleven miles, to cut off part of the Turkish army opposing the 20th Corps, which would then have only the road from Nablus to Beisan open for their retreat. Further, the coastal plain was the only area in which General Allenby could employ his enormous preponderance of mounted troops to the fullest advantage. The work done on the 20th Corps front had greatly strengthened it from a defensive point of view, and it was the opinion of General Bols, the Chief of the General Staff, that it could be held by two divisions and the Cape detachment, the British West Indians, and the Jewish battalions, if they came well out of their training. This would leave five infantry divisions and two mounted divisions for the attack in the coastal plain, even supposing a mounted division and two mounted brigades with the 20th Indian Infantry Brigade were still required in the Jordan valley. It was not considered necessary to allot troops for the attack on the same scale as for a deep trench system in France. The fight would probably resolve itself into one for the principal fortified localities, and the trenches which connected these were hardly likely to give much trouble unless the Turks largely increased the number of men holding them. Between Jiljulieh and the sea, if three divisions were given to this part of the front, each division would have nearly 5000 yards of front to attack.

CHAPTER 9

Plan of Attack

Ten days before the operations were to start the plan of attack was issued to Corps Commanders by the General Staff. General Allenby's 'Force Order, No. 68' is an historical document. It is very short, and one marvels that the scheme of an operation of so comprehensive a character, which was to produce results so fruitful in their effect on the whole war, could have been compressed into such small compass. Yet absolutely nothing was missing. As one reads the Force Order the very first sentence seems to sum up everything: 'The Commander-in-Chief intends to take the offensive.' There are no 'ifs' and no alternatives. What General Allenby expected is laid down clearly in the direct, plain language of the soldier. The Turkish armies were to be destroyed. The plan by which their destruction was to be completed was set out on a few typewritten sheets of foolscap, and everything, positively everything, was foreseen and provided for. All worked according to plan, and military history contains no better example of how a masterly scheme was completely carried into effect.

The second sentence summarises the effort to be made by the three Corps and the detached force under General Chaytor in the Jordan valley:

> The Army pivoting on its positions in the Jordan valley will attack on the front between the high ground east of El Mugheir and the sea with the object of inflicting a decisive defeat on the enemy and driving from the line Nablus-Samaria-Tulkeram-Cesarea.

The main attack, as has been indicated, was to be in the coastal sector. The 21st Corps with the 5th Australian Light Horse, 60th Division, Détachement Français de Palestine et Syrie attached, would attack the enemy's right, and when his trench systems between Et Tireh and the Nahr Falik had been captured, would advance eastwards to drive the enemy from the line Deir Sharaf-Samaria-Tulkeram. As soon as the crossing over the Falik and the marshes to the east had been cleared of the enemy by the advance of the 21st Corps, the Desert Mounted Corps (4th and 5th Cavalry Divisions and the Australian Mounted Division, less one brigade) would pass round the left of the 21st Corps and advance on El Afuleh and Beisan to cut the enemy's railway communications and block his retreat in a northerly and north-easterly direction. The 20th Corps, less the 60th Division which was allotted to the 21st Corps, were to attack astride the Nablus road to gain possession of a line south of Nablus from which they would be in a position to co-operate with the 21st Corps and to advance to the high ground north and north-east of Nablus. The date of the attack was not known when the Force Order was placed in the hands of Corps Commanders, but on 'Zero' day the 21st Corps were to start operations from Umbrella Hill to the sea. There was to be no preliminary bombardment. The infantry would advance to the assault under an artillery barrage put down at the hour the infantry left their positions of deployment. Immediately the trench systems between Et Tireh and the Falik had been gained, the Corps, pivoting on the right, would wheel to the east, clearing the Kalkilieh-Tulkeram road, and seize the high ground east of the railway between Deir Sharaf and Attara, being prepared to pursue the enemy in the direction of Jenin. One division of the Corps, with the 5th Australian Light Horse attached, would advance from the position of the captured trenches *via* Tulkeram and Attara, blocking the railway line between Samaria and Jenin as early as possible. The right division of the 21st Corps were not to advance further east than a line drawn north and south through Bidieh unless required to assist the 20th Corps operating on the right.

During the twenty-four hours preceding the attack Desert Mounted Corps were to move to positions of readiness behind the 21st Corps front, and the cavalry were to begin advancing to the Afuleh area immediately the infantry had broken through and had secured the crossings over the Falik and the Zerkiyeh marsh. The cavalry's first objective was a line through Kakon and Jelameh to Tel ed Dhur and Hudeira, and they were to go forward with the utmost rapidity to Afuleh by the Jelameh-Sumrah and Lejjun and the Hudeira-Abu Shushe roads, and to prevent the Turks removing rolling stock by cutting the railway lines from Jenin and Haifa to Afuleh at the earliest possible moment. Then, while keeping sufficient troops in the Afuleh, Jenin, and Lejjun areas, General Chauvel was to close the Turkish lines of retreat to the north and north-west, and to send out in an easterly direction a considerable body of mounted troops to close the roads which converge on Beisan from the Jordan valley and Nablus. Two torpedo-boat destroyers were to co-operate in the attack by denying to the enemy the use of the coast road south of Haifa. The date on which the 20th Corps would begin their attack on the front Mugheir-Rafat depended on the progress of the 21st Corps, but a division had to be concentrated ready to attack by 6 p.m. on the day after the attack in the coastal sector, two groups operating on the left and right flanks converging on an approximate line Akrabeh-Zeita-Jemmain-Kefr Haris. General Chaytor's force was responsible for the defence of the front from the northern end of the Dead Sea to the Ghoraniyeh and Aujah bridgeheads, Musallabeh, and Nejmeh. It was quite possible that the enemy, to assist in the defence of his line in the Judean hills, might reduce his force in the Jordan valley, and should he do so General Chaytor might be required to advance as far as the Jisr ed Damie ford, or to send a detachment east of the Jordan to join forces with an Arab army moving from the south, but the force was not to be committed to an advance, although General Chaytor was to take measures to make the enemy believe that attacks both east and west of the Jordan were imminent, and so prevent the enemy from concentrating troops in a position from which they could attack the 20th Corps.

The rôle of Desert Mounted Corps was the all-important one of getting behind the enemy, of cutting his railway communications, and, by occupying the country through which his roads passed, to prevent his escape. Theirs was a big task, and it could only be performed by cavalry in a high state of efficiency and in first-class condition. The instructions to the Desert Corps Commander laid it down that the long marches which had to be undertaken, and the necessity of conserving the cavalry's full strength, made it imperative that nothing should allow the cavalry to be drawn into the infantry fight south of the wadi Falik, and after the cavalry had made the passage of that stream they were not to be diverted from their objectives by the presence of hostile troops in the Tulkeram-Et Tireh area, which would be dealt with by the forces of the 21st Corps. The advance from the position of readiness would be regulated by the progress made by the infantry of the 21st Corps, but Desert Mounted Corps Staff was responsible for providing that the line between the Zerkiyeh marsh and the mouth of the Falik should be crossed at the earliest possible moment. In the early stage the field was to be given to the infantry, and the cavalry were not allowed to interfere with the movements of the 21st Corps, or to do anything which would mask the fire of that Corps' artillery.

There was always a possibility that the enemy would endeavour to retire on Haifa, but if the Turks moved in that direction the Desert Mounted Corps was only to detach sufficient troops to keep in touch with them and to protect its lines of communication.

As much of the mounted force as was possible had to be kept for Afuleh and Beisan, to gain which great vigour and rapidity must characterise their action, as it was essential that the cavalry should reach those places before the enemy could withdraw his rolling stock and material, or assemble troops for the defence of the railway. On arrival at Lejjun, General Chauvel's orders were to send a brigade south-east to Jenin to block the roads and railway passing through that place and to gain touch with the 5th Australian Light Horse Brigade, which would be directed by the 21st Corps on that town from the south if the situation permitted. From Afuleh a detachment must be sent to seize the road and railway bridges over the Jordan at Jisr Mejamie, a few miles south of Semakh on the southern edge of the Sea of Galilee, and while the railway bridge was to be prepared for demolition it was not to be destroyed so long as we could hold it. In fact demolitions on the railway were to be limited to such as could be easily repaired, as, when a further advance was ordered, the line and rolling stock in our hands would be an important factor in solving the problems of supply. The Corps Commanders, working within the instructions laid down in the Force Order, were given a free hand, but acting in conformity with the regulations framed throughout the campaign for the protection of all the Sacred Sites, General Allenby was emphatic in his orders that the City of Nazareth was on no account to be bombed or shelled during the operations. We knew perfectly well, and had long known, that General Liman von Sanders, the Commander-in-Chief of the Turkish Army, had his headquarters at Nazareth. He probably knew that the City was a sanctuary as far as we were concerned.

Just prior to the attack our Intelligence branch reported that the enemy knew neither the date of the offensive nor the plan.[1] The Turks were still very busy on the work of improving their system of trenches to protect Es Salt and Amman. Reinforcements amounting to at least three battalions, and possibly to six, with a full complement of machine guns, had come down as reserve to the Turkish 7th Army front, but there were some indications that a portion of these infantry units had been broken up to form drafts for battalions in the line. Three of these battalions had come from the Caucasus. The enemy artillery had been reinforced by 35 guns and 12 howitzers, bringing the total of

1 See Appendix C.

guns to 367. In the months of July and August the ammunition passing through Rayak from Aleppo was twice the amount which went to the front in normal months. More machine guns were reported in transit. The 191st Regiment—about 650 rifles—was believed to have reached Tulkeram for the east of the Jordan, and three or four German battalions were in the Bidieh area in reserve for employment in an emergency. There were elements of German units about Tulkeram, and a German battalion was still stationed near Falik.

For the ten days preceding the commencement of operations nothing was normal behind our lines. The very fact that we were hiding signs of movements from the Turks during the daylight hours made the situation abnormal. There was an enormous amount of work to be done, but we could not do it so long as the sun was up, and while all were enjoined to support the appearance that stagnation, if not stalemate, reigned on this front, all knew they were sitting on the fringe of a volcano about to burst into eruption. Men took their rest by day; there was no time for sleep at night. No sign of confusion marked the strenuous activities which sprang into life when the sun went down. Road makers and road repairers were out in thousands. The accumulation of stores went on apace. The additions to the ammunition supply accounted for a vast amount of road transport. Columns with food for men and horses, stores for engineers, for the signal branch, for the big Army Service Corps trains, and so on filled the roads, yet the traffic control was as perfect as that of the City police outside the Mansion House. At every cross-road and corner, at every deviation of a track, a road marshal was stationed, and his orders were obeyed. The traffic scheme was worked out with splendid skill, and where hesitation or indecision might have created chaos there was good road order and absence of noise, and a strenuous effort by all to get a night's programme completed before dawn. All worked by the clock and carried on with clockwork precision. As I have said, the date of the attack was not known when Force Order No. 68 was issued. The Army had to be prepared to be ready by the morning of the 19th, and it was ready. There were finishing touches, of course, but if the Commander-in-Chief had decided that he would attack at dawn on the 17th, a day's notice would have been sufficient, and the victory would have been just as overwhelming.

CHAPTER 10

September 19

The night of September 18-19 was—until the approach of dawn—
just an ordinary summer night on the Palestine battle front. A brilliant moon threw a powerful light over the country, and positions a
thousand yards or so away were magnified and distorted, and bushes
and vegetation appeared like moving bodies of troops. Only eyes that
had been trained to understand the country under the moonbeams
could appreciate that all was stationary. Occasionally a gun was fired
on either side, but that was a customary challenge and indicated nothing. As the moon was beginning to go down the enemy discharged
magnesium lights to try to ascertain if we were preparing local raids,
of which he stood in awe. For a few months raiding parties had put
terror in his heart. I started away from G.H.Q. soon after half-past
one, at which hour the steady roar of the engines of a Handley-Page
aeroplane told me that our one big bomber had gone away to open
the battle. It was a gorgeous night. The air was almost still, and the
faint movement of a sluggish breeze gave a touch of autumn freshness
which was invigorating and prepared one for the exertions of a long
day. I went out past Ramleh and through Ludd, where loaded motor
lorries near the vast depôts stood waiting for the signal to proceed
beyond the lines we had held for more than nine months, out into the
open to victual men and guns made hungry by the chase. Very little
moving traffic was upon the roads, in itself a proof that concentration
was wholly complete and up to time.

Abandoning the idea of proceeding by the Ludd-Jaffa unmetalled
road for fear of getting mixed up in the divisional trains which would
proceed in the wake of troops, we swung northwards through the
orange and olive groves and travelled some distance by the side of
the new railway track which our railway engineers had laid months
before in preparation for an advance. They had gone boldly into an

area within range of Turkish guns, and only stopped when precious lives had to be saved. Crossing this line to the left we passed through the village of Wilhelma, where a German colony had thrived until our Army's arrival. Their houses had been sadly damaged by Turkish artillery, and no one bemoaned the condition of German-owned property which had been ruined by the action of their allies. Then turning towards the sea we moved for several miles in a north-easterly direction, till in the gloom we got into the thick of the force which that day was to add another bright page to the record of British arms. Our view-point was a knob of a hill around which there had once been some stern fighting, and the Turks, with bitter memories of a bloody day, occasionally seared its head with heavy shells. There were craters all over the place and their circumference gave a good indication of the size of the projectiles. They had usually fallen behind the trenches, and the observation post on top, which doubtless had been the Turks' target, was never touched. From it I saw the action on some fifteen miles of front during the greatest battle ever fought in the Holy Land. It was an unforgettable picture and it was a privilege to take part in it, if only as a recorder of events.

The moon set at 3.55 a.m. The attack was timed to start at half-past four. So long as the moon shed any light on the land nothing was stirring, and in the peaceful surroundings it was difficult to bring oneself to believe that within a brief space of time the thunder of guns and the tap-tap of thousands of machine guns would open a battle which was to have a momentous bearing on the tide of the world-war. With the knowledge of what was to happen that deep silence was profoundly exciting, and one almost counted the minutes during the tense period of waiting. I remember having a feeling of irritation when a beautiful horse in a signal section champed its bit and became playful. It seemed out of keeping with the surroundings. But once the moon had dropped beneath the horizon this sleeping world seemed to spring into life. In the thirty-five minutes before the boom of hundreds of guns and trench mortars was to announce the fate of the Turk there was much to be done. The tens of thousands of gallant infantry were to spring out of their bivouacs and shelters and deploy in silence for their attack on a front which all felt the enemy had occupied too long. The troops marched along guiding lines of tape, so laid down as to ensure that they formed up at right angles to the line of advance. The necessary gaps had been cut in our wire to admit the passage of our infantry and of the artillery and Desert Mounted Corps later on. Every officer carried a compass, and to provide against fog, darkness, and the dust and smoke caused by our bombardment, the bearings of each unit's objective had been taken beforehand. General Bulfin had omitted no precaution, and the whole Army owes to him and his staff a great debt for the perfection of detail which, with the gallantry and self-sacrifice of the troops he commanded, brought glory to British arms an assisted to end the war.

The battle, as I have said, was to begin at 4.30 a.m. Ten minutes before that time we were startled by a sudden rattle of musketry and a few rounds from guns far away on our right. Was it a sign that the enemy had learned our intentions and had forestalled us? Had his forward posts discovered a concentration in front and was he trying to disperse what he believed was a raiding party, and would he precipitate an action along the whole front and put his gunners and infantry on the *qui vive*? Or had some watches in a division gone wrong? It was an alarming situation where everything had been planned to work by the clock. But everything was all right. I did not know until some time afterwards that it was arranged that the 54th Division in the foothills were to go out ten minutes earlier than the remainder of the front-line troops to secure certain points before the enemy had warning of the advance. There was not much time to get anxious about what they were doing. A pink flush showing above the ragged edges of the Judean hills was already heralding the approach of dawn, when at half-past four the thunder of our three hundred guns gave us a message of hope for the issue of the battle. A sporting fellow near me simply said 'They 're off.' and turned to take his part in the columns waiting to pass through when the time came for work in the open. Neither he nor any one else in the Palestine Army had any doubts about getting through, and a long experience of war had so taken off the edge of his curiosity that he did not care about seeing a truly wonderful scene of war from the best view-point. So he went to a lower level to watch and wait for orders. There was no preliminary bombardment. The first flash from a gun was the signal for infantry to move. The heavy artillery were occupied with counter-battery work. Instantly the battle began the well-served 60-pounders and the big howitzers engaged enemy batteries, and put down such an intense volume of fire that the Austrians and Turks were in many cases unable to reach their guns, and there was comparatively little artillery fire from the enemy's side. Some guns were active, of course, but during the early stages of the battle the foresight of our heavy gunners unquestionably saved many lives, and we found later on that quite a substantial number of the batteries we

101

captured had not fired a round because our shells prevented enemy gunners coming up to their guns. A few heavies and howitzers on each divisional front took as targets certain brigade and divisional headquarters and paid particular attention to telephone exchanges, the position of which we knew. The 18-pounder batteries were employed to bombard the enemy's front line while the infantry were marching up to it, and when they arrived and drove the Turks out of their trenches the fire of the field guns had lifted and formed a creeping barrage in front of the riflemen up to the limit of their range. Then the teams were hitched to the guns, and forward they went to begin again. The 4.5 howitzers fired at selected points farther back. Right well did the gunners do their work. They had difficulties to contend with. The light breeze had died down before the moon had disappeared, and the high-explosive shells exploding on impact lifted clouds of dust from the sun-baked edges of the Turkish trench systems. Then again from the fringe of the Zerkiyeh marsh in front of Et Tireh and almost to the foothills a low-lying bank of fog made observation difficult. Shrapnel could be seen bursting above it, but it was only rarely one could see the bursts of high-explosive shells beneath the fog-bank. If one did not know where the enemy's main defences were it would have been easy to pick them out that morning by the flashes of bursting shell. Clearly registration had been as accurate as it was thorough, and all along that grim line of wire and sandbags and sangars thousands of vicious bursts of flame told that the guns were giving loyal support to the waves of glorious infantry moving to overthrow the enemy.

Before it was quite daylight the favourable progress of the battle was apparent. We knew infantry had won trenches, for we saw the barrage lift, an through glasses could watch it raise clouds of golden sand near the sea and thin red dust on the fringe of the plain. What was happening on the rising ground was harder to understand, for there we could make out a fiercer artillery duel, and guessed that if in that locality the surprise had been quite as complete the enemy had not had his traditional stubbornness overborne by the heavy nature of the attack. The Turks' anti-aircraft fire had been directed against aerial observers above the foothills, though it was doubtful if they could see the planes, and they certainly did not drive them away. Where the enemy put down a barrage he showed us he was hopelessly at sea. The element of surprise, so important a factor, was complete, and the Turks were so utterly mistaken in their estimate of what we intended and what we were doing that the majority of their shells fell in the rear of our infantry. The infantry in fact had advanced so rapidly that the supporting line as well as the front wave were actually in fronts of the enemy's barrage and very few casualties; indeed were caused by it. I saw a belated barrage put down in front of Mulebbis when the infantry were from three to four hundred yards beyond it. I do not think the enemy was searching for our guns for there were no batteries near, but it is possible he was trying to reach some emplacements which had long since been evacuated. When dawn broke the day was ours. We had already won. We had passed through many of the trenches and were in the open, and the Turks were trying to get away. There was heavy fighting still to do before the whole of the trench systems were captured, and though some time had to elapse before the signal could be passed for the cavalry to move, a way had been cut for them long ere the sun appeared. As a matter of fact the determination and dash of the infantry had taken them through several points of the enemy's trench system by 4.40 a.m. So that it can be said with truth this all-important battle was won in the first ten minutes. Nothing the Turks could have done would have given them the ground they had lost in ten minutes. They had no opportunity of trying to regain it, for they were kept on the run, and the movement to the rear begun that morning was continuous right up to the date of the Armistice. Right well had the divisional commanders taken to heart the injunction of General Bulfin that Time was the enemy more than the Turk. General Bulfin urged them to break through the enemy lines with the utmost determination, to leave all side-issues alone, to set their faces towards the foothills, and to call for the utmost exertions from their men to push forward to secure the destruction of the enemy's forces. The commanders were told they were expected to take risks, and when acting boldly with their leading troops could leave their reserves to meet unexpected eventualities. General Bulfin put this on record two days prior to the attack, and every divisional commander knew that if through carrying out these orders he had got into difficulties, the Corps Commander would have stood loyally by him and have given him his full support.

This was the plan of attack: Before the operations began the 20th Corps took over the extreme right of the 21st Corps line from Berukin to Rafat, reducing the front of the 21st Corps from $25^{1/4}$ miles to $21^{1/4}$ miles. The formations taking part in the attack and the frontages allotted to them were:

French detachment	5,900 yards
Colonel P. de Piepape, C.B.	
54th Division	9,500 yards
Major-General S. W. Hare, C.B.	
3rd Lahore Division	11,300 yards
Major-General A. R. Hoskins, C.M.G., D.S.O.	
75th Division	1,900 yards
Major-General P. C. Palin, C.B., C.M.G.	
7th Meerut Division	5,500 yards
Major-General Sir V. B. Fane, K.C.I.E., C.B.	
60th London Division	3,300 yards
Major-General J. S. M. Shea, C.B., C.M.G.	
5th Australian Light Horse Brigade	
Brigadier General C. Macarthur Onslow	
placed under the orders of the 60th Division	

The big differences in the frontages allotted to the divisions were due to the fact that the fronts of the 54th and 3rd Divisions included the wide gap between Mejdel Yaba and Ferekiyeh which was only watched by the two divisions. It was never proposed to attack along every yard of the length of the Turkish line but against the various important tactical points of the defences, and this plan enabled us to avoid an advance over bare open ground which could be swept by artillery and machine-gun fire from both sides. All the formations were employed in the initial attack, and there was no Corps reserve, but each division had a strong divisional reserve varying from one to two brigade groups. Taking the line from the sea to the foothills, the disposition of the divisions and the work they were set to accomplish was as follows: The 60th Division was given the left of the line, and the Londoners thus achieved the honour in this campaign of being the first division to attack at Beersheba, the division to win the trench system covering Jerusalem from the west, the first troops to cross the Jordan, and the first to rush through the trenches north of Jaffa and to open the coast road for cavalry to carry on and capture northern Palestine and Syria. Their rôle on the morning of September 19 was to drive the Turks from an intricate trench system three lines deep near the coast north of Arsuf, the scene of *Richard Coeur de Lion's* victory over the Saracens in 1191, and then to trek on and overcome a number of small posts south of the wadi Falik and establish a bridgehead north of the wadi. They had to build three bridges over the wadi, for which purpose No. 13 Pontoon Train was placed at their disposal, and when cavalry had passed over these bridges—if there was too much water in the wadi to allow of horsemen fording it—the division was to march to Tulkeram. On the 60th Division's right was the 7th Meerut Division which had some nasty ground to cover. The division had been in this area several months, and the British and Indian troops composing it had had many opportunities of looking over the country about to be conquered. In it were numerous trenches and cleverly fashioned posts for machine-gunners and gun emplacements, and though there were other difficult places on the front there was none prepared so strongly. Between the lines the land was broken by many watercourses running usually from east to west, but apart from these there was little cover, and the enemy trenches were so placed that troops advancing against them could be caught by enfilade fire. Once through the trench system the 7th Division were instructed to advance along the wadi Hurab el Miskeh, which flows from north to south, to the western edge of the marsh called Birket Ramadan, a big swamp separated by a narrow neck of more or less firm ground from the impassable marsh of Zerkiyeh. When past the soft ground the division was to face eastward to capture the Et Tireh defences, which were some 8000 yards from the spot where the swamps were crossed. Following behind the right of the 7th Division was the 5th Australian Light Horse Brigade, which that day carried out a big task with great success, and once more proved the enormous strength Australia mounted troops added to General Allenby's Army in operations which taxed to the uttermost the physical powers of all ranks. As soon as the path had. been cleared through the defences by the 7th Division General Shea was to issue orders to the 5th Light Horse Brigade to move on to Tulkeram, and when the Tireh defences had been carried the 7th Division were to close to their right so as to leave the long road from Zerkiyeh to Hudeira entirely to the troops of the Desert Mounted Corps.

The 75th Division was on the right of the 7th Division, and on its narrow front there was a mass of wired-in trenches and troublesome pits for riflemen and machine guns. General Palin's Division was directed to push through to beyond the Et Tireh line as rapidly as possible, and a battery of armoured cars and a squadron of cavalry were placed under his orders to round up the enemy retreating from Et Tireh and to capture guns. After the pursuit the squadron was to return to the village of Miskeh, to provide an escort for heavy-artillery batteries proceeding to Tulkeram. The 75th Division was then to come into Corps reserve, and the armoured cars were to go forward to join the 60th Division. The 3rd Lahore Division were to advance with their left on the road from Hadrah to Et Tireh. Two hard nuts to crack lay in their path. One was Brown Hill about 200 yards east of the road, and the other Fir Hill 2000 yards farther east. Both were deeply entrenched and connected up by various ways cut into the earth, and behind them the Jewish village of Sabieh had been made a strong place by an elaborate trench system east and north-east of the village. After capturing the two hills and the Sabieh defences the 3rd Division were to move eastwards against the villages of Jiljulieh and Kalkilieh, the latter between two and three miles north of the former. Jiljulieh was covered on the west by a strongly fortified rise known as Railway Redoubt, about three-quarters of a mile long. Subsequently the 3rd Division was to link up with the 54th Division in the foothills. The 54th Division and the French detachment had Kafr Kasim as their first objective. This was a village on a bold rocky knoll with a number of posts in front of it, while to the north-east there were trenches covering the wadi Kanah in an almost continuous line. The Division had to cross this wadi to secure the high ground on the northern side, and then to face eastwards to form a flank and to wait until the 3rd Division were in a position to advance with them through the hills in an easterly direction.

When the sun appeared the noise of the field guns in front of my point of observation had to a large extent stopped. The field-artillery batteries were moving forward, and that fact alone was sufficient to indicate that the whole line had been carried in one grand impetuous rush, and that the day was ours. The heavies and howitzers were still engaged in wrecking batteries and positions in the enemy's rear, and their thunder drowned the rifle and machine-gun fire which was paralysing the efforts of small enemy parties to stem the tidal wave that had overtaken them. On my left rear I could see columns of cavalry waiting for orders to advance; men of British yeomanry regiments, Australian Light Horsemen, the pukka cavalry of India, standing by their horses ready to mount and be off on a long sweeping movement which was to cut off the escape of the flower of the Turkish Army by closing the exits on the Plain of Esdraelon and on the Beisan road. Behind these grand columns of horsemen were enormous supply trains with food for men and horses who would have to live in a country yielding little to sustain the Army. These columns furnished wonderful targets for enemy aeroplanes, and my eyes frequently searched the heavens for German aircraft, which I felt certain would take full advantage of a great opportunity. Yet not one of them appeared that day, for the reason that our airmen prevented their getting off the ground. But that is anticipating a story I shall tell later on. The position a little after seven o'clock, when the sun had conquered the fog, and the dust of conflict had subsided over the Turkish trench system which German engineers had thought was impregnable against a force the size of General Allenby's Army, was more favourable to us than the most optimistic could have prophesied.

CHAPTER 11

The Great Blow

The 60th Division on the coast had done everything expected of them, and had done it splendidly. They attacked on a one-brigade front. The honour fell to the 180th Brigade, under Brigadier-General C. F. Watson, D.S.O., which had been first in Jerusalem and first over the Jordan. But it was not the same brigade. Battalions had been sent away to the Western Front to show what fighting spirit the Cockney possessed, and General Watson now had with his 2/19th Londons the 2nd Guides, the 2/30th Punjabis, and the 1/50th Kumoan Rifles. Those fighting men of India lived up to the traditions of the 60th Division. The 2nd Guides on the left and the Kumoan Rifles on the right, with the Londons in support and the Punjabis in reserve, attacked on a 2000-yards front. In ten minutes the Guides and Rifles were in the first of the three lines of trenches, and in another half-hour they had taken the second line. Then the artillery put up a creeping barrage behind which the Indian warriors went forward in perfect style, and by twenty minutes to six the third line of trenches was their own. They had had to fight for each line and the best men won. At the third line the Londoners passed through the Guides and Kumoan Rifles, and the Cockneys' hearty recognition of their comrades' gallant work was cordially reciprocated throughout the ranks of the Indians. The Londoners had to clear up some works as they advanced, but they got to the Nahr Falik by moving up the shore at half-past six, and had crossed the wadi and formed a bridgehead by a quarter to seven. The Falik is a deep cut by which the inland marshes drain into the sea, and as it was four miles from the starting-point it was a grand effort to have reached it in two hours, considering that a substantial trench system had be crossed. The wadi was found to be dry in places, and the infantry went over by a ford at the mouth without waiting for bridges. The 180th Brigade were soon over and

108

the 179th and 181st Brigades rapidly followed. The pontoon section began bridging at once, and causeways and bridges were-built in an astonishingly brief time, but the infantry, having found they could get across without bridges, sent back word to the cavalry who were quickly seen moving up the soft beach to get over the wadi. Some of the regiments actually galloped across at half-past seven, and the whole of the 5th Cavalry Division were over and streaming away to the north by nine o'clock. The 4th Cavalry Division followed in the wake of the 7th Division, and long before noon the two cavalry divisions had surmounted what was believed would prove a big obstacle. Indeed, before that hour the transport of the 5th Cavalry Division was being moved up to the bridges which were then ready for it. The rapid work of the 60th Division had opened a barred gate for the cavalry, and a great deal of the big advance made by the mounted men that day was due to infantry swiftness in cutting a wide gap through which the cavalry could pass. Some assistance had been given to the 60th by the shell fire from the destroyers *Druid* and *Forester* which pounded away at small enemy parties moving up the shore and sent them inland.

The 7th Division had been quite as successful as the 60th. The 19th Brigade, under Brigadier-General G. A. Weir, D.S.O., attacked with splendid determination, and the 1st Seaforth Highlanders, the 28th Punjabis, the 92nd Punjabis, and the 125th Napier's Rifles absolutely crushed out all opposition in the trench system. They pushed across the swamps in remarkably quick time on a narrow front, and then facing eastwards literally ran over and by seven o'clock captured that part of the Et Tireh defences allotted to them. The 7th Division thus lived up to the records it had won in Mesopotamia and had added to in Palestine. They were all grand fellows, from the Divisional Commander downwards, and I was glad a few weeks later to be able to congratulate Sir V. B. Fane on commanding a division which could boast of having conquered from Tekrit to Tripoli. The 75th Division had made all its objectives and before seven o'clock was in Miskeh. The 3rd Division captured the enemy's first system without much difficulty, and the right brigade under Brigadier-General S. R. Davidson, C.M.G., 1st Connaught Rangers, 2/7th Gurkha Rifles, 27th Punjabis, and 91st Punjabis, were moving north-east from Kefr Saba. The 9th Brigade under Brigadier-General C. C. Luard, C.M.G., 2nd Dorsets, 1/1st Gurkha Rifles, 93rd Infantry, and 105th Mahratta Light-Infantry, had reached Hill 283 on the Hadrah road by half-past six and then changed front eastwards.

Bombed Turkish transport near Anebta

On our right the 54th Division had captured Kefr Kasim and Jevis Tepe with Crown Hill to the east and west of the village, and the French detachment had done very good work by taking a ridge west of Rafat and an obstinately defended position farther west known as Three Bushes Hill, and they were advancing on Deir el Kussis, a village surrounded by trees across the wadi Ayun. At eight o'clock the 7th Division, by wheeling to the right, had left the ground clear for the 4th Cavalry Division, and the 5th Australian Light Horse Brigade began its advance on Tulkeram.

By this time the resistance of the enemy on our right had increased considerably. He had recovered from the first shock of surprise, and in the rear of the first positions he had collected his forces and tried to put up something in the nature of a counter-attack. Here we could see the influence of the German battalions in this area. The French detachment had been shelled off Deir el Kussis, and the 161st Brigade (Brigadier-General A. B. Orpen Palmer, D.S.O.)—the 1/4th Essex, 1/5th Essex, 1/6th Essex and 1/7th Essex—after advancing to Sivri Tepe and Semer Tepe, two hills north and north-east of Kefr Kasim, had been forced by heavy machine-gun fire to retire over a mile to Kefr Kasim village and the woods about it. Farther west the 3rd Division were meeting a very stubborn foe in Jiljulieh and the Railway Redoubt, and they had to prepare a methodical attack on the redoubt. Field guns were brought within range of the trenches on the mound, and heavy artillery which could reach it was brought to bear, and with reinforcements sent up to the brigade in this area the redoubt was captured with small loss at a quarter-past ten.

By 11 o'clock the 54th Division were once more advancing, and the Turks' effort to hold up the attack had broken down. General Hare had sent the 162nd Brigade (Brigadier-General A. Mudge, C.M.G.), consisting of the 1/5th Bedfords, 1/4th Northamptons, 1/10th Londons, and 1/11th Londons through the 161st Brigade to seize Oghlu Tepe, a hill slightly to the north-west of Sivri Tepe a Semer Tepe, and when they had captured this point at 11 o'clock the 161st Brigade again assaulted Sivri Tepe and Semer Tepe and secured them at 11.15. The 8th Infantry Brigade, consisting of the 1st Manchesters, the 47th Sikhs, the 59th Scinde Rifles, and the 2/124th Baluchistan Infantry, under Brigadier-General S. M. Edwardes, C.B., C.M.G., D.S.O., who had captured Jiljulieh and Railway Redoubt, moved east on Hableh, 6000 yards due north of Kefr Kasim, with the 7th Infantry Brigade on their left, and the 9th Brigade, who had taken Kalkilieh and all the trenches thereabout by ten o'clock, were advancing on Jiyus, a wooded village well in the hills. The 234th Brigade of the 75th Division—the 1/4th Duke of Cornwall's Light Infantry, the 123rd Outram Rifles, the 58th Vaughan's Rifles, and the 1/152nd Indian Infantry, under Brigadier-General C. A. H. Maclean, D.S.O.— swarmed over the enemy's system near Et Tireh at eight o'clock, and then assisted the 232nd Brigade under Brigadier-General H. J. Huddleston, C.M.G., D.S.O., M.C.—the 1/4th Wilts, the 72nd Punjabis, the 2/3rd Gurkhas, and the 3rd Kashmir Imperial Service Infantry—in the attack on Et Tireh village. The 232nd Brigade had reached the outskirts of the village soon after 8 o'clock, but found the enemy determined to hold it, and it was only after three hours of stiff fighting that the place was taken. The 75th Division had then secured all their objectives, and General Palin sent a squadron of the Corps' cavalry and No. 2 Light Armoured Car Battery to pursue the Turks in the direction of Tulkeram. The armoured cars went a long way up the road and eventually joined General Shea's division. They rounded up many prisoners and killed a number of the enemy trying to get away. They also inflicted a large number of casualties on Turkish cavalry, and stopped and disabled some motor lorries full of troops. When about five miles from Tulkeram the leading Rolls-Royce armoured car was put out of action by a direct hit from a Turkish field gun and Captain F. W. Heelgers, the officer in command, was badly wounded.

The 7th Division at eleven o'clock was concentrated at Zerkiyeh, ready to move off to the eastwards into the hills. The 60th Division had left the wadi Falik and were marching rapidly towards Tulkeram, the 180th Brigade leading at first, but the 181st Brigade (Brigadier-General E. C. da Costa, C.M.G., D.S.O.) passed through them later. The going between the Falik and Tulkeram was very bad. The infantry had to march through deep sand in the coastal belt and then across wide patches of light cotton soil, and the forced march under a hot sun was a trying and exhausting ordeal. The Division were instructed to reach Tulkeram if possible by five o'clock. This was sixteen miles as the crow flies from the positions attacked in the morning, and there had to be a long stop and much work done at the crossing at the Falik. I have heard that a distinguished general on this front offered to bet General Shea his men would not get to Tulkeram before dark. General Shea won the bet, for he was in the headquarters of the old Turkish 8th Army at five minutes to five.. Everybody put the best foot foremost. There was opposition but it was not permitted to delay the division. A pocket of 300 Turks with

TURKISH CAVALRY PRISONERS TAKEN NEAR AMMAN

four machine guns was on the right of the line of march and General Shea left a battalion to deal with it and pressed on. As he told me:

> We could see the Turks streaming away through Tulkeram and we were shelled from there, but the whole Division seemed to have their eyes fixed on the white minaret of Tulkeram and nobody stopped.

This was typical of the spirit which won that great day.

The 5th Australian Light Horse Brigade was in the vicinity of Tulkeram before the Londoners but the cavalry were hotly received, and in compliance with orders from the 21st Corps moved round to the north of the town and cut the railway line, taking 2000 prisoners and a vast amount of transport. The cavalry dash was very skilfully carried out, and nothing to the right or left of the brigade engaged their attention if there was a possibility of it delaying them. The horsemen blocked the defile leading from Tulkeram through Anebta to Nablus and stopped everything trying to escape. The booty in Tulkeram included a complete train of twenty-five coaches, which, being of smaller gauge than our standard line, was extremely valuable to us when we brought the Turkish railway into our supply service; fifteen guns, many machine guns, and over 1200 prisoners fell to the 60th Division. I again quote General Shea:

> It was the first day out for the new Division, and the men really did most splendidly. They pressed on to get Tulkeram, though they were dead tired, for some of them had marched over twenty miles and there was sharp but short fighting on the way.'

By two o'clock all the other infantry, except the 75th Division in Corps reserve about Et Tireh, were moving eastwards. The 3rd Division took Hableh at half-past one, and in the field of operations allocated to the 54th Division, Brigadier-General A. J. MacNeill, D.S.O., 163rd Brigade—l/4th Norfolks, l/5th Norfolks, l/5th Suffolks, l/8th Hampshires—had taken Sirisia at three o'clock, and the 162nd Brigade secured the high ground farther to the north-east at half-past six. They continued to go on during the remainder of the afternoon and evening, and at midnight the Division made such magnificent progress that it held the line in the broken hill country from Rafat to the west of Deir el Kussis, beyond Mesha and close to Bidieh, and through a mass of rocky ground near to Thilth, where they joined the 3rd Division, which held the latter village, and Azzun and Jiyus which were not captured until after dark. The 7th Division carried on the line as far north as Taiyibeh. This was an almost due north and south line and was entirely in the hills. During the day the 21st Corps had captured 7000 prisoners, over 100 guns, 170 machine guns, and an immense quantity of war material.

We learned from officer prisoners what a staggering effect the first day's blow had had on them. An officer of the 20th Austrian battery said: 'The advance was so rapid that we were taken completely by surprise. The battery was being fired at by machine guns from all sides.' A staff officer of the Turkish 22nd Army Corps admitted that the 7th and 9th Divisions broke down immediately on the attack being started. 'The 20th Division,' he said 'was thus surrounded and broken up by about 5 a.m. The 144th regiment retired on Miskeh at.' that hour, and the 22nd Army Corps Headquarters moved from Et Tireh to Tulkeram at the same time. The 144th regiment was intercepted and captured at Miskeh and British infantry passed on to Et Tire which fell quickly. The reason for the Turkish debacle was mainly the unexpected rapidity with which the British infantry broke up the 20th Division which was regarded as the best in the Turkish Army.'

CHAPTER 12

Victory in the Air

Before describing what Desert Mounted Corps did on September 19, I will refer to the work of the Royal Air Force. It is true our flying men had secured for General Allenby's Army complete mastery of the air. They had more expert pilots, more machines, better aerodromes, and a much stronger fighting spirit than the German airmen with the Turks. They had thrashed the Germans from the air, or at any rate from that portion of the air which concerned us. For three weeks prior to the grand attack only one enemy plane was seen over our lines, and that at such a great altitude that any useful observation from it was out of the question. This was at a time when it was of vital importance to the enemy that they should have good reports after aerial reconnaissances. General Bulfin, though no one knew better than he that our airmen had proved so far superior to the Germans that the latter disliked flying behind our lines, never imagined that the enemy airmen would exhibit such a lack of enterprise, or he would not have taken the elaborate precautions he did to prevent detection of his concentration. The fact is that the German flying man was cowed and beaten. If there were five of them together they would turn tail at the sight of one of our fighting planes. The Turk had lost all faith in German aviators, and even the German infantry came to despise them, as we have found from captured letters. But granting they had lost supremacy in the air, is there anybody who would believe it possible that on a day when the fate of a vast territory was hanging upon the issue of a battle not a single airman even left the ground? Were the odds ten times or a hundred times as great against him the British pilot would have gone up to bring in an appreciation of the situation. It is only fair, however, to the German pilots to say that airmen were never faced with greater difficulties than they were throughout the whole day of the 19th of September. The Palestine Wing of the

116

Royal Air Force, having got the mastery of the air, were going to use their advantages to the full. Whether in aerial fighting, in bombing, in reconnaissances, or in keeping the enemy airmen to their dug-outs, they set out to utilise their powers as completely as was possible. The programme was ambitious. It was drawn up by General Borton, the chief of the Palestine Wing, a tireless officer whose energy was only equalled by his boldness. Bravery runs in the blood—General Borton's brother won the Victoria Cross. But a greater asset than his courage was this commander's ability to instil his own enthusiasm into all his airmen comrades on the Palestine front. He had only to suggest that such and such a thing should be tried and the men who were to do it would think it the best scheme on earth and would set out to show that it was. If he had had to ask for volunteers to undertake a dangerous job there was no officer in the Royal Air Force who would have got such a response. So when his programme for the offensive was drawn up and circulated the airmen became almost hilarious and said 'It is finished.' The programme had been hall-marked with the approval of Major-General Sir W. G. Salmond, in command of the Royal Air Force in the Middle East, who in days of trial and doubt had always stood by Egypt as one of the best grounds for the training of the pilot. He laboured unceasingly to get adequate provision in Egypt for the aerial education of pilots, and his work was about to show its best results when hostilities ceased. During the winter of 1918-19 more than a thousand pilots would have been turned out of the flying schools in Egypt for service on the Western Front, and they would have received their training at a time when little flying could have been done in Great Britain.

The first of our planes to leave an aerodrome was our big Handley-Page bomber. It was not a machine of the latest type but it served its purpose. The pilot was Captain Ross Smith, who later on was to add to his famous war record by being the first pilot to fly half round the world from England to Australia in his Vickers-Vimy-Rolls. The Handley-Page was allotted to the 1st Australian Flying Squadron as a reward for the sterling work the Australians had done on this front. I may say in parenthesis that both General Salmond and General Borton told me they believed this squadron to be the finest in the whole Air Force, not only because of the quality of the pilots and observers, but because the mechanics were a very highly trained and enthusiastic, efficient lot. The squadron's O.C., Colonel Williams, carried no dead-heads in his crew. The Handley-Page had flown out from England with General Borton as passenger. Ross Smith had taken charge of her at Heliopolis, and, after becoming acquainted with her, brought her to the Australians' aerodrome at Ramleh. At half-past one on September 19 he set out for Afuleh, where the Turks had their chief signal station. Their general headquarters were at Nazareth, on the hills a few miles north of Afuleh, and through the latter little railway town all wires passed from G.H.Q. to Army headquarters at Tulkeram and Nablus, and to Corps headquarters nearer the line. Ross Smith's mission was to destroy these means of communication. He dropped his bombs from a low altitude, and when the cavalry got to Afuleh they found in three bomb craters the broken ends of practically every telegraph and telephone wire between G.H.Q. and the front. A good beginning, surely, and it is plain from what happened afterwards that Turkish G.H.Q. knew very little of the progress of the battle during the day. Just before dawn other planes went out to attack signals at Tulkeram and Nablus, and while I am not certain that all wires were destroyed at Tulkeram, though two hits were scored, it is a fact that a bomb entered the signal headquarters at Nablus and blew, the house to pieces. Divisional headquarters were also bombed with excellent effect, and chaos was created over the whole front. The British squadron stationed near the German colony at Sarona, two or three miles north of Jaffa, had a wonderful day, and its experience was probably unique in this war. The rôle of the pilots in the eighteen machines, which were mostly S.E. 5's, was to prevent the Germans going aloft from their aerodrome at Jenin where they had three two-seaters and eight scouts. Two of our machines went out together, and they sat up above the Jenin aerodrome for an hour and a half at a time until relieved by another couple. The machines were fitted with special bomb racks to carry four twenty-pound bombs, and directly any movement was noticeable on the aerodrome down came a bomb. The aerodrome became as silent as the grave. The German pilots huddled together in their dug-outs, and if one of them did venture out he soon went to earth again, especially if he had chosen the moment when the reliefs were in sight, for then the relieved machines dived down and expended their machine-gun ammunition in the sport of shooting up hangars and damaging everything they could see. This went on throughout the hours of daylight, and to none can darkness have been more welcome than the German pilots and their anti-aircraft gun sections. The squadron which was given the duty of attacking the Germans in their own nest set up a record for a day's flying. Machines of this squadron were in the air $104^{1/2}$ hours in the day, and on the following morning seventeen out of the eighteen machines were reported ready for duty.

That is the supreme test. The previous best record for a day's flying in the Wing was 79 hours. Where every section of the Air Force did superlatively well it is difficult to pick out instances of exceptional work, but the scene I witnessed next morning in the defile between Tulkeram and Anebta struck me as being the most awful example of destructive bombing that could be done from the air. Yet two or three days later this illustration of what airmen could accomplish was completely beaten by a terrible picture on the Ferweh road, where for eight miles the debris of an army lay scattered and shattered by airmen's bombs. That is another story. On that afternoon of the 19th an aerial observer had seen the 5th Australian Light Horse Brigade sitting tight across the road north of Tulkeram and he, being an Australian himself, knew they could not be shifted. He therefore moved above the defile towards Anebta and Messudieh, where he saw that the Turks had crowded on to the road as many guns and as much transport as they had animals to move. As swift as a bird he flew back to his aerodrome, and every available machine followed him out again to block the road. Some of the machines carried twenty-pounders in their bomb racks. Other aeroplanes had boxes fitted to them to carry small canisters of material to make smoke screens under cover of which infantry could advance, and very successful this plan had proved. In place of smoke canisters on this occasion the airmen took Mills hand grenades from which the safety-pin had been withdrawn, but the lever was held in place by tape covered with shellac, and this was released by an automatic arrangement on the grenades being dropped. Where the grenades exploded depended upon the height from which they were released, but in almost every case the explosion happened a moment after they had reached the earth, though some did burst in the air and had the effect of shrapnel. The appearance of the bombing squadron must have appalled the Turks. Not far from the spot where the road takes a right-hand turn north of Tulkeram the bombs fell into the midst of a column of transport. Lorries, general service waggons, guns, field kitchens, water carts, were smashed up and destroyed. Horses, mules, donkeys, oxen, big draught beasts, were horribly mutilated and had fallen with their drivers. That there was instant confusion was proved by the number of vehicles which had scattered to the right and left the road, but these had been brought to a full stop by airmen who, after swooping up the defile to take in bigger targets, found they had a bomb or a few grenades left, and turned to deal with the remnants of the column. And when all the racks were empty the planes came down very low and dealt out death with their machine guns. Stragglers off the road, scores of them, had met their death in this way, and I saw the bodies of three men who had sought refuge from the whirl-wind of bombs beneath the arch of a small road bridge near Anebta. An airman, greatly daring, had come down just over the level of the stony ground to machine-gun these men as they stood beneath the centre of the arch, and had shot them dead.

It might be supposed that the balloon sections were out of the hunt. Not a bit of it. They also accomplished work of much usefulness, as they always did, and the men in the balloons ran risks as great in their way as the fighting men in planes. In the summer I saw three of our balloons brought down in flames, one on the Nablus road and the other two north of Jaffa. Enemy pilots were eager to burn them. It was from the balloons that some of the advancing infantry were able to be located, and divisions kept in touch with each other. Where the forward move-ment was so rapid that signal wire could not always keep up with them, an ingenious system was adopted by which communication could be opened with balloons and messages transmitted through them. In the bright sunlight of September 19 the heliograph could be used at any moment of the day. While the troops were in the flat country there was no necessity to talk through the eyes in the balloons, but once the infantry got into the hills one height blotted out another, and direct communication from brigade to brigade—certainly from one division to another—and with Corps fighting headquarters, which were con-tinually changing during the day, was sometimes impossible. At these times the forward signallers with the helio flashed out messages to one or other of the balloon sections, and when the officers in the baskets were not giving tactical information to the Corps, they were often bus-ily engaged in reading messages from helios and telephoning them to Corps headquarters for retransmission to various parts of the fighting line. As the battle progressed the balloons did not remain in their old positions, and during the afternoon one section was packed up and transported to a spot north of Kalkilieh in an astonishingly short time, and was aloft doing grand work in that advanced position several hours before darkness fell. There was not a branch of the Air Service which did not add to the reputation of the Royal Air Force on September 19, and when those members sought the repose they had earned, they must have had the satisfaction of knowing they had served the Army well on the greatest of all our days in Palestine. But I think few men in the Air Force save the fighting pilots and observers had any rest that night. They were preparing for the morrow.

CHAPTER 13

Cavalry on Armageddon

I now come to the operations of Desert Mounted Corps. It is a question whether in any war cavalry had such an opportunity, and our horsemen could not have made more of their chances. The narrative of the doings of Desert Mounted Corps would be incomplete without some account of the period of concentration, and though brief reference has been made to it fuller details should be given. Infantry are easier to hide than cavalry, and when one can state as a fact that tens of thousands of men and horses were transferred from one end of a sixty-miles front to the other without the enemy having the slightest knowledge of it, and even without the civil population of the two areas knowing anything about it, the highest praise will be accorded to the Corps staff. This is what actually happened. Three out of the four divisions of Desert Mounted Corps had to be moved from the Jordan valley through Palestine to the sea coast, with the artillery attached to them, without the enemy appreciating that anything beyond the normal reliefs was in progress, or that divisions were being moved for any other purpose than for the usual periods of rest and training. The Anzac Mounted Division, with a considerable amount of additional artillery, had been left in the Jordan valley to become what was known during the operations as 'Chaytor's Force,' and with them were two brigades of infantry. Nearly the whole of the artillery in the valley and a considerable number of personnel belonging to other corps had also to be transferred. The difficulties of the concentration were added to by the fact that troops could not remain in the Jordan valley beyond a month or six weeks without serious risk of impairing their health, and the exchange had to take place, therefore, at the latest possible moment.

The reliefs in the Jordan area began on August 15 It was a small beginning, and it was not until September 15 that the whole garrison there had been completely reorganised for the operations. The other three divisions of Desert Mounted Corps had to be brought over to the neighbourhood of the German colony of Sarona. All of them had to march by one road where there was a limited supply of water from Jericho to Jerusalem, and, to keep the enemy mystified, all the marches westward were done under cover of darkness, and all those eastwards in daylight. Dummy camps and dummy horses were put up in the valley for purposes of deception, and demonstrations across the Jordan were carried out to complete the 'camouflage.' Later on we learned how fully the enemy was deceived, and we marvelled at the successful accomplishment of a big task. The Turks were in absolute ignorance of the fact that two nights before the attack there was one of the biggest bodies of cavalry ever assembled in war in one small area, under their very noses, and within easy shelling distance of their long-range guns. By the 17th of September the 5th Cavalry Division were sleeping beneath the leafy trees in the orange groves north-west of Sarona, the 4th Cavalry Division were in the orange groves to the east of Sarona, and the Australian Mounted Division occupied the thick olive groves about Ramleh. The concentration was a masterly achievement. It was complete and perfect to the smallest detail, and everybody could say 'Well done' when they had got to the preparatory position.

The original intention was that, during the night preceding the fight at dawn, the 5th Cavalry Division should be moved across the Auja and be formed up in depth behind the 60th Division on the coast, that the 4th Cavalry Division should be similarly stationed behind the 7th Indian Division, and that advanced cavalry patrols should be actually in the infantry trenches ready to move forward at once when a way had been opened for the cavalry. This arrangement was altered, and the heads of the Cavalry Division were not farther forward than the line of the southern boundary of the 21st Corps' gun positions. On the night before the attack the 5th Cavalry Division were in depth to the west of the village of Jelil, the 4th Cavalry Division were about two miles to the east along the light railway we had built to provision the front line, with the head of the Division at Cromarty Hill, about a mile and a quarter south-east of Jelil, while the Australian Mounted Division were at Sarona in the area vacated by the 4th Cavalry Division. The first work the cavalry were to do, after a way had been cleared by the infantry assault and the 60th Division had swung eastwards towards Tulkeram, was to dash forward at great speed so as to cut in on the enemy's communications a long way behind the Turkish divisions and reserves, and to block all chances of escape from the Jordan, at Beisan, to the sea. The 5th Cavalry Division were directed to reach Nazareth with all possible speed. They had to proceed up the coast to the Nahr Iskanderunieh—an obstacle of which they had little geographical knowledge except that obtained from aeroplane photographs—and, after crossing it, to sweep on to a line from the mound of Dhrur through Hudeira, a substantial village, to the sea; and from this position the Division were to advance by way of Dufeis and Jarak on to Nazareth, where it was hoped they would find General Liman von Sanders, the German commander of the Turkish forces.

The 4th Cavalry Division were to move inside the 6th Cavalry Division, and go up the Musmus Pass *via* Lejjun (Megiddo) on to Afuleh, with Beisan as their ultimate objective. The Australian Mounted Division were to follow the 4th Cavalry Division in Corps reserve, advanced Desert Mounted Corps Headquarters being with the division. At 7.30 a.m. on the 19th the 5th Cavalry Division moved through the enemy's lines behind the 60th Division and crossed the Falik at its mouth. There was not much opposition, but the sand on the beach proved very heavy going. The 13th and 14th Cavalry Brigades were both over the wadi by 9 o'clock and were quickly followed by the 15th Cavalry Brigade, and, picking up the horse-artillery batteries which had been engaged in bombarding the enemy's lines on the 21st Corps front, they moved northward at rapid rate. The speed at which the cavalry travelled may be estimated by the fact that, despite having to deal with pockets of the enemy *en route*, the 13th Cavalry Brigade were at Hudeira by 11 o'clock, or considerably more than twenty miles from their starting-point, and had taken 250 prisoners and four guns. At this time the 14th Cavalry Brigade were also over the Iskanderunieh. The 15th Cavalry Brigade with guns and ammunition column were at Mulahid, five miles south of the wadi, and the Divisional Train, which with their heavy loads found the soft soil a serious difficulty, was being escorted some miles to the rear. When General Mac Andrew reached Hudeira he decided to rest his men and horses till 6 p.m. and then to proceed north to Nazareth with the 13th and 14th Cavalry Brigades without the impediment of wheels, the 15th Cavalry Brigade, which reached Hudeira at 3 p.m., remaining as escort for guns and fighting wheels.

The Jarak road was in a hopeless condition, and after General MacAndrew had gone along it he directed that all the guns and transport should proceed up the road to Beidus and, crossing the old Turkish goods railway at that place, should go up the Musmus Pass to Lejjun, and thence across the Plain of Esdraelon. The 13th and 14th Cavalry Brigades were at Jarak at 1 o'clock on the morning of September

20. Leaving a squadron in Jarak to guard the flank of Desert Mounted Corps on passing through the Musmus defile, the two brigades debouched into the plain, the 13th Brigade moving straight on to Nazareth, while the remainder of the Division rode on to El Mezreh, which was reached at daybreak. The 13th Cavalry Brigade entered Nazareth at dawn, having covered a distance as the crow flies of fifty miles—it was really considerably farther by the tracks they took—in well under twenty-two hours, a splendid feat which only those who have been over the country can appreciate. Nazareth is built on a hill and some of the streets have a much greater elevation than others. When the cavalry got into the lower part of the town they met with little opposition, but later on they found a large number of the enemy, Germans preponderating, in the monasteries and houses on the high ground north of the town. These buildings had been converted into barracks, and from the windows Germans and Turks opened a heavy fire from machine guns and rifles. The cavalry tried in vain to work round to the north to close the exits; the enemy held positions astride the road, and were hanging on tenaciously to the hills. There was a determined effort to envelop the left flank of the brigade, and it became plain that one cavalry brigade was insufficient to secure the whole town. The brigade made a fine fight while some important buildings were being searched, and valuable documents were secured in the Turkish Army headquarters. These threw much light on the condition of the Turkish army and on German pretensions in the East. The 13th Cavalry Brigade's entry into Nazareth was such a surprise to the enemy that some members of Liman von Sanders' staff were captured in their pyjamas. The Germans said that the Commander-in-Chief had escaped the night before in a high-powered motor car, but the story of a European resident was that von Sanders was staying with a friend in the northern outskirts, and got away in a motor ambulance when the cavalry galloped into the town. The Germans' story was believed at first, but the other version has received corroboration and is regarded as accurate. The brigade collected 2000 prisoners, and sent them down the winding road towards Afuleh well in advance of themselves, and when the men of the brigade got to Afuleh they found that their comrades of the 4th Cavalry Division had occupied the railway junction at eight o'clock that morning.

The 4th Cavalry Division at 7.40 on the morning of the 19th began moving up to our front line, with pioneer parties well forward to cut tracks through the wire. By 9 o'clock the Division commenced advancing through the infantry line, and proceeded north by way of the neck between the Ramadan and Zerkiyeh marshes which was badly cut up. The 11th and 12th Cavalry Brigades had crossed the Falik by 10 o'clock, and were moving up both sides of the Tabsor-El Mugheir road, followed by the 10th Cavalry Brigade. An observer's report, dropped on divisional headquarters while advancing, stated that on all roads the enemy was retiring northwards, and that he was burning tents and stores. At 1 o'clock the 4th Cavalry Division was moving on El Mugheir, having met with little opposition, but at half-past two they were on the look-out for 700 enemy cavalry who were reported by the Royal Air Force to have crossed the Iskanderunieh and to be trekking in a south-easterly direction. These horsemen probably receiving information which they did not like from retreating infantry, had swung off towards the east, for they were not seen by the 4th Cavalry Division. The Division were over the Iskanderunieh shortly after six and here they rested awhile. At 10 p.m. they were in the neighbourhood of Hudeira, with patrols as far as the entrance to the Musmus Pass, where the leading brigade had to beat down some opposition. The situation there was soon cleared up and a hundred prisoners were taken, and the whole Division had moved up the defile by daybreak. On descending the steep narrow road from the hills on to the flat, an Indian cavalry regiment made a brilliant charge on the Plain of Armageddon. The 2nd Lancers, the leading regiment of the 10th Cavalry Brigade, came out of the Pass at half-past five, just when it was sufficiently light to see across the patches of cultivation watered by a small stream. The advanced guard and the 11th Light Armoured Motor Battery reported that a battalion of infantry was in front of the road and appeared to be advancing to reach the slopes about Lejjun, apparently in ignorance that our cavalry were already in Nazareth, miles away to their rear. As a matter of fact the battalion had marched from Afuleh to hold the Musmus Pass. The infantry might have given us a good deal of trouble if they had got to the hills: before us, but they were too late. Two squadrons of the 2nd Lancers immediately deployed, and with their shrill voices ringing over the plain they charged full weight into the infantry, killing forty-six with the lance, and accepting the surrender of the whole of the remainder, 470 in all, with their machine guns, automatic rifles, and rifles. Armageddon will take a proud place in the records of the regiment.

Leaving the prisoners to be collected and passed to the rear, the brigade rode across the plain through rank thigh-deep grass and Indian corn, making for the red-roofed buildings and water tower of

Afuleh, the important railway junction, where engines could be seen with steam up to carry away a substantial amount of rolling stock in the sidings. There were eight engines and two made-up trains in Afuleh—a splendid prize. It did not escape us. While the bigger part of the Division remained in Afuleh on the 20th, as they were entrusted with the important duty of assisting to prevent a northward march of the Turks across the plain, a detachment of the 19th Lancers was sent over the hills to Jisr Mejamie, a station on the railway six miles due south of the Sea of Galilee, where a railway bridge crosses the Jordan. It was important to be ready to blow up the bridge and deny the railway to the enemy. The detachment moving across the hills by way of Nein and Endor, had a terrible march through almost impassable country to reach their goal. Led by British officers the Indian cavalry-men made an exceedingly meritorious forced march and got to the bridge before the enemy had the remotest idea of their approach, and had everything ready for destroying the structure by dawn on the 21st. They were ordered not to cut the line unless forced to do so by ex-treme pressure from the enemy, as we should require the railway very soon, and railway-construction troops and materials were as yet a long way in the rear. But this is anticipating.

I now come to the day's work of the Australian Mounted Di-vision. The division was in Corps reserve, and as such it did little more than follow in the wake of the 4th and 5th Cavalry Divi-sions. The Australians were halted just beyond the old Turkish front line till noon and then they advanced to the wadi Iskanderunieh, and, having crossed it, bivouacked for the night, sending the 4th Australian Light Horse Brigade to Hudeira to escort the 5th Cav-alry Division's transport. Next morning the division got through the Musmus Pass without opposition, and at half-past three General Wilson's 3rd Light Horse Brigade and the 11th Light Armoured Motor Battery were ordered to press on with boldness and speed to occupy Jenin, a large Turkish centre ten miles due south of Afuleh, and about the same distance south-east of Lejjun, the Australians' jumping-off place. It was supremely important to hold Jenin. It was on the southern edge of the plain, and through it passed not only the railways from Tulkeram and Nablus which joined up at the junction of Messudieh, but the road systems between those places. Railway and road came through the Dothan Pass. The roads were in quite a good state of repair. German engineers had been busy, and they had changed rough mountain tracks into a good highway fit to carry laden motor lorries. Steep gradients were few, and a lot of masonry work had been done to build sound retaining walls where the road had been cut into the hillside. The enemy's only hope of escape was by this road or, if he came from the direction of Nablus, to descend into the valley and cross the Jordan in the neighbourhood of Beisan or at Jisr ed Damie on the road to Es Salt. The two routes indicated were effectually blocked on the afternoon of the 20th, and we held the enemy from the Plain of Armageddon to the Jordan. Such was the crushing blow inflicted on the Turks and their German military masters. The 3rd Australian Light Horse Brigade carried out their task in the spirit as well as the letter. Their orders were to capture Jenin with the 'greatest boldness and speed,' and three hours after their start from Lejjun the place was theirs, although fighting had not stopped. They moved at a fast trot over Armageddon to a line of defensive works which the enemy had built to cover Jenin from the north-west. The Australians had recently been changed from mounted infantry to cavalry, and had discarded the bayonet for the sword. They went for the Turk with the *arme blanche*. Opening out they drew swords and charged the trenches, overwhelming the defenders in the most decisive fashion, and galloped into a portion of the village beyond the aerodrome, capturing it with thousands of prisoners and an enormous quantity of war material. The Australians' terrific speed prevented any organised resistance, but there was a good deal of fighting among the houses and trees in the dark, and, to do them justice, the, Germans were mainly responsible for it. The 14th Cavalry Brigade from the 5th Cavalry Division were on their way from Afuleh to assist the Light Horse, and as many Turks continued to pour into Jenin from the south, the 11th regiment of Light Horse came from the 4th Brigade to reinforce the 3rd Brigade, and artillery was also moved towards the village. The whole position was cleared up on the following morning, and the 14th Cavalry Brigade returned to Afuleh. The 3rd Light Horse Brigade had one officer and one man wounded, and they sent on to Lejjun 7000 prisoners. More, many more were to follow.

At the moment the 3rd Light Horse were setting out for their triumph at Jenin the 4th Cavalry Division were starting from Afuleh to frustrate any Turkish effort to keep a way open for their army at Beisan. They raced along the valley of Jezreel between frowning hills which might have contained the remnants of an army. If there were any Turks in those hills they preferred hiding to fighting, and beyond an occasional sniper's shot there was no opposition while the column of horsemen moved up to Shutta Station, more than half-way to their objective. This was reached in rather more than an hour from leaving Afuleh, a ten-miles ride. By half-past four the leading brigade were within two miles of Beisan, and in another half-hour they had silenced the enemy and occupied the village, capturing about 100 prisoners and three 5.9 guns. The division had covered a distance of eighty-five miles in thirty-four hours, and having got to the commanding position of Beisan, General Barrow instructed the detachment of the 19th Lancers to withdraw the demolition charges from the bridge at Jisr Mejamie, and, whilst doing so, heartily congratulated the officers and men on their exceptional work. At half-past one on the afternoon of September 21 the 13th Cavalry Brigade marched through Nazareth. They gained the junction of the roads leading from Tiberias to Acre and Haifa without much trouble, and small parties went forward to Kefr Kenna and Safarieh, where more Germans and Turks, who recognised the impossibility of getting away, were made prisoners. While the 13th Cavalry Brigade occupied a line north of Nazareth the other two brigades of the 5th Cavalry Division picketed the country from Afuleh to Shutta Station. Thus, with the 4th Cavalry Division on the east and the Australian Mounted Division on the west and south, there was a long network of troops waiting to gather in a further haul of battalions of the Turkish 7th and 8th Armies.

There was one incident at Afuleh on the 20th which told as well as anything could tell how mazed the Turkish forces had become at the suddenness of the destruction of their power. After the capture of Afuleh our airmen quickly took advantage of the place for a forward landing-ground, and our planes came down on the former German aerodrome. A couple of hours after some Australian machines had arrived the hum of an aero engine was heard, and to everybody's surprise it turned out to be a Hun machine. No one stirred while the plane banked and dived, but when it was seen to be about to land, one of our pilots started his engine and jumped into his seat, in readiness to go up and fight if the German did not get out of his machine. Just as the plane touched earth an armoured car went after it, and then the pilot, doubtless looking about him and seeing the red-white-and-blue rings on our planes, tried to take off. But he was in the trap. The armoured car was on him at once and he surrendered. With the plane we captured two bags containing mail for Turkish headquarters, including letters for Liman von Sanders which the pilot had carried from Rayak, the railway junction north of Damascus. Either the news that we had broken through the whole Turkish line had not trickled through to Damascus (though General von Sanders himself was not far from Damascus at the time), or the full nature of the defeat had been withheld. The latter surmise is scarcely probable, because if the Germans at Rayak had known of the disaster at the front they would not have risked putting letters for the Generalissimo in a bag to be delivered at Afuleh. It would be interesting to know when the news reached Constantinople, and I would hazard a guess that the Turkish Government first heard of the full extent of the defeat from extracts of General Allenby's telegrams published in the London papers. There was no delay in sending our good news to the Continent. We had a real propaganda department at last.

CHAPTER 14

Stern Hill Fighting

It is time to return to the fighting of the infantry corps, and to deal with the operations in the sector immediately north of Jerusalem. The rôle of the 20th Corps, a difficult one with its strength very largely reduced by the transfer of the 60th Division to the 21stCorps, was to drive the enemy from the hills between our front line and Nablus, and to send them into the cavalry's long outstretched arms either at Beisan or Jenin as the Turks might choose. The 20th Corps achieved its aims, and with the 21st Corps and Desert Mounted Corps it shared the credit for the complete destruction of two Turkish armies. The 20th Corps' work in the final phase of General Allenby's campaign was just as masterly as in its turning movements at Beersheba and Sheria, and in the capture and defence of Jerusalem. General Chetwode, the Corps Commander, after considering the problem of an advance on Nablus, had come the conclusion that, whether the force available consisted of two, three, or four divisions, the attack ought to take the form of a converging movement from both flanks towards the general line from Akrabeh, a village five miles east of the Nablus road, to Jemmain, a spot four miles west of the road. This line was approximately eight miles north of the line we held across the Nablus road, and about the same distance south of Nablus. The whole country directly to our front was exceedingly difficult. There was a continuous succession of deep wadis and precipitous mountains with rarely a piece of flat ground. The enemy had concentrated all his energy on building defensive works in the centre of the 20th Corps front which General Chetwode did not propose to assault at all. In carrying out a converging movement, the two attacks from the flanks would be moving either along a watershed on the right, or along spurs on the left with no deep wadis or other obstacles to cross.

The enemy's road systems on the flanks were convenient to the proposed line of advance, and arrangements could be made by previous forward construction up to our outpost line to join up our system rapidly with that of the enemy as soon as the advance began. We had to secure some highway other than the Nablus road because that road had been destroyed in several places between Sinjil and Lubban, and it was believed repairs would take a considerable time. After the raid on the El Burj ridge, which I have already described, the enemy employed a good deal of labour on repairing and strengthening his works, and if he intended to hold them, an advance from the flanks, carried out rapidly, would offer a chance of cutting off and capturing guns and material opposite the centre of the Corps front. A preliminary operation was necessary to get an enemy position on the wadi Samieh, one of those extraordinarily deep clefts in the mountains on the Jordan valley side of the Judean hills, in order that the advance might not be held up by having to take a position which the Turks had arranged well to the south-east of their main line, but General Headquarters decided that the necessary movement should not take place till just before the commencement of the main attack. Only the 10th and 53rd Divisions were allotted to the 20th Corps for the September operations, so that during the period of concentration there was a wide gap left in the centre of the front. The fullest strength of the two divisions would be required for the attacks on the flanks, and General Chetwode arranged a force under General Watson, consisting of the Worcester Yeomanry, the Corps Cavalry regiment, the two pioneer battalions of the 10th and 53rd Divisions, who would be required to repair the Nablus road as soon as it was opened, and a temporary detachment made up of surplus men from the Corps reinforcement camp. Watson's force would fill the gap when concentration took place and prevent the enemy noticing any change in our dispositions.

In preparation for the attack a considerable amount of work was taken in hand. New roads had to be made and others improved. The pipe line had to be extended and an additional 200,000 gallons of water stored, while forward dumps of ammunition and food were arranged for. General Watson's force took over the centre of the line on the night of September 13. The Corps was originally ordered to prepare to commence its main advance on the evening of September 20, but on the evening of September 16 it was decided that the 10th Division should be ready to advance on the evening of the 19th, and this is another instance of how thoroughly the General Staff appreciated the course the battle would take. The preliminary operations by the 53rd Division took place on the night of September 18, in order to advance the right flank of the Corps across the wadi Samieh to Mugheir, two miles to the north of the wadi, and a ridge running westward from it. The importance of this line was that, once it was held by us, the main advance could proceed along the watershed, which ran west of the village of Domeh through Medjel Beni Fadl on to Akrabeh and the high ground to the north, without having to cross any deep wadis, and by securing the wadi Samieh we should obtain and develop an unlimited supply of water in the wadi, Which was essential in view of the shortage in the country ahead of us. It would also enable us to link up our road system in this area with that of the enemy.

The 160th Brigade on the right and the 159th Brigade on the left were employed in the attack. The battalions of the 160th left their positions as soon as it was dark and followed one another in succession across the wadi Samieh. The spurs running up the northern side of the wadi were very steep and hard to climb, but there was only slight opposition and the brigade made good progress till near some works a mile north-east of the wadi, where the enemy resisted and fired heavily with machine guns and rifles. Our guns got on to the works, and after a brief bombardment the 1/17th Infantry assaulted them successfully. The remaining battalions then advanced and secured their objectives, the enemy appearing surprised and offering little resistance when he found his prepared positions turned and attacked from flanks and rear. While the 159th Brigade were winning their first objectives a demonstration was made against Amurieh, and a raid on Turmus Aya, a village near the Nablus road close to Sinjil, induced the Turks to believe that an attack on the whole front was beginning. A hill, which in our Army's nomenclature was called Hindhead, was taken by the 159th Brigade before the enemy had time to man the defences, and Square Hill, not far away, was assaulted and carried after a five-minutes bombardment by the Cape Corps battalion of the 160th Brigade. There was only one point in the line where the Division failed to reach their objectives. This was a redoubt on Abu Malul, a hill nearly 3000 feet high, two miles due west of Mugheir. The 3/152nd Infantry went to the assault three times, but the redoubt was strongly held and after severe fighting the battalion was withdrawn to another hill in the vicinity. However, early the following night Abu Malul was taken. The 53rd Division did very indeed in securing this new line. The 160th Brigade had to follow a steep and difficult road, and took strong positions from the rear with several hundred prisoners at only slight loss to themselves. The brigade was officially reported to have 'carried out a difficult night march with great skill and discipline, and pushed through the attack with dash and vigour.' The 159th Brigade had to make direct assaults on strong enemy works and they met with greater resistance, but this was quickly overcome by the gallantry and resolution of the troops.

The 20th Corps was now ready to carry out its main attack as soon as orders were received from G.H.Q. They were not long in coming. At a little after noon on the 19th, General Allenby, in view of the remarkable success which had been achieved by the 21stCorps on the whole line from the coast to the foothills, decided that the 10th and 53rd Divisions should attack on the night of the 19th. General Chetwode issued orders at three o'clock that both divisions should pursue the enemy relentlessly if there were any signs of a general retreat. The first main objective of the 10th Division was the Furkhah ridge, six miles west of the Nablus road and parallel with the village of Lubban. The ridge was the whole pivot of the enemy's defensive line on this part of the front. It was more strongly fortified than any position opposite the 20th Corps, but here again the Turks had employed all their ingenuity in constructing works to resist an attack from the south. It was a fatal mistake. Since the line opposite Furkhah had been held, the 20th Corps set out to lead the enemy to anticipate that we should assault the position from the south. Nothing was ever attempted against the western spurs of the ridge, and the result was that the Turks left the ground rising up to Furkhah from both sides of the wadi Rashid in a comparatively weak state of defence. Yet the policy of the 20th Corps was always to attack up these spurs. Between two and three miles to the north-west were the Kher Ras ridge and Mogg ridge, where the works were also arranged to resist a direct assault, whereas the intention was to turn and attack them from the east. The advance of the 10th Division was to be done in three stages. In the first place the 29th Brigade were to assault and capture the Furkhah ridge by an attack from the west up the spurs from the wadi Rashid. Having taken the ridge the brigade in the second phase were to march to Selfit, a village two miles to the north-east, while the 31st Brigade crossing the wadi Mutwy, north-west of Furkhah, were to throw out a defensive flank to the north, and then roll up the Mogg ridge defences from the east, thus taking them in flank and rear. The success of the 31st Brigade would place the division on a broad front for the third stage—which was an advance of the whole Division north-eastwards towards Iskaka and Jemain—and bring it much closer to the Nablus road.

General Longley's division had reason to be proud of the brilliant performance of its night's work. Not only had the troops to face the trials of exceedingly bad country and strong enemy works, but the plan as laid down—it was followed to the letter—demanded heavy marches at the cost of much fatigue. The Irish battalions and the Indian battalions brigaded with them were splendid. The attack on Furkhah was a double disappointment to the enemy. It came from a direction the Turks had not provided for and it fell on them at a most unseasonable moment. The enemy troops on the front of the attack had received orders to retire at eight o'clock; the 29th Brigade's attack was timed a quarter of an hour earlier, and instead of the enemy surprising us by leaving empty trenches on our front, our bombardment and machine-gun barrage pinned him down to fight it out. The 1st Leinsters advanced on the right and the 1/151st Infantry on the left, and footed it up the steep rocky slopes with the agility of strong men. They were stoutly opposed at first but nothing could stop them. The speed with which they gained the trenches made the Turks realise that they were irresistible, and the opposition soon broke down. The battalions forged ahead from the ridge, and at four o'clock next morning held a strong line from Selfit along a track to the small village of Senameh, a mile and a half to the north-west. While the Turks on Furkhah ridge were being suitably dealt with the 31st Brigade were moving by on the west. The 2nd Royal Irish Fusiliers crossed the wadi Mutwy at ten o'clock and took the Khan el Mutwy from the east, meeting with slight opposition. The 74th Punjabis went over the Mutwy at a point farther to the west and, attacking the defences from the flank and rear, soon became possessed of the works at Fakhakhir and on Mogg ridge. The other two battalions of the brigade moved over the wadi next morning at two o'clock, the 2/42nd Deolis pushing on to Jaly and Ras Aish, both north of Selfit, and the 2/101st Grenadiers making for Kefr Haris and Sheikh Othman, important points west of Jaly. Two battalions of the 30th Brigade which were in reserve had in the meantime commenced to make a road to connect with the enemy's road system at Ain Mutwy, and they completed three and a half miles of good track by noon next day.

The rapid advance of the Irish Division gave promise of good results in this sector in the next day or two, but very heavy fighting was before them on September 20, and the formidable resistance met with was doubtless due to the fact that the Turks in this sector knew nothing of the disaster on their right. The position to which the enemy had retired when Furkhah was attacked was one of enormous strength. It ran from Ras et Dar on the Nablus road through Iskaka to Kefr Haris, and was held by four battalions which included many

Germans, with a large number of machine guns. Throughout the day the enemy fought with the greatest determination, and always showed a readiness to counter-attack. Whereas the enemy was well placed, the 10th Division had all the difficulties of the country to contend with. It seemed impossible to move field artillery, and only one mountain battery was available, but after superhuman efforts the field-gunners, who frequently had to manhandle their guns over rocks and up mountain sides, managed to get into action in the afternoon. By seven o'clock in the morning the 29th Brigade were attacking in the direction of Iskaka and Merda, and for a time made some progress in the hilly ground, but their further advance was stopped by artillery and machine-gun fire. At half-past eight the 31st Brigade, which had been delayed by the terrible state of the tracks, attacked towards Haris and Kefr Haris, two villages a mile apart. The 2/42nd Deolis got to Ras Aish, about a mile south-east of Haris, and made a magnificent effort to secure the crest of a hill to the north. Nine times they tried to get a footing on the top of the hill, but on each occasion they were driven back and they had heavy losses, The 2/101st Grenadiers managed, to reach Sheikh Othman but they could get no farther towards Kefr Haris, and owing to the failure to drive the enemy from his positions about that village, the road which had been made during the night by the 30th Brigade with such skill and rapidity was under fire and could not be used for artillery or transport. Therefore another 5000 yards of road up a wadi had to be constructed and, guns being brought up along this new path, the attack was continued in the afternoon and the whole of the Kefr Haris system was won after heavy fighting. The casualties had been considerable among the attacking infantry, but despite the fact that they had been marching and fighting continuously in bad country for nearly twenty-four hours, they proved still capable of a great effort. j

On the other side of the Nablus road the 53rd Division were only able to make slow progress during the day. A hill called Jebeit was captured by the Cape battalion early in the morning, but a tremendous counter-attack drove them off, and the men from the Cape, who throughout the operations behaved with the greatest gallantry, suffered heavy losses. The counter-attack was delivered by the Turkish 109th regiment, which had only recently arrived from the Caucasus and had not previously been observed by contact on the Palestine Front. The advance of the 158th Brigade should have been started early in the morning, but the concentration was late, and when a forward movement began it was held up by enemy rearguards in strong positions with machine guns. Soon after noon the 1/17th Infantry of the 160th

Brigade assaulted Jebeit and took 150 prisoners, and away on their right the 159th Brigade had obtained possession of Ras et Tawil, but as the 158th Brigade were still unable to make progress against the hill of El Kust, General Mott postponed the attack till dusk.

General Watson's force were told on the evening of the 19th that the enemy opposite their front might retreat during the night, and a patrol stood by to move up the Nablus road at daylight, the remainder of the Worcester Yeomanry being held ready to proceed at an instant's notice. The patrol went out at six but was fired on from both sides of the road. The regiment was then ordered north to clear the ridge to Lubban, supported, if necessary, by the pioneer battalions, but after they had reached a point a couple of miles ahead of our front line, heavy machine-gun and artillery fire stopped them. The cavalry found that the damage to the road was not so serious as reported, but they discovered seventy-eight unexploded mines on the way and removed them. The situation on the Corps front by nightfall of the 20th was that, while considerable progress had been made, the resistance of strong enemy rearguards had not been broken down, owing to the difficulties of ground which prevented artillery giving close support to infantry. In these circumstances progress during daylight against an enemy well supplied with machine guns and artillery was bound to be slow, as the force available was not sufficient to press the enemy on a front broad enough to enable the turning of his strong points.

CHAPTER 15

Infantry Secure the Railway Junction

To return to the XXIst Corps front. It will be remembered that the 60th Division on the 19th were in Tulkeram before sundown, and that the 7th, 3rd, and 54th Divisions were well in the foothills in an easterly and north-easterly direction, the 75th Division remaining in Corps reserve.

General Bulfin ordered a further general advance eastward to be started at 5 A.M. on the 20th. During the night the 5th Australian Light Horse Brigade had got so far across the hills north-east of Tulkeram that they were able to destroy half a mile of the Turkish railway about Ajjeh, but there were far too many troops in their path to enable them to reach Jenin and they returned to Tulkeram. The 54th Division moved out from Bidieh, and the French detachment, after getting to Arara and Zawieh, joined up with the right of the 163rd Brigade. When the 8th Infantry Brigade of the 3rd Division started their forward movement they were hotly opposed by strong German rear-guards, and although the left of the 54th Division gave them assistance, seven hours' fighting only took the brigade to a point one mile east of Azzun. The opposition against the 7th as well as the 8th Brigade continued to be stubborn until late in the afternoon when it weakened and both brigades pushed rapidly on to El Funduk, where they captured 250 prisoners, fifteen guns, and a large quantity of war material. The 9th Brigade met with less resistance, and passing through Baka at noon got to Kefr Kaddum and Kuryet Jit before it was dark. The 7th Division had the worst of the country and marched over tracks which nowhere deserved the description of roads. The 21st Brigade took what was called on the map the Felamieh-Kefr Zebad road. The 19th and 28th Brigades went along the Kefr Sur road, but these roads were found to converge at a spot near Kur, and from this place forward the whole Division was on one bad narrow stony track, with the 19th Brigade leading.

All wheels were left behind—a general service wagon would have been held up in a hundred places along the track—and only mountain guns could be moved with the infantry, but so physically fit were the men of the Division that the leading troops were within 1000 yards of Beit Lid by 11 o'clock, having crossed some ten miles of broken mountainous country in six hours with all sorts of obstacles in their path, to say nothing of an active enemy. Beit Lid is a village on the side of a hill which dominates Messudieh and the railway junction at that place. The enemy on Beit Lid had many machine guns and was supported by artillery. The Seaforth Highlanders attacked the hill twice without success, and had substantial losses from machine-gun fire as they attempted to crawl up the slopes. It was decided not to attack again at once but to wait until the 21st brigade had made a detour and had marched round the high ground at Khed Deir, a mile to the east. The brigade got on to this ridge at half-past five, and the completion of this turning movement enabled the 19th Brigade to carry Beit Lid an hour later. The 179th Brigade of the 60th Division (Brigadier-General K. T. Humphreys, D.S.O., who at one time was the B.G.G.S., XXIst Corps) moved up the Tulkeram-Messudieh road, and on reaching Anebta took to the hills and got to Jebel bir Asur in the evening. The Turks had tunnelled this hill for their railway, but as the line had been cut by the Australian Light Horse it was feared the enemy would try to destroy the tunnel. The Londoners found fifty boxes of gelignite packed into the southern end of the tunnel, and these they removed. Thus by the evening of the second day of the battle the cavalry had closed the principal exits through which the Turks could escape on the north, and the infantry of the XXIst Corps were almost in a position to form a barrier against them farther south, while other infantry of this Corps and the two divisions of the XXth Corps were gradually pressing what remained of the two Turkish armies into the net. It was a situation which filled the Palestine Army with enthusiasm. The men were to be called upon for fresh sacrifices, but tired as they were by trying marches unrelieved by short snatches of sleep, they would cheerfully have done twice as much as was asked of them.

The 28th Brigade of the 7th Division after making a hard march during the day did a fine night march. They moved past Beit Lid and over the wadi Eshi Shair, and got on to the Tulkeram-Nablus road at Ramin by half-past one. They then turned eastwards and advanced on Messudieh station, which they occupied at three in the morning, capturing an engine, sixteen railway wagons, and a complete Turkish hospital train in the station containing 400 sick Turks. Two German

SAMARIA

hospital nurses also surrendered. They had had an awful experience. When the Arabs had blown up the railway near Deraa they made a descent on a train which could not proceed and, so the nurses said, killed every man in it. The nurses escaped and, footsore and weary, managed to get to Messudieh, where the 7th Division took care of them. Soon after the occupation of Messudieh station an Indian battalion in the bright moonlight stalked Sumaria Hill to the south-east of the station, taking the garrison completely by surprise, and capturing 200 prisoners and a number of machine guns without suffering a single casualty themselves. Leaving a detachment in the station, the 28th Brigade pressed on farther to the east, and by an admirable disposition of his force Brigadier-General Davies took Samaria with slight loss. The 3rd Division also reached their objectives in good time on the 21st and linked up with the 7th Division. On the night of the 20th General Onslow had orders to march on Nablus from Tulkeram with his 5th Light Horse Brigade, reinforced by a squadron of the Corps Cavalry regiment and No. 2 Light Armoured Motor Battery. The brigade passed through the 179th Brigade near Anebta on the morning of the 21st and occupied Nablus soon after noon. The inhabitants were keen to show them how truly our airmen aimed in bombing the Turks' headquarters, but those troops which entered the town on duty did not remain long, for there were cases of cholera in the place. The Light Horse sent out a squadron to Balata on the outskirts of Nablus. Having gained touch there with the XXth Corps, they were recalled and ordered to march with the whole brigade to Jenin to rejoin the Australian Mounted Division. The brigade had had a stirring three days.

I have remarked upon the splendid fighting powers of the 60th Division. A tribute must also be paid to the 7th Indian Division which broke through the enemy's defences on Tabsor Hill, one of the strongest points in his line, and fought their way over a series of trenches to the Et Tireh system, a distance of 5½ miles in two and a half hours. It was a magnificent feat which could have been accomplished by none but the best troops. The Division was then reorganised and marched eastwards to Felamieh, 8½ miles away, which was reached at 6 P.M. The advance was continued at 5 A.M. on the 20th over exceedingly difficult tracks. In spite of serious opposition at Beit Lid the Division took Samaria on the morning of the 21st, having covered 30 miles in forty-eight and a half hours, fighting practically all the way. One part of the training of men of the XXIst Corps during the summer consisted of instruction in the use of captured weapons. This proved very useful in the 54th Division when men of the 1/8th Hants, by the skilful employment of captured machine guns, so increased the volume of fire that they materially assisted in the advance of their battalion. Kefr Kasim's capture in the initial stages of the battle was effected at light cost by the bold handling of Lewis guns which were pushed forward to deal with enemy machine guns. The 1/10th Londons of the 54th Division reached the high ground overlooking the wadi Kanah as two 5.9 and one 4.2 howitzers were being limbered up. A section of the 162nd Machine Gun Company immediately came into action at 1500 yards and with their first burst shot down the gun teams. Under cover of this machine-gun fire and of Lewis-gun fire the leading company of the battalion then charged and captured the three guns with their detachments. During the advance of the 181st Brigade north of Et Tireh enemy machine guns were very active, and held the brigade in check until a single 18-pounder was brought into action within 1500 yards of the enemy and in full view of them. The gun was fired over the sights and dispersed the machine-gunners. Another instance of the handiness of Lewis-gunners was furnished a little later during the advance of the 60th Division. When the 2/152nd Infantry got to Irteh they saw seven of the Turks' 77-mm. guns moving along a track. The fire of Lewis guns was at once brought to bear on the teams, and these were shot down and the guns and detachments captured.

The public have only a vague impression of the difficulties attending the provisioning of a big army in the field. Chapters might be written giving statistics of the hundreds of thousands of tons of supplies for men, horses, and guns, of the appetites of tractors, of lorries, of motor cars, and aeroplanes which consumed vast quantities of petrol, and yet the figures, staggering as they are, would convey but I small idea of the task thrown on the officers who controlled the desert railway from its terminus on the Suez Canal at Kantara to the railheads. They had a limited supply of rolling stock. Some of it was lent by the administration of the Egyptian Government railways, the remainder was drawn from British railway lines which had no surplus. The contribution from England could ill be spared, but we would have welcomed twice the quantity, and the fullest use would have been made of it. Very few trucks were idle for twenty-four hours. There was a sufficiency of labour, thanks to the far-sighted policy of General Sir Walter Campbell, and the good support given to it by Egyptian Government departments. At Kantara large gangs of Egyptian Labour Corps unloaded ocean-going steamers at the wharves, and worked in the railway depots, and at Ludd and Jerusalem the happy, singing

Ruins of the Church of St John the Baptist, Samaria

Egyptians, under sympathetic British and some excellent Syrian officers, were willing helpers of British troops. They were handsomely paid, far above the labour rates in Egypt, were better fed than at home, and had good allowances of leave. Heavy trains ran for many weeks before the battle started and they kept excellent time. The best was also got out of the light lines which ran from Ludd to Jaffa, and across the river Auja, and that which we built from Jerusalem around the hills to the west of the Holy City and on to Ramallah saved an immense amount of lorry traffic on the Nablus road. These light lines prevented the Quartermaster-General's department from having to apply for additional motor-lorry companies which were required for the Western Front, and they did much to help to solve the supply problem during an anxious period.

Water was as important as food and ammunition, and it gave as much trouble to the Chief Engineer, General Wright, as anything. Behind our front the water supply was developed wherever there was any sign of a yield, and one of the blessings our occupation conferred on the people of Palestine was the legacy we left of many new wells and many others repaired and cleaned out. But the reports of agents told of a shortage of water in front of our line and the information was accurate. Therefore preparations had to be made to carry water during the advance, as well as to supply the additional infantry and divisions of cavalry brought into the XXIst Corps for the attack. The majority of these troops being concentrated on the coast, there, just about Jelil, a pipe line was laid to give an output of almost 20,000 gallons per hour. Along the beach as many as forty-five wells were sunk, each of them giving a yield of 3000 gallons a day. To provide water for the troops operating in the foothills, where wells were few and far between and in poor repair, two water convoys were organised. Each convoy consisted of 2400 camels and donkeys carrying *fanatis*, flat rectangular tanks holding from ten to twelve gallons when camels carried them, or in case of donkeys, round receptacles of smaller capacity. These convoys were trained in the back areas, and crossed to the north of the Auja a few hours before the guns began to speak. It is obvious that if it could be arranged to refill the tanks some distance north of the line we held prior to the battle it would greatly lessen the journeys of the convoys, and the Chief Engineer of the XXIst Corps, General Hawksley, therefore had everything in readiness to extend his pipe line to a central delivering spot immediately the infantry crossed the enemy's trenches. His men actually laid 7000 yards of pipe line in eight hours, and were ready to supply

4000 gallons of water per hour at Jiljulieh early on the afternoon of September 19. It is admitted that without these convoys neither the 3rd nor the 7th Divisions could have continued their advance on the 20th. The hills in front of them were found to be practically waterless, and the Turks, knowing this from sad experience, must have been astonished at our perfection of detail.

A great deal of energy had also to be expended on road making. Between our front and the road system of the Turks, which only came south about as far as Jiljulieh, there was nothing except a few mud tracks. These were all in a bad state and the first rainfall made them quite useless. With scores of thousands of men and horses launched on a long attack, it was vital that the two road systems should be linked up as soon as possible, and that the new road which was to connect the two should be fit, not merely for general service wagons holding comparatively light loads, but for lorries filled to their utmost capacity. The main railway line had been built out to Ras el Ain, a Crusader ruin which stood out like a grim mediaeval fortress in the distance, but the line was under shell fire and was not used until the advance began in earnest. A road had to be built from Ras el Ain to Jiljulieh, and this would form the XXIst Corps' main line of supply until the railway was extended. The engineers and road-makers stood by to make the road when the battle started, and they actually began their work while the battle was going on round them. They worked with a will, and by half-past three in the afternoon had the four miles finished to Jiljulieh, and supplies were going over it at that hour.

I have often turned over in my mind the events of that glorious day, to decide which was the most wonderful of all the extraordinary scenes on the battle front. Sometimes I think it was the furious bombardment over more than twenty miles of the line, and the attacks of the infantry close behind and, in some cases, right into our barrage of shells. It was the most thrilling spectacle, certainly, but was it more magnificent than that mighty mass of cavalry waiting for the signal that the infantry were through, and then speeding away, heedless of hazards, as fast as their gallant chargers could take them to complete thoroughly what the splendid infantry had so well begun? Then again he would be lacking in patriotic fire who did not feel the blood quicken in his veins at the sight of large bodies of disarmed prisoners coming back to behind our old positions within a couple of hours of the guns first boom. That went on all day. As I passed over a portion of the field from left to right, on ground we had just wrested from the enemy, I met many such parties. It seemed almost ridiculous to see hundreds of men escorted by half a dozen infantrymen. One lot of prisoners had only two Light Horsemen as escort, one in front, and the other in rear trying to keep the stragglers from falling behind. Officers as well as men seemed downcast, as if the surprise of defeat had taken the spirit out of them. But I think the movement of lorry columns that afternoon gave me greater pride in our Army than the capture of thousands of prisoners. The lorries moved forward over a country which but a few brief hours before had been roadless, its shallow wadis veritable traps for all wheeled vehicles, and its uneven cracked ground needing to be levelled and made sound, and watching that stream of traffic so swiftly set going one felt that the organisation of the Army was all right, and that the fighting men were to get all the support that it was possible to give them.

CHAPTER 16

Wrecking an Army

The Desert Mounted Corps, arriving at Afuleh and Beisan, blocked all roads of retreat for the defeated armies except that from Nablus down the wadi Farah to the Jisr ed Damie crossing of the Jordan. It was therefore imperative that the troops of the XXth Corps should reach Nablus and the high ground north and north-east of the town as rapidly as possible to cut off this last line of retreat. General Chetwode accordingly issued orders on the late afternoon of the 20th that the 53rd Division should press on after dark to reach the neighbourhood of Nablus early on the following day, and the 10th Division were directed on the town itself. The Worcester Yeomanry were to keep touch with the enemy on the main road during the night and to advance at dawn, and the 10th Heavy Battery and the 205th Siege Battery were under orders to be prepared to occupy positions about Sawieh by daylight. General Chetwode spoke to both divisional commanders and urged upon them the necessity of blocking the road to Damie, instructing them to take bold action to brush aside resistance. He ordered them to push on absolutely regardless of fatigue of men and animals. Both divisions had a long way to go. The 53rd starting at midnight got to Kusrah at 4 A.M. and close to the road at Telfit at dawn, a single Lewis-gun team of the 5/6th Royal Welsh Fusiliers capturing 150 prisoners and some machine guns. Then there was a rapid advance on Akrabeh, which was entered at 10 o'clock, and by evening the Division had made Beit Furik and Beit Dejan, an advance of some 15,000 yards during the day. However, they were still a considerable distance from the wadi Farah road. The 10th Division had a very trying time in appallingly bad country, but the Division's attack that day was one of the finest performances in the whole operations. The 29th Brigade were directed to proceed by the Iskaka-Yasuf track towards Kuzah, two miles south of Huwarah, and the 31st Brigade went by

Jemmain-Ain Abus road to Mazar abd el Hakk. The 30th Brigade was ordered to concentrate at Selfit by half-past nine on the 20th, and follow in rear of the 29th Brigade till the latter reached a line south of Kuzah, when the 30th Brigade with the 68th Brigade R.F.A. and a mountain battery were to pass through and at their best pace make for the high ground beyond Nablus. It was intended that the 31st Brigade should follow in support, the 29th coming into divisional reserve. The road from Selfit to Iskaka is very narrow and full of rocks, and with transport as well as troops coming through the first-named place it was impossible to avoid congestion and delay. The troops however willingly responded to a call to make up the stoppages, and the Kashmir Imperial Service Infantry, the rear battalion of the 30th Brigade, covered three miles at the double to catch up the brigade. Yet these grand fighting men had been marching and fighting since the operations began and had had practically no sleep for three nights.

At half-past eight on the morning of the 21st the 30th Brigade had passed through the 29th and were debouching into the plain between Huwarah and Nablus. The plain is a wide flat stretch of country almost entirely enclosed by hills, those on the north being higher than the hills on the east. The most prominent hill on the north appeared to be Gezerim, but that was only because, from the point at which the Irish Division entered the plain, Gezerim was nearer to us than Mount Ebal, the noble height on the other side of the pass which held Nablus, the Shechem of old. On Gezerim and the nearer hills the Turks were waiting to hold up the advance, and the nearer hills certainly appeared an obstacle which nothing but a methodical attack supported by guns could surmount. The enemy had many machine guns here and on other hills fringing the plain on the west, and when our infantry came into the open machine guns enfiladed them. The brigadier, true to his orders to press on, paid no heed to them, but opening out his battalions into widely extended lines he swung the whole brigade over to the eastern side of the plain out of range, leaving a field battery in action south of Huwarah to protect his flank, with a mountain battery following in close support behind his right flank. Machine-gun sections were immediately behind the leading battalion. This was a bold stroke, and much valuable time was saved by not attacking the craggy hills, and forcing the Turks out of them by manoeuvre. The 30th Brigade were out of range, and their rapid advance was threatening the Turks' line of retreat, so the enemy left the hills and his rearguards resisted but little longer.

The Turks did attempt to make a stand at Rujib, two miles south of Nablus, but it lasted no more than an hour, for another outflanking movement from the east drove them off at eleven o'clock, and the enemy thereafter became a disorganised rabble. The Worcester Yeomanry then took up the pursuit and got as far as Askar, north-east of Nablus, where they were

stopped by machine-gun fire. The 31st Brigade also made a fine march to the hills south of Nablus, while the 29th Brigade having followed the 30th Brigade, on the initiative of its commander went on to Balata where many prisoners were taken. In a warm appreciation of the performance of the 10th Division General Chetwode said: 'The spirit and endurance of the troops and the resolution of the commanders resulted in the final collapse of the enemy's resistance. The Division had fought and marched continuously for two days over more than twenty miles of difficult country.'

* * * * * * * *

When the 10th Division got to Balata and fighting stopped, some of the men saw, away to their right, one of the most remarkable scenes of wreckage in the war. They had been very curious as to the object of an extremely rapid burst of gun fire on their left earlier in the day. The guns of a battery of the 68th Brigade R.F.A. had come into action near the road slightly more than a mile south of Nablus, and were firing across the 30th Brigade's front. The black smoke of H.E. shells had risen in clouds above a depression, and the volume of fire suggested that there was a substantial target. The guns' work was soon over and then there was silence, except for an occasional rifle shot or a distant burst of machine-gun fire. The artillery had finished a job that the airmen had almost completed. Generals who had spent years on the Western Front told me they had never seen such a picture of destruction. An airman it appears, who was out on reconnaissance early in the morning of the 21st, went to see what was happening on the road leading from Nablus to the Jisr ed Damie crossing, the only route by which the enemy could escape. He came back to his aerodrome and reported that the enemy was streaming down the road, and that from near Balata onwards on the road, as it passed through a defile to Ferweh and along the wadi Farah, there was a column of guns and transport stretching from five to eight miles. This information was instantly telephoned to the headquarters of the Palestine Wing, and General Borton at once organised a scheme to stop the column. The speed with which it was put into operation was evidence of the efficiency of the Air Force. Every aeroplane on the front which could be spared for the work was brought into the plan. From the aerodromes at Jerusalem, Junction Station, Ramleh, and Sarona (many of the planes which had been stationed at those places had gone to forward positions) machines went out at intervals so arranged that there should be two bombers over the Ferweh road every two minutes, and an additional flight of six machines each half-hour.

The airmen worked to a timetable and the times were well kept. The result of the bombing was awful. The road was narrow and enclosed. There were few places where a lorry or waggon could turn., Beyond Ferweh there were cliff sides falling to the wadi Farah on the right-hand side of the road, and steep slopes on the other side which threatened destruction to anything leaving the highway. The first pair of bombers attacked the head of the column. Their bombs dropped with unerring accuracy, and, smashing up guns and teams, they blocked the road as effectually as if a stone wall had been built across it. They then came down and machine-gunned men and animals before hurrying off home to get a fresh supply of 'eggs.' The next pair made certain that the first airmen had made no mistake and dropped a bomb or two to complete the wreckage at the head of the column before continuing to work towards the centre of the halted transport. The enemy drivers, escorts, and gunners took to the high ground, for they saw escape was hopeless, and it spelt death to remain with their teams. Nothing could be done for the animals, and this immovable mass had to be left to be destroyed at the airmen's will. Our pilots took chances in doing their work thoroughly and, dropping their bombs mostly from a height of two hundred feet, they were always under the fire of machine guns and riflemen from the high ground. Two of them were brought down and killed, but there were others to carry on, and from eight o'clock in the morning till nearly midday there was a continual succession of explosions in and about the column. Then some of the airmen got so sick of the awful havoc they had created that they asked to be relieved of the duty, and it was left to the gunners to smash up the rear of the column and to leave what remained of the booty to be collected at leisure.

I did not see the road till next day. It was horrible. Thousands of dead animals already made the air offensive. Horses, oxen, mules, and donkeys had met sudden deaths as they stood anchored in that long-drawn-out column of transport. There were signs of panic, for some beasts had swung out of the line and had hurled themselves with their loads over the precipice into the bed of the wadi, while other frightened creatures had made a desperate effort to haul the vehicles attached to them up the rocky hills. There was scarcely anything standing on wheels except guns, and not all of these had survived the bombs.

A whole army's papers were distributed to the four winds, and it was astonishing to find what an amount office work the Germans had introduced into the Turkish army.

There seemed to be papers and books for recording everything, and with the rubbish was an immense quantity of propaganda literature printed in Arabic and containing excellent illustrations, which was designed to make Arabs believe in the might and majesty of the German Empire and its mighty army. The All Highest of course appeared in many a picture.

Old uniforms, ragged and dirty, camp equipment, officers' kit of German manufacture were strewn everywhere and were heaped with the hard flat cakes of bread which formed the staple portion of the Turks' rations, dried beans, and some canned meat. Field kitchens, serviceable no longer, and water carts drained dry through many a hole torn in the tanks, had been tossed about by the shock of high explosives, and guns, limbers, and lorries were hopelessly destroyed. Before I entered the defile I was told it would be difficult for a camel to pick a path along the road. That was true. The moment the first bomb dropped on the head of the column the whole of the transport was doomed, and when the airmen had ceased there was not one vehicle the enemy could move away. It was a repetition of the scene on the Tulkeram road near Anebta, but the destruction and the horror were magnified twentyfold.

Between Balata and Ferweh we counted 74 guns, a number of them 5.9s, 11 motor lorries, 683 four-wheeled wagons, and 75 two-wheeled carts, and lower down the road where it followed the course of the wadi Farah we found 13 guns, 44 motor lorries, 154 four-wheeled wagons, 4 motor cars, 20 water carts, a number of field kitchens, and an enormous amount of stores of which the enemy was greatly in need. The Turks could not replace those 87 guns. On the morning of the 23rd September a brigade of the 10th Division was sent up the road to clear it, but the task was beyond one brigade's powers and a second brigade went to its assistance. All the guns were drawn out by lorries and a vast quantity of material was burned. The Worcester Yeomanry patrolled the roads to Tubas and Beisan to gain touch with the 4th Cavalry Division parties south of the latter place. They met with some opposition, but the Turks had lost heart and, by the evening of the 23rd, 150 of our Midland yeomen had collected

1500 prisoners. More were brought in on the following day, and then the Corps' cavalry made a sweep of the country between the Beisan road and the Jordan. During the operations commencing on September 19, the XXth Corps had 9 British officers killed and 32 wounded, 60 British other ranks killed and 222 wounded, 4 Indian officers killed and 19 wounded, and 152 Indian other ranks killed and 989 wounded, whilst 18 men were missing, making a total of 1505 casualties. The enemy's casualties in killed and wounded were infinitely greater, and great numbers of prisoners were taken.

CHAPTER 17

The Cavalry's Net

It is impossible to exaggerate the importance of the work which fell on Desert Mounted Corps during the operations. So far from the cavalry's labours being lightened by the complete annihilation of the Turkish 7th and 8th Armies, they were enormously increased. The War Cabinet, recognising the vast influence which the victory in Palestine would have on the whole war, were urging that our great success should be exploited to the fullest extent, and wished for an immediate advance on Aleppo, some three hundred miles to the north. Aleppo was always within the sphere of General Allenby's ultimate achievements and his plan included an advance as early as possible from the line he had won, but he advocated caution. A precipitate advance might have involved a check, and though he had already moved troops northwards before London asked his advice about a dash on Aleppo, the Commander-in-Chief pointed out the difficulties of such a venture, and the War Cabinet, having absolute faith in his judgment, trusted the man on the spot. But the cavalry had far more to do than to keep closed the Turks' lines of retreat. The rounding-up of every Turk who might again come into action against us if he escaped needed ceaseless vigilance, and while the majority of the enemy seemed willing enough to surrender when they saw there was no chance of reaching Damascus, many of them, especially when Germans were with them, fought desperately in their efforts to get away. Our troops invariably proved that they were the masters of the situation, but they were called upon to fight hard, and the impression which somehow or other seemed to have gained support at home, that the Palestine Army was having a military promenade through a bright, picturesque and historical country, was altogether wrong.

Desert Mounted Corps had much to do besides capturing Turks on the road and searching villages and caves for them. It had also to secure points which were vital to us as jumping-off places for the next stage in the advance. Haifa was one of the most important of these. As a port there is not much to be said for it. The roadstead is completely exposed to winds which blow strongly from the north and north-west, and these are the prevailing winds in winter. But we had to get Haifa and make the utmost use of it as a base for supplying the infantry who would march up the coast, and to help to provision Desert Mounted Corps when in a day or two the cavalry should again leap forward. Accordingly it was decided to take the town on September 23. Natives had reported on the previous day that the enemy had evacuated it. That, like a great deal of native information, was inaccurate. Brigadier-General A. D'A. King, D.S.O., who had served as chief artillery officer in Desert Column and afterwards continued in a like capacity when the column was converted into Desert Mounted Corps, had been appointed prospective military governor of Haifa, and on the 22nd he left Lejjun for the town with No. 12 Light Armoured Motor Battery and No. 7 Light Car Patrol. On nearing the town the party were heavily fired upon by field guns, machine guns and infantry, and could not proceed. Indeed some of the party narrowly escaped capture. The Light Car Patrol, however, secured and brought in 64 prisoners, and captured an enemy demolition party in the act of trying to explode a charge under one of the road bridges. The charge was withdrawn.

The Australian Mounted Division relieved the 5th Cavalry Division at Afuleh and Nazareth at dawn on the 23rd, and this left the 5th Cavalry Division free to attack Haifa and Acre, orders for the march having been issued on the previous day.

In the early hours of the 22nd some of their outposts north-west of Nazareth had had a brisk hour or two. About 700 Turks, making a forced march from Haifa to Tiberias along the Acre-Nazareth road, came upon our outposts and vigorously attacked them. They were beaten off, and the 18th Lancers organised a counter-attack which was well pushed home, 311 prisoners and four machine guns being taken and many Turks killed.

At five o'clock on the morning of the 23rd the 5th Cavalry Division advanced in two columns, the right consisting of the 13th Cavalry Brigade, with No. 11 Light Armoured Motor Battery and No. 1 Light Car Patrol, by the main Nazareth-Acre road. They entered the walled town of Acre at one o'clock after slight opposition, capturing two guns, nine officers, and 250 other ranks. The left column took the Jebata-Jeida road, a trifle to the south of the main Nazareth road, the 15th Cavalry Brigade (less the Hyderabad Lancers), and 'B' Battery

A VIEW FROM SAMARIA

H. A.C. leading, followed by Divisional Headquarters and the 14th Cavalry Brigade. At Jebata a contact aeroplane dropped a message that 200 Turks were holding Haifa railway station, and that it had been fired on by machine guns at Jidru. Shortly after ten o'clock the leading troops of the advanced guard, having crossed the railway at the edge of the plain and proceeded to the Mount Carmel range, got to a spot about a mile north of the village of Duweimin, some five miles due south of Haifa, and it was soon apparent that our entry into the town would be stoutly resisted. It would be hard to imagine a place more easy to defend. On the east there is low-lying ground cut up by numerous wadis and swamps with quicksands in many places. To the south of the town, where the Jewish and native quarters are on a low level, the approach is over a series of hills which are steep and rocky, and Karmel-heim, the German colony, is on a hill about a thousand feet above the level of the sea, and reached from the town by a zigzag road. The place was taken by a brilliant, dashing piece of fighting, although held by a force stronger in men and infinitely stronger in guns than the regiments put into the attack. To secure the place in face of many disadvantages and at small cost was highly creditable alike to the commander and to his officers and men.

At one o'clock our main body had halted at a point east of the Haifa-Afuleh railway opposite Yajir, four miles south-east of Haifa. One squadron of the Mysore Lancers was on the Haifa-Acre railway two miles east of the town, two squadrons were about a mile and a half farther south, and another squadron was between them and the main body. The Sherwood Rangers were on the way to join the Mysore Lancers, and the Jodhpur Lancers were behind the line held by the Mysore Lancers, ready to gallop through them and attack. Close up with the Jodhpur Lancers, 'B' Battery H.A.C. was in action. Patrols reported that two enemy guns and eight machine guns were placed on the north side of the wadi which flows from south to north a mile east of Haifa railway station, and that they could not reach the wadi because of these guns and machine guns, the latter being hidden among palm-trees near the shore. The enemy kept up a desultory fire, to which the H.A.C. replied when the gunners could obtain targets. The Jodhpur Lancers at two o'clock moved across the wadi Mukutta to a position of readiness a quarter of a mile north-east of the Haifa-Nazareth road near Beled esh Sheikh, and at a quarter to three the Jodhpurs went off at a trot in column of squadrons in line of troop columns and made for the south-and-north wadi on the east of the town. They had to face very heavy machine-gun fire, the intensity of which had prevented

155

a reconnaissance of the wadi. This was found to be impassable, and two of the ground scouts who had got into it disappeared at once in the quicksands. The Jodhpurs immediately changed direction left, the leading squadron being directed on machine-gunners and riflemen to the west of the road and railway. These they killed and made the passage of the defile possible. Another squadron worked up the road and got west of the troublesome wadi, when they rushed on to a mound near a soap factory and took three guns and two machine guns. The other two squadrons were close behind and, Colonel Holden leading them, charged straight into and through the town, where they were joined by the remainder of the regiment, one squadron which had passed south of the town along the lower slopes of Mount Carmel capturing two guns *en route*. Considerable fighting continued in the streets for some time. Meanwhile a detached squadron of the Mysore Lancers under Lieut. Menin had advanced through the sand dunes after being held up machine-gun fire, and, galloping along the flat soft beach, they caught the Turks near the mouth of the wadi Mukutta and charged with the lance, killing many and taking 110 prisoners, two guns, and two machine guns.

At the same time as the mounted attack from the east, a weak squadron of the Mysore Lancers under Lieut. Horseman, which had worked rapidly on to Mount Carmel, made a stirring charge on the enemy's positions one mile north of Karmelheim. When the Mysores' machine guns and Hotchkiss rifle had come into action on a flank, the squadron numbered fifteen all told, but neither the very rocky ground in front of them nor the good position of the enemy deterred them, and the little band were rewarded for their valiant charge by taking seventy-eight prisoners, a 6-inch naval gun, two mountain guns and two machine guns. A portion of the Sherwood Rangers moved in support and took another fifty prisoners. The Germans and Turks were staggered by the violence of the attack, and in half an hour the fighting was over and General MacAndrew and the remainder of his division were in Haifa. The Bedouins had commenced looting, and energetic action was taken to protect property from the natives, who here, as in many places we occupied, seemed to think that our arrival gave them the right to seize whatever had belonged to our enemies or their nationals. They were quickly disillusioned and taught that we regarded private property as sacred and would protect it. Often when I was proceeding through the country and had bivouacked at sunset, an officer of the detachment near by would send and ask me to camp close to his men, 'as he was not certain of the natives in such and such a village.' One slept with an automatic pistol near at hand. It was not easy to drive off these Bedouin marauders. As I was on my way to join the Desert Mounted Corps in their advance on Damascus I selected a pitch for the night at Lejjun where the Corps had had their headquarters. A pile of material captured from the Turks was awaiting transport, and the small guard taking care of it was kept busy by the natives. All through the early morning shots were fired to drive away the thieves, but when day broke a score of them remained searching the dumps for any stuff they could carry away. The guard was made up of Australians, who, when they saw the Bedouins, made them drop what they had collected in bundles and sprint off at their best pace to get out of reach.

The captures at Haifa were one 6-inch naval gun, four 4.2 guns, eight 77-mm. guns, four camel guns eleven machine guns, two German officers, 35 Turkish officers, and 1314 German and Turkish other ranks. On the day after the cavalry had taken Haifa the 28th Brigade of the 7th Division left their bivouacs at Messudieh to take over that town and Acre as well, so as to leave the cavalry free to rejoin Desert Mounted Corps. One of the battalions was sent on in motor lorries and found the road as bad as it had been painted, and the men who stood in the lorries as passengers were thankful when they got round the headland into the town.

I will now swing over to the other side of Desert Mounted Corps' front to describe the action of the 4th Cavalry Division which, it will be remembered reached Beisan on the 20th after riding and fighting for a distance of eighty-five miles in thirty-four hours On September 21 a column of Turks, 1500 strong, was reported to be four miles south of Beisan and approaching our lines, apparently having no knowledge that we occupied Beisan and that the road was closed to them. Acting under instructions from G.H.Q. strong patrols were sent down the Beisan-Nablus road, and, on the east of the Jordan, down the Merka-Jisr ed Damie road, and during the night of September 21 they took 3000 prisoners, and small parties were still coming in. Late on the evening of September 22, orders were issued for a brigade to be sent down the Jordan valley on the west and east banks to operate against formed bodies reported to be crossing the river in various places, and with this object the 11th Cavalry Brigade moved off at six o'clock on September 23 to cut off the retreat of the remnant of the 7th Turkish Army. The left patrol of the 29th Lancers were fired on from the direction of Makhadat abu Naj, where a strong enemy rearguard of 1000 infantry and thirty machine guns were holding a position covering the ford and the passage of the enemy's troops across the river. The 29th Lancers had made a rapid march of eight miles through patches of cultivation and scrub, but they lost no time in routing out the enemy from positions on the edge of the broken ground alongside the river. Two squadrons of the regiment charged the enemy and rolled them up from end to end, capturing 800 prisoners and the whole of their machine guns. Meanwhile the Middlesex Yeomanry had moved south to turn the left rear of the Turks' rearguard, behind which some of the enemy were seen to be attempting to get over the river. On the east bank the Turks were in strength, and two attacks made by the 36th Jacob's Horse against the ford on the east bank could not be driven home. The Hants Battery R.H.A. came into action at eleven o'clock to assist the attacks, but they drew an accurate fire from two batteries of field guns south-east of the ford, and all the Hants guns were hit. A squadron of Middlesex Yeomanry managed to find a fordable place across the river about five thousand yards farther south, and Colonel Fred Lawson's Middlesex men, working up quickly through the rough ground, deployed and brilliantly charged the guns, putting them out of action. The enemy, seeing he could hold the Abu Naj ford no longer, withdrew at three o'clock, suffering very heavily indeed from machine-gun and automatic-rifle fire, and abandoning an enormous amount of material. Our men and horses were tired from their incessant exertions, and the brigade bivouacked for the night near the ford. The determined resistance of the enemy at Abu Naj was made to enable the commander of the Turkish 7th Army to escape. He succeeded in making his way to Ajlun with his headquarters, but the brigade captured some 3000 prisoners.

By the afternoon of the 23rd September 660 officers and 11,932 other ranks had passed through the Desert Mounted Corps' cages, and it was known that thousands of others were being sent in. The prisoners entailed an enormous amount of work when every man was wanted to carry on the advance. They had to be sent by march route to Ludd, and it took days to get them to our railhead. Very large compounds were prepared for them with admirable hospital and sanitary accommodation, but great care had to be exercised by our medical authorities, as the prisoners' quarters were not far from our own depôts, and we knew there had been cases of cholera in the Turkish army. It was difficult to get some of the sick prisoners to Ludd, and a number of other Turks were in bad condition for marching. Escorts had a trying time with stragglers, but on the whole the Turks suffered comparatively little during the march, and, though the supply branch

MOSQUE AT SAMARIA

had a heavy task in provisioning our own fighting troops, the Turks had more food and water than they had received for months with their own army. They got fat and lazy in confinement. If one did see some painful scenes by the way these were unavoidable in war time, and the Turks seemed to take less notice of them than their escorts.

On the 24th September the 5th Cavalry Division were occupied in assisting the Military Governor of Haifa to arrange for the administration of the town. They searched all the houses and found many prisoners in hiding. The division also sent out a reconnaissance over a wide stretch of country to Tantura, to ensure that it was cleared of the enemy, and so relieved the infantry of an arduous duty when they occupied the neighbourhood.

The 4th Cavalry Division had another lively day. A party was sent to Maleh to bring in 2000 Turks who had intimated that they wished to surrender, and during the day the 11th Cavalry Brigade got in among the enemy several times in their wide sweep east of the Jordan. Whenever the Turks showed a disposition to fight the cavalry charged them, and in frequent hand-to-hand encounters more than 300 Turks were killed and 500 were taken prisoners. Four camel guns, two complete batteries of field guns and fifteen machine guns were captured, and when the brigade rejoined the division at Beisan next day they reported that the foothills east of the Jordan were covered with abandoned transport and war material. The debris of wrecked and broken armies now covered hundreds of square miles in which, six days previously, the enemy felt secure in strong defensive positions. The regiment at Jisr Mejamie sent in a message that in the course of the night a train had run into Samakh on the southern edge of the Sea of Galilee, and that it was still there at 11 a.m. Patrols were sent out towards the station and came under fire of two 4.2 guns from the north-east of Samakh, but they were able to report that there was a dump of 5000 rails in a yard near the station, information that was cheering to the railway engineers.

During the 24th the Australian Mounted Division made plans for attacking Samakh next morning. General Grant's 4th Australian Light Horse Brigade marched in the evening with orders to surprise the enemy at dawn, and to push patrols up the Yarmak river. The brigade had a big fight to secure Samakh, but the casualties would have been very small had it not been for the treacherous action of Germans and Turks alike, in firing on them after showing white flags. While approaching Samakh in the dark at half-past four the Australians were met by intense machine-gun fire and rifle fire along the whole front.

The enemy's position covered an open plain for seven hundred yards south of Samakh, the flanks being in the hills on both sides of the town. The officer commanding the 11th regiment A.L.H., who had not expected this fire, decided to go straight into the town, and sent two squadrons from the east covered by the machine-gun squadron in action on the south of the town, one squadron to charge along the railway into the place and the other to advance on the northern side of the railway, through the left flank of the enemy, and thence into the town. A supporting squadron occupied a point on the east flank watching the railway from Deraa and in readiness to assist if the resistance in Samakh proved stubborn, while a squadron of the 12th A.L.H. Regiment attacked the west flank. The machine-gun squadron came into action very quickly with all twelve guns, and two guns worked round the right flank and opened fire near the sea. The light was bad and the enemy could only be located by the flash of his machine guns. The squadron which moved along the railway found the town strongly held, especially at the railway station buildings, in which there was fierce hand-to-hand fighting, a number of Germans supporting the Turks. The 11th regiment's squadron on the right galloped into the town and charged dismounted, whilst the machine guns closed in and had the town surrounded. The enemy nevertheless continued to fight most determinedly, using bombs and automatic rifles. Our machine guns were successful in neutralising the enemy guns and in demoralising the Turks, but targets were difficult to find owing to the buildings and the enclosed surroundings of the town.

The enemy now showed several white flags from the station buildings, but as the Australians approached to disarm them they were heavily fired on. From the time of the charge it took one hour's hard fighting to overcome the defence, and it was broad daylight when the station buildings, the last place to surrender, were in our hands. More than twenty dead Germans and Turks were found in the station, but some of them had been killed before the display of white flags and not sufficient of them met the fate their treachery merited. Two motor boats were moored at a stage by the shore. One of these escaped and the other pushed off with its engine running, but it was fired on by the Australians with a captured Turkish field gun, and a Hotchkiss-rifle team set the boat on fire. The occupants jumped overboard and, swimming ashore, were captured. Prisoners said the attack was expected and the garrison had asked headquarters if they could withdraw, but orders were given them to hold Samakh at all costs. Our casualties were seventeen killed, including three officers, and seven officers and fifty-three other ranks wounded. Seventy-seven horses were killed. The prisoners taken were 150 Germans and 239 Turks, and a train with steam up also fell into our hands. Strong patrols were sent up the Yarmak valley, but they found the enemy guarding every bridge. Thirty men at one bridge caused us some casualties, and at another sixty Germans occupied a redoubt with an engine and tender. Five hundred infantry and one gun were found to be occupying the Ain en Nimir mountain, a rugged hill 1800 feet above the level of the Sea of Galilee, and less than two miles from its southern edge. After the occupation of Samakh two squadrons from the 3rd and 4th Australian Light Horse brigades proceeded north along the shore road and entered Tiberias at three o'clock in the afternoon, and here fifty-six prisoners, nearly half of them Germans, were taken, and some Turkish army papers were found in an hotel.

CHAPTER 18

Amman at Last

This is a suitable place to break off the narrative of the doings of the cavalry in order to call attention to the force in the Jordan valley, whose operations resulted in the capture of over 10,000 prisoners and an immense quantity of guns and war material. This force General Allenby entrusted to Major-General Sir E. W. C. Chaytor, the commander of the Anzac Mounted Division, whose capacity as a leader and as a general had been proved over and over again. General Chaytor was a veteran in this theatre of war. He came to Egypt with the first contingent sent by New Zealand, and, after serving on Gallipoli, returned to Egypt in command of the New Zealand Mounted Rifles Brigade, which was a part of the Anzac Mounted Division. The division's operations for many months in the Sinai Desert, when an incessant watch had to be kept on a wide front continually being crossed by the enemy who showed considerable enterprise, won for them a reputation which made the King's Dominions under the Southern Cross justly proud of their fighting men. They had good reason, for troops who could retain their first-class fighting form in the fearful heat of the desert, where water was scarce and rations were of the iron variety, were a big asset of the Empire. General Chauvel commanded the Anzac Division in those trying days, and on his promotion to the command of Desert Mounted Corps, General Chaytor succeeded him. He had to carry out many heavy tasks, but none of them was so important or yielded such great results as the duty of watching the right flank of General Allenby's Army, and of advancing over Jordan to complete the destruction of the enemy's forces which was begun on the coastal plain. These operations were carried out with supreme success, and in working out a scheme to meet all possibilities of a situation which was   continually changing, General Chaytor showed generalship of a high order. His force consisted of the Anzac Mounted

Division, the 1st and 2nd battalions of the British West India regiment, the 38th and 39th Royal Fusiliers (Jewish battalions), and the 20th Indian (Imperial Service Infantry) Brigade.

General Headquarters gave instructions that at the commencement of operations this force should not move forward, but should keep a careful watch on the enemy and actively patrol all along the line by day and night. If the enemy dropped back from any of his forward positions they were to be occupied at once. On the enemy's southern or left flank bodies of cavalry watched the tracks leading to Madeba. The line of the foothills running to Shunet Nimrin and north of it were strongly entrenched, and advanced posts on Kebr Said, Tel er Rame and Mujahid, hills which covered the poor track leading from the Hajlah ford to the Moab plateau, were entrenched and surrounded by wire, and were difficult to approach owing to the thick scrub which gave opportunity for enemy ambushes. From a point 8000 yards north of Nimrin, a line of trenches and redoubts facing south, ran across to the Jordan to a spot about half a mile south of the Umm esh Shert ford, which was some eight miles north of Ghoraniyeh, and between four and five miles north of our Aujah bridgehead. Behind this line was Red Hill, a bold mound near the scene of the fighting in April when we lost nine horse-artillery guns. This hill was entrenched and was the principal artillery observation point against our line. The entrenched line continued in a north-westerly direction on the northern side of the Mankattat el Mellaha, behind which was rough broken country covering the Jordan. The defences here were a series of redoubts, all wired-in and having a splendid field of fire over absolutely open ground. The line then continued across the western side of the valley to Bahr ridge, at the beginning of the hills leading up to the Judean range, and north of this was a strong position of well-built sangars with wire entanglements at Baghalet on the old Roman road from Jericho to Nablus. The enemy's lack of enterprise was not helpful. He made no trench raids and very seldom had parties out in front of his entrenched positions. For this reason it was difficult, without incurring some loss, to keep a close watch and make certain that he was not reducing his numbers, but information was given by a large number of deserters.

The Turks believed we could not remain in the Jordan valley all through the summer months. It is a horribly depressing region, with pests of all kinds, but our men stuck it out, while the percentage of enemy deserters grew with the approach of autumn. The Turks devised schemes for preventing desertion, and any one caught in an attempt to reach our lines met with the severest punishment, but they could not stop it and the wretched fellows who came in were helpful to our Intelligence officers.

On the night of September 17 there was close patrolling of enemy positions, and from the bridgeheads a regiment of the 2nd Australian Light Horse Brigade made a demonstration, and the 1st Australian Light Horse Brigade went out from their camp at Tel es Sultan towards the Jordan. On the morning of September 18 an enemy long-range gun opened fire on the Anzac Mounted Division headquarters which were near Jericho, and afterwards shelled the town of Jericho. This gun was christened by the Anzacs *Jericho Jane*, and its position was located, beyond reach of any of our own guns, in a fold of the hills close to the wadi Shaib, about three miles east of Nimrin. It was a long 5.9 naval gun with a mobile mounting, and was firing at a range of some seventeen miles. Very few casualties were caused by its fire, which was at times quite wild, but it frightened the natives. The following week we found it capsized in the wadi, with the bodies of two Turks so mutilated as to indicate a direct hit by a bomb dropped from an aeroplane. Nobody was sorry for *Jericho Jane's* fate. She was a noisy, wayward wench, and the shriek of her shell as it passed in a tired fashion overhead, always brought out a number of men ready to bet where it would not burst.

On the night of September 18 the activity of our patrols alarmed the enemy. Wherever a patrol appeared it was received by heavy machine-gun and rifle fire. A few cavalry who showed themselves southeast of Baghalet were thought to be preparing a raid and the enemy wasted much ammunition by putting down an artillery barrage in front of them. The next morning the Turks had ground for their agitation. The 2nd British West India regiment made a fine attack on lofty ground south of Bahr ridge and gained it. The Turks rightly believed it to be in too close proximity to their main positions and heavily shelled the West Indians, who, however, behaving with exemplary courage, securely dug themselves in while they were the targets of the enemy's artillery. Next morning they used their newly-made trenches as a stepping-off place for Bahr ridge itself, and again they did credit to themselves in resolutely driving the enemy away from well-planned positions. They did not stop long here, pushing on to Chalk Ridge, from which they could see small enemy parties retiring. The 1st British West Indians also won their spurs that day. They occupied a hill named Grant, after the brigadier of the 4th Australian Light Horse Brigade, and went on and captured Baghalet. These places they consolidated under a heavy fire from Red Hill which was kept up throughout the day. The 38th Royal Fusiliers found the trenches along the northern side of the Mellaha strongly held. The enemy showed no inclination to leave that portion of the line, but early on the morning of the 22nd there were signs that the defence was weakening, and the battalion forced its way into the trenches and occupied the line overlooking the Umm esh Shert ford. Two companies of the 39th Royal Fusiliers were brought up into positions vacated by the 38th, and the latter battalion proceeded to take the ford at daylight, and then continued its advance up the Mankattat el Mellaha.

General Ryrie's 2nd Australian Light Horse Brigade was a long way east of the Jordan at seven o'clock and occupied Tel er Rame, and General Meldrum's New Zealand Mounted Rifles Brigade in the western valley surrounded the garrisons at Makhruk and Kadir across the road leading from the hills of Judea to the Jisr ed Damie ford, taking the G.O.C. of the Turkish 53rd Division and 600 prisoners. Jisr ed Damie, however, was still strongly held, and the enemy began to concentrate about Jozeleh, lower down the river, and threatened the flank of the New Zealand Brigade. General   Cox's 1st Australian Light Horse Brigade, with the Inverness Battery R.H.A., was therefore ordered up to Fusail to be in readiness to fall on the Turks if they attempted to envelop the New Zealanders' flank. General Meldrum was not going to permit this threat to his flank to interfere with his intention to drive the enemy from the Jisr ed Damie ford. The 1st British West Indians had made a fine march across country and had joined up with the New Zealanders. Between them they captured the whole bridgehead. Under cover of machine-gun fire they charged the enemy who were holding the bridge, and there was some desperate hand-to-hand fighting. It did not last long, and a bridgehead was gradually established east of the Jordan, though the enemy continued to close the exits from the eastern bank with machine-gun fire.

No troops were more delighted than the New Zealanders at the way the British West Indians acquitted themselves. Like most Dominion troops the New Zealanders did not estimate the fighting powers of coloured troops very highly, but after they saw the dash of the West Indians and their race to the Damie bridge, grinning broadly in their desire to get at grips with the enemy, they regarded them as sterling brothers in arms. The West Indians had found themselves. There was a time when they were given garrison duties only. They cleared up a mess behind the lines, furnished sentries and so on, but the pestilential heat of the Jordan valley affected them less

'JERICHO JANE' CAPSIZED IN A WADI

than white troops, and they longed for a chance of showing they could fight. They made the most of the opportunities in the Jordan valley rout of the Turks. A distinguished New Zealand officer told me there was something almost humorous in the West Indians' magnificent charge at the bridge. The tremendous effort they made to get in front of the New Zealanders created much amusement, and when the King's coloured soldiers got to work with the bayonet, still laughing aloud, it was a 'great exhibition of blood and teeth.' The 2nd British West Indians took two officers and 77 other ranks prisoners in another part of the valley, and the total captures by Chaytor's force for the day amounted to 33 officers, 685 other ranks, four machine guns, four automatic rifles, and many waggons, horses, and stores. Just before midnight the enemy was seen to be retiring, and orders were circulated to press him and inflict as much damage as possible on the following day. The 2nd Australian Light Horse Brigade were to move from the neighbourhood of Mujahid and Rame, sending one squadron towards Nimrin, to which place the mobile part of the 20th Indian Infantry Brigade were to march. Colonel Patterson's column, consisting of the 38th and 39th Royal Fusiliers, were to concentrate at the Aujah bridgehead and to follow the 20th Brigade, while the 1st Australian Light Horse Brigade were to press the enemy across the Jordan opposite Mafid Jozeleh and attack into the foothills. General Meldrum was to leave one battalion of the British West Indians and a squadron of New Zealanders to hold Damie, and, followed by the other battalion of the British West Indians, to force the enemy back into the hills, moving by the Damie-Es Salt track.

Early on September 23 the 2nd Light Horse Brigade went up the tracks to Ain es Sir, in very different weather from that experienced the last time they were in the district, six months earlier in the year. All the ground west of the Jordan was now cleared of the enemy, but the 3rd regiment of Light Horse and the 2nd British West Indians found that the Turks had destroyed the bridge at Jozeleh. The 1st Light Horse Brigade accordingly crossed the Jordan by the Umm esh Shert ford, and cantering across the valley, proceeded into the hills by the Arseniyet track. By six o'clock in the evening the 20th Indian Infantry Brigade were at Nimrin with a squadron of the 2nd Light Horse Brigade in front of them, and soon afterwards some of the horsemen saw *Jericho Jane* for the first time. The New Zealand Mounted Rifles Brigade made light work of the journey over the rough hills, and entered Es Salt for the third time at seven in the evening, the only opposition they met with during the morning being from a wired-in post with machine guns across the Damie track. This the Canterbury Mounted Rifles outflanked, and they then rushed the post and captured it. On the march and in Es Salt the brigade captured 312 prisoners, two machine guns, two 4.2 guns, and a 77-mm. Patterson's column had to leave the 38th Royal Fusiliers behind during the day owing to the exhaustion of the battalion due to the heavy work among the clay hills in the Jordan valley, but the 39th Royal Fusiliers continued their march towards Nimrin.

At night Chaytor's force received instructions to harass the enemy further, to cut off his retreat north of Amman, and to get into touch with the Arab army. Early on the morning of the 24th the squadron of the 2nd Light Horse Brigade moving up the Es Salt road, sent back a message that the road had been blown up and badly damaged a short distance from Howeij. It was of vital importance that it should be rapidly got into some sort of order, for it was the only possible route by which motor lorries and waggons could ration the force, and the 20th Indian infantry Brigade were awakened in their bivouacs to furnish working parties with picks and shovels to repair the road. I went up it during the afternoon, and can speak of the excellent work the Indian troops had done. The damage was at an elbow where a precipice overlooks the wadi. The Turks had drilled deep holes in the rock a foot or two below the road bed, packing therein a considerable amount of explosives. Some of the charges were unexploded, but half of the roadway was blown up and the damage was not easy to repair. However, the Indians had worked with vigour, and they skilfully built up the side of the road with big blocks of rock jammed into the cavity. I was advised not to go near the edge as it might not be safe for a light car, but I saw laden lorries take the corner quite comfortably, and there was no doubt the Indians had made as sound a job of it as sappers would have done. In going up the road we felt grateful to our airmen for winning the mastery of the air. The gradients were very steep and the surface was several inches thick with dust. With the road full of every type of supply-vehicle and guns an enemy plane would have had an easy target, and a well-placed bomb would have blocked the way for hours. But no German pilot dared approach Es Salt, and we were left in security to toil up the narrow winding ascent, choked with dust and feeling quite satisfied with a progress at the rate of three miles an hour. It was hard travelling for the lorry drivers, and my driver, who had steered a Ford car over many thousands of miles of bad country during the campaign, always regarded this trip to Es Salt as the worst in his experience.

I was invited to bivouac with Divisional Headquarters Staff that night near Es Salt, but as those seasoned warriors had chosen a place close to the spot where our flying men had bombed the Turks during the morning, and the carcases of scores of horses and cattle and the bodies of many men were making the air foul, my driver and I selected a cornfield three miles nearer Amman, where we would have obtained sleep to fit us to appreciate the fighting for Amman the following day had not an Australian supply train come into the same field to outspan. It was an education to see those Australians prepare themselves for the night. Did they ever sleep? They came into the field at midnight when I had finished a frugal meal and had got beneath a blanket. Three or four men cut up wood for a fire and were soon preparing tea for the entire train. Every white man got a full allowance, and then fresh water was put on to the fire for the Egyptian drivers, and by the time their coffee or tea (I forget which) was ready they had off-saddled and fed the horses. The Gyppies had as liberal a ration as the white men, and it was interesting to hear how careful the cooks were to see that no man was missed. The Australian treated his Egyptian driver like a man who was doing the same job as himself, and if he discriminated between the white and coloured man the advantage was certainly in favour of the latter. I am inclined to think that the Egyptian who did service with General Allenby's Army had during the war the best time of his life. He was a willing, if sometimes stupid, fellow, but he did not grouse or agitate, and to all appearances he was quite contented and moderately happy. He was drawn from the fellah class, and was very unlike the young dandily-dressed Egyptians who, after growing rich out of the war in the country we had made safe for them, proceeded to agitate for independence. Their ideas of government would be to grind as much as possible out of the fellaheen. Let us hope we shall save the fellah who did duty with us from that sad fate. By the evening f the 24th the 38th Royal Fusiliers had got to Nimrin Mid the 39th Royal Fusiliers were following up the Es Salt road as rearguard to the force. The 20th Indian Infantry Brigade and the remainder of the force, less that portion of it watching the Jordan valley, were concentrated about Es Salt, the New Zealanders, who had met with opposition at Suweileh, and the 2nd Light Horse Brigade, who had been shelled by field guns near Es Sir, having pushed through.

The 25th September sealed the fate of the Turkish force east of the Jordan, and on the line of the Hedjaz railway. It was a hard and exciting day, with almost continuous fighting in one or other part of the field, but by the energetic action of all three brigades of the

Anzac Mounted Division a great success was scored, and the way was opened to taking this grain-growing country out of the dominion of the Turks and incorporating it into the new kingdom of Arabia. May the new rule be more in accordance with the wishes of the population than that which it has superseded. During the night a party of the Auckland Mounted Rifles marched to the railway and cut a substantial part of it near Kalaat ez Zerka, and the removal of any rolling. stock or material north became impossible. In any case it would never have reached Damascus, for the 4th Cavalry Division was about to give another proof of its energy in the region of Deraa, and Colonel Lawrence and the Arabs were damaging the line north of that junction. Mounted troops began their advance on Amman at daybreak. The New Zealand Mounted Rifles Brigade proceeded along the main Es Salt-Amman road. The word ' road' is quite misleading. There are patches of metalled highway, but for the most part the surface is one of mud with large masses of rock protruding through it. Shallow water courses cross the road, but there are some rude short bridges in places to prevent it becoming impassable in wet weather. The cavalry as a rule merely took the so-called road as an indication of their line of march and rode beside it, and I found that my Ford waggon made better progress across the cultivated fields than on the highway. General Ryrie and his men of the 2nd Australian Light Horse Brigade proceeded from Es Sir to operate from the west, and General Cox's 1st Australian Light Horse Brigade moved behind the New Zealanders and kept a watch from the north. Quite early in the morning General Ryrie chased and captured 105 cavalry with four machine guns, and prevented their giving information of his approach. The cavalry were mounted on small wiry ponies which looked unfit to carry a man and equipment, but they were hardy little mounts, sure-footed in the hills, and lived practically on what they could nibble. The New Zealanders were directed against the defences north-west of Amman, and at eleven o'clock the Canterbury Mounted Rifles were ready to gallop the defences opposite them but were brought up by a steep cliff. The only other route they could take was between two hills held by enemy machine-gunners and infantry, so General Chaytor ordered mountain guns to come up to their support, and then, with other brigades moving up to assist, directed that the attack should be pressed home.

The town of Amman lies in a hollow with a line of hills running from the north-west to the south-east of it. Well before noon we had secured most of these hills. The 2nd Light Horse Brigade had the high ground on the south-west and were only waiting for the clearing up of the line in front of the New Zealanders to gallop into the town and to get on to the famous 3039 hill to make the capture of the railway station and all that was in it a certainty. The New Zealanders' goal was the old citadel near the fine ruins of buildings which an ancient civilisation brought into the land. The raids of March and April taught the Turks the importance of holding on grimly to Amman, and they had given time to the making of trenches sited near the citadel. These were not easy to take, but pressure and the knowledge that we had been victorious in all sections of the field in Palestine had their effect, and at three o'clock the Canterbury Mounted Rifles had passed over the trench system and entered the citadel. The method of defence by nests of machine guns made progress difficult, and it was only by galloping to points of vantage and by bringing fire to bear on the flanks of the machine-gunners that the position was finally taken. From a hill overlooking Amman on the west, and easily within range of the Turkish guns, General Chaytor saw the Turks' resistance collapsing, and while the light was still good he had the welcome news that Amman was ours. General Ryrie, who had his brigade headquarters on a hill about a mile south of Force headquarters, had sent his brigade in to seize the town, and then to cross the wadi Amman and capture Hill 3039. In my despatch to the London newspapers describing the operations about Amman I gave the credit of winning the place to the New Zealanders. That was wrong. It was easy to make the mistake. They captured the citadel, and from where I stood I said, as I thought, the New Zealanders advanced into the town itself. I made a hurried visit to Amman, but had to leave in the darkness to begin a bad journey back to G.H.Q., some seventy miles away, to send off my message to London. Let me make amends. The New Zealanders, the best and most modest fellows in the world, never claimed they had taken Amman, and were delighted to speak of it being won by their Australian comrades. It was General Eyrie's men who first entered the town and gave us secure possession of it by driving the enemy off Hill 3039. The 1st Australian Light Horse Brigade also got across the railway well to the north of the town and captured several guns which were being hauled away.

Having secured an important strategic point General Chaytor proceeded to make the most of his success. There was a large enemy force to the south, and he determined not only to put them in the worst possible position should they intend to attack him, but to make it extremely hard for them to escape capture. He therefore brought his 20th Indian Infantry Brigade to Amman, leaving one battalion to hold

Suweileh, a rather nice little oasis on the Es Salt road, and ordered the 2nd Australian Light Horse Brigade to proceed as far south as they could to blow up the railway. To try to get away the Turks would either have to march over the hills in an endeavour to reach the Jordan valley (where they would have been out of the frying-pan into the fire) or to take the Darb el Haj road and pass east of Amman. If the Turkish commander did not choose to attack Amman, and it was improbable that he would put his head into that hornet's nest, it was to our advantage to make his march as long as possible, and to increase his difficulties in watering his troops. If he selected the Darb el Haj, the nearest water from Kastal, a station nearly twenty miles south of Amman, would be in the wadi El Hamman, some ten miles north of Amman, and to deny him this supply the 1st Australian Light Horse Brigade were directed to secure and hold it. In case the Turks tried to gain the Jordan valley the troops at Nimrin, Es Salt, and Suweileh were ordered to entrench those places strongly, and the 2nd Light Horse Brigade to watch the country closely between the railway and Naaur, through which a track proceeds north to Es Salt, and to have a strong detachment waiting at Es Sir ready to drop into the Jordan valley and harass tired troops. The 1st Light Horse Brigade, after reconnoitring the wadi Hamman, had a short action at Zerka, taking 105 prisoners and one gun, and reported that enemy cavalry and infantry were moving south. Up to the evening of September 26 the captures at Amman were 2563 prisoners, three heavy guns and seven field guns, and many machine guns. On the morning of September 27 the 3rd regiment of Light Horse met a strong party of the enemy north of the wadi Hamman. One of our aeroplanes flying over the district notified the presence of the enemy to the regiment's commanding officer, and then directed the regiment on to the position where the Turks were entrenched. As the troops attacked the aeroplane came down low and machine-gunned the enemy, who so disliked being between two fires that over three hundred of them with two machine guns held up their hands and surrendered.

The 2nd Light Horse Brigade met some Turks south of Lebban station, and they learned from a prisoner that the garrison at Maan had evacuated that town and were marching on Kastal. The prisoner put the number of the force at 6000, but this was a slight exaggeration. Early next morning the Royal Air Force located the southern force at Kastal with three trains in the station, and General Chaytor decided to give the commander an opportunity of surrendering without bloodshed. It was clear that the force could not get away, and

Es Saw

taking a humane view of the situation General Chaytor informed the commander that all possible water he could reach north of Kastal was in our hands, and that, while refraining from bombing the force that day, our aeroplanes would be over Kastal next day for that purpose if the troops did not surrender. By nine o'clock next morning no answer had been returned to this message, and arrangements were made to bomb the force in the afternoon. At noon however, when the 5th regiment of Light Horse were across the railway south of Lebban, negotiations were opened. The situation was a peculiar one, and called for tact and not a little consideration for the position in which the Turkish commander found himself. He was a reasonable fellow and wished to give all the protection he could to his men, but hanging on to him was a large number of Arabs, well armed with military weapons, some of them of our manufacture and some of them German rifles we had taken from the Turks and had sent to Arabia for the use of Arabs in revolt against Ottoman rule. These Arabs surrounding the Turkish force were intent on looting, and so fierce was their hatred of their enemies that there is no question that, if they had got among them, they would not have stopped at mere plunder. The Turkish commander, Kaimakan AH Bey Whakaby, said that if he surrendered his force to one regiment of Light Horse and his men were disarmed, the regiment would not be numerically strong enough to protect so large a number of prisoners. Any sign of a white flag was likely to precipitate matters.

As soon as this situation was communicated to him General Ryrie at once started for Kastal with the remainder of his brigade, and the energetic steps he took to protect the Turks undoubtedly prevented a considerable portion of the enemy falling victims to the Arabs. By dark there had already been two collisions owing to the Arabs pressing in on the Turks, but General Ryrie, on arriving at Kastal, placed a cordon round the enemy and told the Arabs plainly that any attempt to rush in on his prisoners would be met by force. The position was very uncertain, and General Ryrie allowed the Turks, or a majority of them, to retain their arms, of course on the understanding, which was honourably observed, that they were to be used against the Arabs in defence only and not in attack. Even after our troops were placed as a shield for the Turks the Arabs attempted to get to the Turkish hospital and had to be driven off. The Turkish commander was sent by car to report to General Chaytor. At dawn next morning the Arabs had not given up hope of being able to loot the army which, despite many attacks, had held Maan against them for years. It may be that this stubborn defence caused the Australians to have a soldierly admiration for the Turks, but in any case chivalry demanded that while they were there as guards for prisoners no harm should come to them, and above all that the numerous sick should be protected. The Arabs saw their hopes disappear when the New Zealand Mounted Rifles Brigade arrived at Kastal, and in face of this increased force they gradually drew off. The 2nd Light Horse Brigade were relieved by the New Zealanders in the line of posts around the Turks, and during the morning those of the enemy who were able to march proceeded towards Amman. Large numbers of sick were left behind at Kastal under guard, but these were subsequently brought in. The captures at Kastal included 4068 prisoners, among them 502 in hospital, twelve guns, thirty-five machine guns, and two automatic rifles. The sum-total of prisoners captured by General Chaytor's force from the commencement of operations to September 30 was 10,322, and a large number of Arabs and local inhabitants who had been serving with the Turks deserted to their homes. The artillery taken from the enemy consisted of one 5.9 one 5.9 howitzer, thirty-two 77-mm. guns, six 75-mm guns, two 3-inch guns, one anti-aircraft gun, and ten 10-cm. guns, as well as two of the 13-pounder guns lost in the Jordan valley in April by the Honourable Artillery Company which were recovered. This gave a total of 55 guns, and the force also took 132 machine guns, 13 automatic rifles, one Hotchkiss and one Lewis gun, two wireless sets, 11 locomotives, 106 railway trucks and carriages, 142 vehicles, and an immense quantity of shells and small-arms ammunition.

All over the country we found German-made motor lorries whose engines had been smashed when there was a prospect that they would fall into our hands. The wheels were shod with iron, and the state of the tyres of the Turks' motor cars was proof of the shortage of rubber in Germany. We had a further example of this later on when we captured a heavy armoured car south of Aleppo. The car had a powerful engine, but its speed was handicapped by strong metal rims to the wheels, and though it bumped its way over rocky ground as fast as our Rolls-Royce cars, it had not a fourth of the speed of our cars on the smoother earth tracks. A comparison of our losses during the operations of September in the Jordan valley and in the hill country east of the Jordan shows that our total casualties were fewer by far than the Turkish killed. Chaytor's force had 3 officers and 24 other ranks killed, 10 officers and 95 other ranks wounded, and 7 other ranks missing, a total of 139. Against this we took 10,322 prisoners—a marvellous tribute to good leading as well as an eloquent illustration of the utter demoralisation of the Turks. In his report to G.H.Q. General Chaytor drew attention to the way all ranks in his force worked to keep a careful watch on the enemy, so that any attempt at withdrawal could not escape notice. He particularly mentioned the steadiness under fire of the 1st and 2nd British West India regiments, and spoke of their dash when called upon to attack, especially at the Jisr ed Damie ford, and their extremely good marching powers up the steep hills to Es Salt and thence to Amman. The 38th Royal Fusiliers did very good work in continually pressing the enemy along the Manhatat el Mellaha, and in taking advantage of any weakening of his line by seizing his trenches overlooking the Umm esh Shert ford. Another noteworthy performance was the rapid march of the New Zealand Mounted Rifles Brigade, and particular praise was given to the Canterbury Mounted Rifles for rapidly and effectively dealing with a body of Turks opposite them on the Damie track on September 23.

CHAPTER 19

Advance on Damascus

In six days the Turkish 7th, 8th, and 4th Armies and the Maan garrison, to give the force in the order of battle from the coast to the Hedjaz railway, had either been utterly destroyed for any effective fighting purposes or were in a position from which they could not extricate themselves. Of course some small parties had got away. That was inevitable, but they were absolutely negligible quantities, and if they reached Damascus—most of them did not—their only use would be by absorption in other units. Their moral was completely broken, and however brave a man may be it is not possible for him to be a witness of the overwhelming of his army and still remain a good soldier. Military outlook alone does not direct the strategy of campaigns. Political considerations enter largely into a commander's strategy, and General Allenby, having already crushed the military power of Turkey so as to place it beyond redemption in this war, could not hope by making a long march through Syria to do more from a military point of view than reduce still further the numbers of the Turkish army. But it was of great importance at this critical period of the war, when the enemy, whether German, Austrian, Bulgar, or Turk, knew he was beaten, that we should show the world that we were conquerors. We had to consider the situation in Persia, and it was vital we should occupy Aleppo, which would render it impossible for Germans and Turks to fulfil their prophecies, made through propagandists working assiduously among Mahomedan peoples, that they would retake Bagdad. Yet before Aleppo could be won we should have to take Damascus, and the influence which the capture of that ancient city would have on hundreds of millions of people in Asia and Africa could not be exaggerated.

The soldier's grasp of the situation was sound, and until he had crushed out of existence the armies which he had surrounded, political considerations took but a secondary place in General Allenby's strategy, though they were always in his calculations. But once he had secured his main object he put into operation that larger scheme which, conceived by a bold master mind, and executed with the swift precision of a cavalryman, will go down to history as one of the greatest feats of war.

The Commander-in-Chief made no mistake. While paying heed to suggestions from the War Cabinet that Aleppo was a goal which would have a far-reaching effect on the Allied cause, General Allenby decided that he would not reach it by a mere cavalry raid. The War Cabinet were willing to take all the risks involved. The victory gained on September 19 had an instantaneous effect in the Caucasus, and, news travelling unaccountably fast, was already having an influence in North-West Persia at the beginning of the fourth week of September, and it is not difficult to understand that Ministers with a wide appreciation of the world's affairs were anxious that Turkey should cease to be a belligerent. The loss of Aleppo would make her crave for peace. The Bulgar was anxious for it; Austria would cry 'Enough' when she saw that Turkey and Bulgaria had laid down arms. If a cavalry raid on Aleppo had been successful Turkey might have obtained an armistice two weeks or three weeks earlier than she did. But what would have happened if the raid had been unsuccessful, or only partially successful? Would it have given the enemy heart to continue? Would he have gone through another winter? No, the risk was not worth taking, and though he was freed from all responsibility General Allenby chose the prudent course of proceeding by stages, and actually obtained all the War Cabinet wished for in hardly two weeks longer than it would have taken his cavalry to raid Aleppo. The War Cabinet received General Allenby's view that the suggested raid was not feasible on September 26. They accepted his arguments in their entirety, and showed sound common sense in doing so. Aleppo is 300 miles from Nazareth and if there were no fighting of consequence it would take three cavalry divisions three weeks at the very least to reach it. Such a march would involve very heavy wastage, and when the cavalry arrived they would be tired and in poor condition to meet the Turkish troops—some 25,000 fighting men—in the Aleppo and Alexandretta areas. Moreover, before the cavalry had travelled 300 miles the enemy in those areas would have been reinforced by many troops of good quality who had set out from Anatolia when the news of the break-through in Central Pales; tine had reached them. Unless the War Cabinet were prepared to embark on a combined naval and military

NAZARETH
TO ALEPPO

Statute Miles
0 5 10   20   30   40
Kilometres
0 10 20 30 40 50 60
┼┼┼┼ Railways
──── Principal Roads

MEDITERRANEAN

SEA

Antioch

Orontes

ALEPPO
Khan Tuman
Karas
Seraikin
Khan Sebil
Maarit en Naaman

Ladikiya

Khan Shaikhun

Taiyibe
Orontes
Hama

Homs

Kusseir
Orontes

C.Madonna
Tripoli

Lebwe
Anti-Lebanon

Baalbek
Nebk

Ras el Kelb Junie
Zahle
Rayak Ali

BEIRUT
Moallaka

Bar Elias Zebdani
Ain Jedeide
Dumar Duma
Saida
(Sidon) Khan Meizelun
DAMASCUS
Khan Dimez Meidan
Kaukab Kiswe

Tyre Khan esh Shiha
Sasa

Ras en Nakura
El Kuneitra
Jisr Benat Yakub

Acre
Safed
Sheikh Miskin

HAIFA
L.of Tiberias
Nazareth Tiberias

Kishon ToNablus
Deraa

operation on a large scale at Alexandretta, and to maintain by sea the military forces employed in it, the only sound policy was an advance by stages. With the experience of Gallipoli fresh in their memory the War Cabinet were not willing to risk another landing.

An advance on Damascus was already being prepared before London put the Aleppo suggestion before the Commander-in-Chief. The three cavalry visions with Desert Mounted Corps were all concentrated by the evening of the 25th with a view to commencing the advance to capture Damascus, and to intercept that portion of the Turkish 4th Army which had not been dealt with by General Chaytor's force. The operation took the form of a parallel pursuit. Part of the Turkish 4th Army was retreating from Amman to Damascus, and the 4th Cavalry Division were ordered to intercept it at Deraa, in co-operation with Emir Feisal's Arab army which was in the neighbourhood, and to pursue and harass the Turks and drive them into the hands of the Australian Mounted Division and the 5th Cavalry Division, who were to make a rapid march on a converging road west of Lake Tiberias to Damascus. Some day, no doubt, a full record of this advance will be written, and, with accompanying maps, it will form a valuable work for the study by soldiers of the art of war. It will well deserve its place in military records, for the operation was carried out to complete success, and the movements of divisions working up widely separated roads were so timed that they came together almost at the minute arranged. Everything planned was accomplished, nothing went wrong, and the Staff work was carried through so thoroughly that it might well serve as a model. And Desert Mounted Corps can be proud to leave what it achieved as the best possible evidence of the soundness of General Allenby's scheme for conquering by stages. No cavalry 'raid' would have attained the same results. The concentration was complete on September 26; on the morning of October 1, Desert Mounted Corps had won Damascus and captured 20,000 prisoners in and about the city.

The 4th Cavalry Division concentrated at Beisan, with one brigade at Jisr Mejamie and patrols out east of the Jordan trying to get in touch with the Arab forces. The Australian Mounted Division were about Tiberias and had advanced parties thrown out towards Safed, to the north. The 5th Cavalry Division had concentrated at Kefr Kenna (Cana of Galilee), leaving a regiment and a squadron at Haifa and Acre respectively until the troops of the 7th Indian Division should arrive at those towns. At six o'clock on the morning of the 27th the Australian Mounted Division left Tiberias and the 5th Cavalry Division started their march from Kefr Kenna. The road from Tiberias followed the western shores of the Sea of Galilee for several miles, and then proceeded north-west through land which, being well watered, gave abundant crops. The water overflowed the road in places, and the culverts were in bad order and were broken in by the weight of lorries. The mounted men were not delayed at all, but supply columns were held up occasionally until the water could be diverted and culverts filled in with stones. The Australians made excellent progress. The advanced guards had cleared the road for many miles ahead and the highway was good going in parts. There was a stiff climb up a track with a number of hairpin bends in it until close to Safed, an important Jewish colony two miles west of the road and about eight miles from the point where the Jordan was once more to be crossed.

Another Jewish colony, Rosh Pina, near to Safed, illustrated how an industrious people could prosper if provided with a settled form of government. Their houses were comparatively comfortable and the village was planned with a good idea of artistic effect, while their fields and vineyards, if showing traces of the scourge of war, were well tended. It is probable that Rosh Pina is quite itself again. On a second journey I made from G.H.Q. to Damascus in the second week of October I noticed a remarkable change. When Desert Mounted Corps first bivouacked in the vicinity, villagers stood by as interested spectators wondering if we should have the success they hoped for. They had seen something of armies, and until they were certain we were going to relieve them of the Turk they would not trouble to turn a spade in the soil. But a fortnight later all was changed. Instead of the indolence which was foreign to their natures, they were out again in the fields, labouring hard to make up for time lost, and the appearance of the countryside showed a marked improvement. They were satisfied that the war had passed beyond their area and that the blighting influence of the Turk was at an end. They knew it because they had seen many thousands of their old enemies, and large numbers of Germans with them, passing through their area as prisoners. War is a horrible thing, but these people thought there was some good in it, and in this fair spot happy faces told us that the people were thankful we had come to their deliverance. When the Australian Mounted Division first passed through the village the inhabitants were still doubtful about their progress, if the Australians were not.

The Turks had blown up the Jisr Benat Yakub bridge (the Bridge of Jacob's Daughters), which for four hundred years had spanned the boulder-strewn bed of the Jordan about 2000 yards from the place

A Turkish Road

where the Sacred River flows out of Lake Hule. It was a picturesque old bridge which had borne the stress of many a flood and tempest, but its years were numbered, and perhaps the Turks did not do the inhabitants a bad turn when they exploded charges of gelignite beneath the centre span. Something stronger would take its place. The enemy thought that the destruction of the bridge would hold up our advance. They were once more in error. They had hurried from Damascus nearly a thousand Germans and Turks in motor lorries, and some field guns to hold the crossing, and these men would have been very hard to dislodge by a frontal attack. The east bank to a depth possibly of three miles is one mass of lava boulders. There is scarcely any vegetation and to penetrate into the country beyond one had either to go up a road which was covered two feet thick with large loose pieces of lava, or climb over the boulders. No trenches were necessary in this place; a machine-gunner or rifleman could find a position at every yard. In a direct attack nothing but high angle fire would turn the enemy out, and, as the bridge was broken down, a frontal attack exposed to a wide field of fire was hopeless. General Hodgson did not intend to put his Australians into this trap. He ordered the 3rd Light Horse Brigade to try to cross the river at the southern end of Lake Hule, and the 5th Light Horse Brigade, save one regiment detached to hold the front, were to endeavour to effect a crossing at El Min, nearly two miles south of the damaged bridge of Jacob. The 5th Brigade made no mistake. They rode hard to the top of the steep bank down which they led their horses through marshy ground to the water's edge. There was no ford. Between Benat Yakub bridge and the Sea of Galilee there is a drop of 650 feet and the Jordan tears along over a rocky bottom. The Australians had to swim with their horses, but all got across very quickly, and the enemy, taken by surprise on their left flank, abandoned their positions and fled towards Damascus. Unfortunately the cavalry were in extremely bad country for horses and, until they had moved out of the stony region by the Jordan's banks and could get on to the road, infantry could get to their lorries parked in the rear twice as fast as they could be followed. The 3rd Light Horse Brigade crossed the river after dark, and did wonderfully well to get over the worst part of the rough country in the darkness. They pursued the enemy as far as Deir es Saras, where fifty men who could not get into lorries to return to Damascus were captured, with three field guns and some machine guns. The explosion had badly shaken the old bridge, and it was doubtful if the pillars supporting the remaining arches were strong enough to allow lorries to cross when the arches had again been spanned, but the Australian engineers belonging to the Corps Bridging Train buttressed the bridge with heavy baulks of timber, and armoured cars and supply lorries were going over it next morning.

The British lorry driver in Palestine and Syria was used to bad roads. He had negotiated mud tracks, mountain roads, and so-called metalled roads in wet and dry weather, and he kept a cheerful countenance when things were going very badly for him. He was a Never-say-die, and was always ready to dig himself out of any difficult position. But the road from Benat Yakub bridge to Saras nearly beat him. It is doubtful if there ever was a worse road in the world. The gradients were very steep, the road was narrow, and almost every turning was a right angle. These difficulties could be got over on most roads, but here the surface was abominable. The Turks had simply piled some two feet of soft stone over the road and left vehicles to crush it in. If the stones had been broken it would have been comparatively easy driving to get over them, but they varied in size from a man's head to a camel's body, and until there had been some levelling and breaking nothing on wheels could move. Quartermasters with their regiments miles ahead were asking for rations, and it seemed they would not get them for days, but a road party did a really amazing feat in clearing the big stuff away and in enabling a long train of lorries to get up the road in a few hours. The lorrymen helped, as they always did when there was road trouble, and when we were in Kuneitra on the afternoon of the 28th, preparing to set out on the night of the 29th to march on Damascus, we saw the lorries of two divisions roll up. Colonel Farr, General Trew's assistant in the 'Q.' branch of Desert Mounted Corps, was an optimist, but there was a look of wonderment on his face when the M.T. columns were reported. If they had only got in next day they would have done well.

While General Chauvel was at Kuneitra a deputation of Druse sheikhs came to him. The chief sheikh after offering a welcome, made many protestations of friendship, which were doubtless quite genuine. He asked permission to fight for the British, and said all his Arabs were anxious to go to war by our side against the Turk. They were deeply grateful that we had come to deliver them. During this audience some pot shots were being taken at Australians from a neighbouring village, and our troops found that Circassians were again the culprits. The country between Kuneitra and the Jordan was full of Circassians and had to be treated as hostile. The Australia Mounted Division and the 5th Cavalry Division had a night's repose at Kuneitra, a village of stone-built houses which looked picturesque at a distance. There were unwholesome smells about it which the fresh night air blowing from Mount Hermon distributed over the bivouacs, and no one was sorry to leave that unsavoury spot. The whole country was gaunt and bare as Hermon itself. Rock protruded everywhere, and the Royal Air Force took risks in selecting Kuneitra as a forward landing ground. But the airmen kept as close as possible to Corps' headquarters, and right through the cavalry advance the pilots always managed to improvise an aerodrome within a stone's throw of the corps or divisions. Their co-operation was complete and their service of the highest value.

When the Australian Mounted Division and the 5th Cavalry Division were getting to Kuneitra, the 4th Cavalry Division were moving round the other side of the Sea of Galilee. The 10th Cavalry Brigade started from Jisr Mejamie on September 26 for Irbid, but the road which agents had reported as good was found to be in a deplorable state. They had opposition on the road, but Irbid was reached after a trying march of fifteen miles. The 11th and 12th Brigades followed the 10th Brigade into the town. Next day the 10th Brigade again led the way, fighting a good deal but always keeping the enemy rearguards on the move. The Turks attempted to make one stand, but it did not last long as the Dorset Yeomanry delivered a fine charge and rounded up over 200 prisoners and twenty machine guns. The 10th and 12th Cavalry Brigades were at El Remte that night, and gained, touch with the Arab forces. The next day the whole of the 4th Cavalry Division were in Deraa, the important railway junction on the Hedjaz line. There were no Turks there. The place was in utter confusion. Our airmen had repeatedly bombed the station and railway depôt, creating havoc everywhere, and the fires and piled-up debris told of the effect of the Air Force's work. Before we arrived the Bedouins had been through the place and had looted everything they could carry away. It is hardly necessary to say, therefore, that there was not much worth collecting when we got to Deraa. On the 29th the division, with the Arabs operating on their right, got into touch with the retreating Turkish 4th Army in the Dilli area, and thereafter it became a chase and rounding-up of remnants of that ill-fated, tired mass of disorganised troops. The 4th Army was on a march of 120 miles to Damascus with water at long intervals.

The advance on Damascus from Kuneitra began after sundown on September 29. The Australian Mounted Division led. As the cavalry set out on their night march they presented a weird and wonderful spectacle. After the sun had ceased to cast a light above the mountains of Lebanon, thousands of horsemen passed out into the darkness with no sound other than the regular hoof-beats, the occasional jingle of arms and accoutrements, and the rumble of gun and limber wheels. There was no moon, but the heavens sparkled with a million stars, and the only part of the land which was visible in the gloom was where the irregular crest line of Mount Hermon blotted out the stars. Special instructions were issued with regard to securing the Beyrout railway, cutting telegraph lines, and avoiding entering Damascus, if that were possible. The Australians had marched about six miles and had passed over a wadi bridge, which to our surprise was intact and fit for wheels, when they were held up by the enemy on a hill, north of Khuriebe, a mound of stone between the wadi Mughanize and Sasa. On this hill were a number of Germans and Turks, and they had three field guns and many machine guns. It was a hard place to attack in the dark, the hill being covered with masses of lava deposits, and the stony nature of the surrounding country made it impossible for men to move across it mounted. To add to the difficulties the enemy's right flank rested on an impassable bog. The 9th and 10th Australian Light Horse regiments forced their way through the position astride the road, but they could not pass on and leave the remainder of the division exposed to machine-gun fire from the hill. They therefore had to extend to the east and attack the hill, an operation which lasted till three o'clock next morning, when they took two field guns, seven machine guns, and twenty-five prisoners. The Germans got away, but during the march in daylight they were found at Shiha and were galloped down. They were a weary lot, well fed but footsore with their long hurried tramp across stony country, and their mud-splashed legs and wet feet told us they had walked through stream and marsh in taking a bee-line for Damascus and, as they hoped, security. Some of them had thrown away their rifles, and in their anxiety to get away they had actually abandoned loot which, in their modesty, they preferred to call 'souvenirs.' As I went through Sasa just before the Australians had brought the Germans to heel, an Australian officer showed me a beautiful Arab sword he had picked up on the road. It had a magnificent damascene blade, and the scabbard was richly chased and ornamented with gold bands. It was a fine example of Oriental workmanship, and the Hun who dropped it must have been hard pressed to throw away such a prize.

The day was bright and warm, and we soon got into a well-watered region with an abundance of vegetation, refreshing alike to man and horse. It prepared us for the more glorious picture of the afternoon. Between nine and ten o'clock General Chauvel had a report dropped on his headquarters by aeroplane—which, so rapid was the advance on the wide front, was almost the only means of quick communication between the wings of the force—that 3000 Turkish infantry and 1000 cavalry were seen moving up the road from Deraa, apparently making for a gap in the hills between our road and the track the 4th Cavalry Division were taking. General Chauvel took no hurried steps to deal with this body, for he knew the time it would take the Turks to reach Damascus, and that they were in the good and safe keeping of General Barrow's division, which was timed to reach Damascus at the same hour as the column proceeding on the western route. The 14th Cavalry Brigade were detached to intercept this enemy column.

Opposition had to be dealt with in front of us. There were fires and explosions in Damascus. We could see three great columns of black smoke long before the high slender minarets of the city's mosques came into view, and it was obvious the Turks in front of us intended to delay our advance to permit the destruction of war material. To prevent the enemy getting away—he had his railway open to the north by way of Rayak, and to Beyrout—General Chauvel decided on fierce, unrelenting pressure, and right gallantly did his troops support him.

The enemy held a powerful position at Kaukab—reputed to be the site of the conversion of St. Paul—and the ridge east of it, a little more than ten miles south-west of Damascus, with 2500 infantry, some guns and many machine guns, and it was determined to make their defence as short as possible by attacking with mounted men. General Hodgson gave the attack to Lieut.-Colonel Bourchier with the 4th and 12th regiments of Light Horse, which had passed through the 3rd Light Horse Brigade on the road. Colonel Bourchier tried to work round the enemy's right but found it would entail too many casualties, and he therefore decided to make a mounted attack under cover of a bombardment. The guns of the Notts Battery R.H.A. and 'A' Battery H.A.C. opened a rapid fire on the position, and under cover of it the Australians made a perfect charge. The 4th regiment galloped to the ridge from the front, and the 12th regiment, which had worked round to the enemy's left, charged him in flank. The timing was well coordinated and both regiments got into the position at the same time. Not many of the enemy waited for them, but the few who saw that escape was hopeless were not unwilling to be taken prisoners. The majority streamed away to the woods of Daraya near one of the railway lines from the south, but they had no prospect of getting away and practically all of them were captured. The Australians pressed on on both sides of the western road, and soon after high noon were on the barren flat which separates the mountain range from the cultivated area on the south-western fringe of Damascus. They did not get to their position without encountering trouble. The hills west of El Mezza had many machine guns and some field guns upon them, and the 19th Brigade R.H.A. had to come into action to drive them out. The hilly position was very difficult to force because the steep ground and wadis made the space too narrow for a frontal attack in face of so many machine guns, and the French regiment dismounted and moved along the line of hills to silence the opposition. We then got on to the flat and obtained our best view of Damascus. What a scene it was. There, lying in a vast semicircular frame of brown, sterile, rocky hills, was an oasis of surpassing loveliness. Gardens of the brightest green brought forth memories of home, and to the eyes of these warriors from the Southern Cross in particular, who had spent years campaigning in the hot sands of the Sinai Desert, and had had their vitality lowered by long stretches of fighting and watching in the awful atmosphere of the Jordan valley, they were a grateful relief.

Away in this green setting, the minarets and white-walled buildings stood out like pearl in the dancing sunlight, and if the picture was blurred and marred by the smoke of fires, the prospect was certainly the most delightful since we had looked over Jerusalem and Bethlehem for the first time: months before.

We did not know what was happening in Damascus, but we were certain the Turks were there. Snipers and machine guns lay in those gardens, and none of our troops became trespassers. Bedouins were just as dangerous. Like vultures which hover about a dying animal, the Bedouins had swarmed towards Damascus in the hope of looting the rich quarter and the world-famed bazaars, and these wild men were armed, and fired without discrimination upon Turk and Briton. It was apparent by three o'clock in the afternoon that, if Damascus was not surrendered, the city would not be entered that night, for the Arab army was some distance away, and General Hodgson made his dispositions to prevent the enemy leaving by the western exit to gain the road across the mountains leading to the plain between the Anti-Lebanon and Lebanon ranges.

This road passes by the suburb of Salahiye, and enters the hills by a steep pass dominated on both sides by two high hills. It is the best road out Damascus, and it is the route chosen by French engineers for the railway which connects Damascus with Beyrout, and joins

189

Rolls-Royce armoured cars crossing the Jordan by the Bridge of Jacob's Daughters

the Aleppo line at Rayak. The Turks had not counted on the length of the cavalry's arm. They never believed we could advance so fast, and during the afternoon, when they found we were at the doors of Damascus, they made a panicky attempt to get away a portion of their forces. Some went by road on foot, others crowded themselves in motors, and a number of the ram-shackle vehicles which, during the war, plied for hire in Damascus streets were requisitioned. It was *sauve qui peut*. Into a train were packed the Turkish Army's war chest and archives, and, with officers and officials filling it far beyond its normal capacity, it steamed out of the city. It was too late. As the train passed into the Abana gorge our guns opened fire on it, leaving marks on trucks and coaches, but without stopping it. But there was an effective block on the hills overlooking the road and railway. The 5th Australian Light Horse Brigade were astride that road. With General Onslow's brigade was the French cavalry regiment, the *Chasseurs d'Afrique*, under Major Lebon; whilst the 14th Light Horse regiment and New Zealand machine-gun detachments were on the hills. They turned the defile into a shambles, and in a few minutes after they opened fire it became a more ghastly scene of war than the Ferweh road after our airmen had bombed it. The Australians were south-east of Dumar, three miles from the heart of Damascus. They first turned their attention on the train and brought it to a standstill. Then they caught the head of the column on the road and so raked it with their fire that the whole surface was strewn with dead and wounded. Men tried to return to the city, vehicles endeavoured to turn and were upset, and in two or three minutes there was pandemonium on the road. Officers and men fought in a mob to cut a way back to Damascus, but they were checked lower down and had to surrender. They could not find a way out over the wrecked transport and, recognising that their capture was inevitable, over 4000 gave themselves up to what was little more than a handful of men. They were brought round to the south-west of Damascus, to remain as quiet as lambs for the night within earshot of the Australian Mounted Divisional headquarters. The Beyrout road next morning was a horrible sight; hundreds of dead lay on all sides but the Australians quickly cleared it up, burying 375 bodies and sending many wounded into the hospitals.

While the Australians were making it certain that the enemy could not escape through their screen, firm and gallant work was being done to the south of Damascus. The 14th Brigade of the 5th Cavalry Division, sent from the western column of Desert Mounted Corps to cut off the Turkish 4th Army moving through Kiswe to Damascus, hit the enemy very hard. I was standing at the khan of Shiha when the order was issued to the brigade, and if all the men had been already in the saddle they could not have got away more quickly. They moved off to the east between us and Kaukab well before the latter place had been charged by the Australians, and one could follow their rapid movements between the woods and the red-roofed station of Kiswe by high pillars of dust raised by galloping horses. They had guns with them, and while these put in a hot fire, the brigade seized the hill Jebel el Aswad astride the Kiswe-Damascus road and cut the enemy column in half. Leaving the rear portion to be dealt with later by the 4th Cavalry Division they went after a disorganised mob of Turks running to the hills on the north-east and down the main road to Damascus. They captured almost the whole of the leading portion of the column, including the remnants of the 3rd Turkish cavalry division with its divisional commander and staff. The Essex Battery R.H.A. shelled the enemy in the hills, while the men on the road were taken by squadrons who had frequent gallops to round them up. A little after midday, when the brigade were having a strenuous time with a force they had scattered over a wide stretch of country, some of it hilly and some of it full of trees, a message was sent back to Desert Mounted Corps' headquarters that a portion of the rear part of the column was breaking back and moving up the wadi Zabirani towards the khan at Shiha. The remaining brigades of the 5th Cavalry Division were sent to deal with this force, and headed it off towards the 4th Cavalry Division. The 13th Cavalry Brigade reached Kiswe at five o'clock, and after Blight opposition took 675 prisoners and four guns. The brigade then advanced and bivouacked for the night in the southern outskirts of Damascus, with patrols at Kadem station, the main Damascus depôt for the Hedjaz railway.

An admirable effort was made to secure the German wireless installation. It was a high-powered plant, and by its means the Germans were in constant communication with Constantinople and Berlin. A great deal of German propaganda in the East passed through this station, and we should have liked to capture it intact. Captain Lord Apsley was sent on a special mission to secure it. He took with him two troops of the Royal Gloucester Hussars Yeomanry and, leaving after the 14th Cavalry Brigade started for the Kiswe road, they arrived at Kadem station at half-past four. The wireless station was close by, but the German operators had taken no risks. They had prepared the whole equipment for demolition, and on the Gloucesters' approach the great standards were blown up, and a party of Germans and Turks were seen completing the destruction. The Gloucesters charged this party in the hope of saving some of the apparatus, and three Germans and seven Turks were killed with the sword. The remainder surrendered, but before they could be marched away they were reinforced by a considerable number of Germans, and the two troops had to withdraw by a different route from that which had taken to enter the military area of Damascus. They joined the Australian Mounted Division in the evening. If the two troops had been two divisions they could not have prevented the wreckage of whole plant, and the Gloucesters' fine action served better luck.

CHAPTER 20

A Night of Fireworks

All day long the 4th Cavalry Division had been engaging the 4th Army. They were continually firing into, breaking up, and capturing large bodies of troops, and their advance would have been more rapid than it was if the Turks had not been a tired and extended column. Having to collect a large number of stragglers and to protect them from Bedouins, it was remarkable that the division were able to keep so well to the time-table arranged for the march and to get into touch with the remainder of Desert Mounted Corps on the night of September 30–October 1. The 13th Cavalry Brigade had seen the division about two miles from Kiswe when they were capturing Turks there, and when the troops bivouacked that night it was as certain as anything could be in war that British troops would take the surrender of Damascus next morning. Twelve days of fighting and hard marching, during which every man had covered 150 miles and some a much longer distance, sent the troops to their blankets after horses had been fed and a rough trek supper eaten. But no one could sleep. The enemy gave us the finest display of pyrotechnics we had ever seen. He had burned a considerable portion of his military stores during the day, and we had become anxious lest

the fires should spread into the city. There was a similar alarm in the city itself, for the report had got about that the Germans intended that we should only have the shell of the place. For four thousand years Damascus had been coveted by martial kings and the tide of battle had often surged round her, but so fair a jewel was the city that barbarian rulers and their hordes had never destroyed her. She was the oldest living city in the world, and when watching the fires we wondered if we were going to witness her first destruction. It would have been in keeping with the bad record of the Turk if by his action, aided by Germans, the fires should spread into the city. There was a high wind, and many of the houses were of wood. Fortunately observers, who had taken bearings on the columns of smoke, reported that they all continued to issue from the same spots, and when at sundown the wind dropped it seemed that Damascus would continue to live.

Those of us who had halted near Australian Mounted Divisional headquarters were preparing to seek repose wrapped in a blanket on the hard sunburnt earth, when there was a vivid flash as of lightning followed by a violent concussion, and we knew an ammunition dump had gone up. For a couple of hours there was no sleeping man in the force. Explosion followed explosion, and, heightened no doubt by the dark green fringe of the encircling orchards, the effect was as of vivid lightning continually stabbing the sky as one pile of ammunition was fired after another. The hills accentuated sound, and after the report struck us it was caught by the hills and passed backwards and forwards in wonderful echoes. Every eye was centred on this enthralling scene. One burst of flame followed another, and the lights increased in intensity as if the enemy were working up interest in his fireworks and keeping his biggest dump to the last. Sometimes there were double explosions, the first a fraction of a second before the other, and occasionally high up in the smoke clouds you would see two or three large shells burst like rockets. Small-arms ammunition was blown sky-high and burst like golden rain, and one blinding flash suggested that the whole of the enemy's reserve of signal lights had been destroyed in one second. The Turks kept the main dump near Meidan station for their finale. It went up in a mighty column of flame which lost itself in a smoke cloud and then reappeared a couple of hundred yards higher. We waited for the roar. It came upon us in a stunning crash, and scarcely had the shock passed over us than it came back from the hills, modified, of course, but still so violent as to send a feeling of awe throughout an army which had grown accustomed to all the sounds of war. When the echoes had died away an Australian described the last big report as the 'crack of doom,' and it certainly spelt the approaching end of Turkish resistance. I was on the Rand in 1896 when fifty-six tons of dynamite went up in a suburb of Johannesburg, but that explosion, raising a mighty mushroom-shaped column of smoke, was small compared with the thunderous report which followed the destruction of the main dump in Damascus. After the explosions had ceased we rested in as much quietude as was permitted by the coming and going of despatch riders seeking the location of signal headquarters, and of horsed supply columns anxious to deposit precious food, and no one felt refreshed when an hour before dawn the troops stood to in readiness to complete the work begun on the previous day.

The situation in Damascus did not become clear until late in the morning. I was on a hill close to Salahiye talking to Major-General Hodgson when Captain Dray, Intelligence officer with Desert Mounted Corps, came up and asked if he could proceed into the city as he had orders to get into touch with the Governor. General Hodgson had had no report that the city had been occupied, and he told Captain Dray he could either go under a white flag or in an armoured car. I left to find my way in, and was diverted from the main road by a military policeman who said the road was blocked by snipers in the orchards. I then took the track which led down to the Abana Gorge. It was an awful track, very narrow, with gradients in places of about one in three, and a right-hand turn at the bottom leading to a rickety wooden bridge over a fast-flowing stream. Preceding me was a Rolls-Royce armoured car which pulled up when it was found the bridge would not carry its weight. An officer came to me and said he had an urgent message from G.H.Q. to deliver to General Godwin, the B.G.G.S. of Desert Mounted Corps, and was ordered to go through the city with turrets closed and his machine gun ready for action. As his car was held up he accepted my invitation to travel with me in my Ford car, but he had to leave his escort behind. We got into the town safely, though snipers were still active and there were many Bedouin gentlemen blazing away more ammunition than was good for the skins of the inhabitants. We went to the municipal building, and found that Captain Dray had already installed himself there and was doing good work, for the local authorities were in need of a strong guiding hand, and from him we learned that Australians had taken the city and had passed through it hours before.

What had happened was this. Some patrols of the Australian Mounted Division were in the northern outskirts of the city during the night, and they spied out the land to see if it was possible to get round Damascus on the north to reach the Aleppo road, which was the only route the Turks could take since the Beyrout road had been closed to them the previous afternoon. No track fit for horses was found on the north, and Brigadier-General Wilson, who was ordered to proceed with his 3rd Australian Light Horse Brigade to cut off the enemy reported to be trekking northward, decided that he must make a dash through the city, whether it was surrendered or not. The brigade galloped into Damascus. They started at five o'clock in the morning down the Abana Gorge. A mass of wrecked transport had to be hauled off the highway to make a path for cavalry, but they could not wholly clear it; in fact it took 300 German prisoners a fortnight to remove the debris. At the bottom of the gorge the road was clear, and a West Australian regiment put their horses to their best pace. As they were riding beside a mud wall enclosure they met a heavy burst of musketry and the officer charged a body of Turks. He then rode on to the municipal building, and, finding that organised resistance had ceased, gave directions for the preservation of order. Instantly half of Damascus came into the streets. The people gave the Australians an amazing welcome. They clapped their hands in truly Oriental fashion, threw flowers and branches of trees on the road, and showered gifts of fruit on the victors, while those in possession of firearms blazed away in their joy that the Turk no longer held sway over them. Outside the city hall a surging mob of citizens, the rich in the bright colours of the East, and the poor in rags, greeted them with the wildest enthusiasm. The Governor, suave and dignified, assured the officers that their orders would be carried out, but begged them to think lightly of the discharge of firearms as it was merely a sign of the people's delight that we had arrived. He offered coffee and cigarettes, as if time was of no consequence, and repeated his assurance that all would be well. An Oriental official preserves a wonderful calm in moments of stress.

The 3rd Light Horse Brigade left sightseeing and demonstrations of the citizens' goodwill to a future occasion, and proceeded with the task of getting at the enemy. Obtaining a good guide, General Wilson took his column of horsemen at a rapid rate through the city, and, passing the old English hospital, got on to the Aleppo road, taking another train *en route* and 483 prisoners, thirty machine guns, and eight field guns. The brigade then advanced up the road, and when in the neighbourhood of Duma, about six miles from the outskirts of the city, came upon many parties of the enemy. The district was a cultivated area with vineyards and many trees, and Germans were hiding in houses with machine guns to cover the retreat. They fought a hard rearguard action, but the 10th Light Horse regiment charged the rear of a column, and then, by continually outflanking the machine-gunners, the cavalry reached Duma, after killing a large number of the enemy and taking 600 prisoners and thirty-seven machine guns. They continued the pursuit till dusk, by which time they had reached the guard-house at Kusseir, where they secured one hundred Germans and more machine guns. The admirable way in which the machine-gunners were captured, by working round the flanks and taking them in rear, unquestionably accounted for our light casualties. While the brigade were occupied in routing out the enemy from the cultivated area they had one period of anxiety. A patrol brought in news that a column estimated to contain 3000 mounted men was advancing down the Aleppo road on Damascus, and the order was given to deal with the utmost energy with the machine-gunners so as to be ready to meet the larger body. However this proved to be the annual caravan proceeding from Aleppo to Mecca under the escort of a thousand armed Arabs. During the war the Turks had allowed this caravan to pass unhindered to the Holy Place, and the Arabs showed great interest and not a little satisfaction when, after meeting retreating Turks, they fell in with Australian troops who could assure them that Damascus had passed through the ordeal of war without any damage, and that right through the Hedjaz down to Medina Turkish resistance had ceased.

The 3rd Light Horse Brigade bivouacked on October 1 at Duma, where, at half-past seven next morning, General Wilson was informed that a large party of the enemy was retiring through a wooded district north-east of him. There was little time to spare. The enemy were five miles from the cavalry when the report came in, and if they could get another two miles on the road it would be impossible for the Australians to follow them, because of a range of hills on which a few machine guns could sweep the open plain. The Light Horse were sent off at their best pace and they had a hard gallop of six miles to head off the column. They reached the Turks in the nick of time, and, drawing swords, charged them in flank, capturing a divisional commander, 1500 other prisoners, two field guns, a mountain gun and twenty-six machine guns. While the charge was taking place a handful of Australians went ahead and posted six machine guns across the road to close it. These guns opened fire at 700 yards, and all the Turks then surrendered. There was only one casualty in the brigade. Thus all exits from Damascus were effectually closed, and hardly a German or Turk who had waited in the city till the British arrived got beyond the reach of our far-flung cavalry line. General Liman von Sanders had the soldier's insight, and left Damascus for Aleppo four days before we were seen in the open about the city.

When General Chauvel heard that Australia troops had passed through Damascus he, with Brigadier-General Godwin, motored to the Governor's official residence to arrange for the civil administration. This was on the morning of October 1. Near the Serai General Chauvel met Colonel Lawrence, who with a small following of

Arab horsemen had ridden in behind the advanced troops of the 14th Cavalry Brigade. Colonel Lawrence introduced General Chauvel to Shukri Pasha, to whom the Commander-in-Chief's instructions with regard to civil administration were communicated. The people greeted the Desert Corps' commander most cordially, and they seemed to be only slightly less interested in his Rolls-Royce car. A Briton entering the city on the day of its capture, who did not have his emotions stirred by the welcome of the Damascenes, must have been without a spark of national pride. Having moved through the country with the cavalry and having seen some Circassian villages display a lukewarm, unconcerned attitude at our victorious advance against the Turks, I was under the impression that in Damascus the Arabs would show their usual unemotional demeanour and would accept our appearance as *Kismet*, and, while appreciating the \ prospect of a change from bad to good government, would receive us with their customary immobility of feature and give us no outward or visible sign of their true feelings. But so far from that being true, the welcome given to any one wearing British uniform was amazingly cordial. The population did not take our victory as an ordinary incident of life. The inhabitants threw off their stolid exterior and received us with great joy, closed their shops and bazaars, put on festival dress, and made holiday. They acclaimed the day as the greatest in Damascus during her four thousand years of history. Only a few British officers came into Damascus on October 1, but each of them was welcomed with the same wholehearted fervour.

At Jerusalem the British Army was received with deep feelings of thankfulness by all sects and creeds, but the condition of the people, rendered pitiable by slow starvation, prevented the welcome being so demonstrative as in Damascus, though it was at least equally, and probably more, sincere. When a soldier appeared in the streets he was surrounded by excited and delighted crowds, and when I was stopped by an English-speaking Syrian who asked for news, the throng was. so persistent in getting the Syrian to translate what I told him that it was very hard to make myself heard. I spoke of the latest victories on the Western Front. The people, of course, had not heard of them; indeed, they had been led to believe that the Allies in that theatre of war were on the point of collapse. Then I told of Bulgaria's plight and that aroused warm enthusiasm, for, with evidence before their eyes that Turkey was beaten, the people began to realise that the war was nearing its end. They crowded round me for details of our army's gigantic stride through Palestine and Syria, and when I mentioned the enormous captures of men and guns, of which the people had no conception, they asked me to repeat what I had said, possibly fearing they would detect an exaggeration. But I merely stated plain unadorned facts, and there was no need to do more. There were cries of 'Finish the Turks,' 'Settle our accounts'—at least this is how the cries were interpreted to me by the Syrian. I thought there were one or two persons in the crowd who were sceptical, not about our victory, because it was obvious we had triumphed or we should not have reached Damascus, but about the extent of it. I had two parcels of newspapers in my car. The Intelligence Department in its wisdom had arranged for the distribution of newspapers printed in the language which the people could read in the conquered territory, and before I left G.H.Q. the Chief Field Censor, knowing it to be my duty to get as far forward as possible, asked me to hand them out when I got to the front. I kept them all for Damascus, and I think I did right.

One paper which above all others is regarded in Syria as a faithful conveyor of news is the journal *Al Mokattam*. It is printed in Cairo, and is published by Syrian gentlemen of high standing who have always warmly supported the British. Its area of circulation extends from the north-west of Africa in a continuous line through Persia to the borders of Afghanistan, and its reputation is so high that during the war it was a deadly crime in the eyes of Germans or Turks for any one in Syria to possess a copy. Some of them dropped by aeroplane helped our propaganda. Now I had a couple of hundred copies of the *Mokattam* in my car, and I asked the crowd if they would believe the news I had told them if they saw it in that journal. There were loud shouts of agreement, and I proceeded to distribute copies. My driver warned me I was risking the car. It proved I risked more than the car. So great was the desire to possess a copy that the mob in their excitement got hold of me, and, if I had fallen, I should have been under a hundred feet. I had to throw the papers into the crowd and let them fight for them and tear their clothes in doing it. While I was getting rid of the last copies there were literally thousands of people rushing from all the courts and alleys of an overcrowded quarter to take part in the scrimmage. The papers were more than a week out of date, but they had got the news that the people desired, namely that the Turkish armies had been overwhelmed and were in full retreat. They had seen the rest. They also learned the truth of what I had told them about our victories in France. Wherever you went you saw a knot of people listening to some person reading the *Mokattam*. British prestige stood very high that day in Damascus.

The rejoicings lasted all day. They reached an extraordinary height when sections of the Arab army came into the city. The Emir Feisal had had his agents in Damascus and they had sown good seed. Colonel Lawrence had come in with a small following, and the people recognised the small brave English scholar who had turned soldier to influence Arabs to fight to throw off the Turkish yoke. Colonel Lawrence wore the head-dress, robes and sword of an Arab chief of high degree, but this was not a complete disguise, and if the Damascenes had not been told they were to expect him they certainly very readily identified this gallant gentleman, who, more than any one else, had striven through good times and bad to put Arab pressure on the Turkish garrisons at Medina and Maan, and to spread Arab disaffection throughout the Turkish Empire. The good report of Colonel Lawrence's work had filtered through the land. The Turks had great fear of him, a personal fear as well as a dread of his influence, for they knew he had led scores of raids and had marshalled the Arabs for battle. On the head of this heroic figure they had placed a price of £50,000, but no Arab desired to gain such a reward. There was a scene of remarkable enthusiasm when Colonel Lawrence rode into the city. The Arabs came in at a fast trot, and in the narrow winding streets, badly paved and neglected so that the tramway. rails were in places nearly a foot above the level of the road, there was not sufficient room for demonstration. But as the party rode towards the city, firing at the heavens, as Arabs will in their moments of rejoicing, the people received them delightedly, throwing sweetmeats in Colonel Lawrence's path and showering upon him the perfumes of Araby. All this happened an hour or two before I arrived, so I did not witness the welcome, but I was told it was a remarkable scene and was a tribute as much to Colonel Lawrence's work as to the popularity of the cause he had supported with such wonderful succes.[1]

But I was in time to see the entry into Damascus of a larger body of the Arab army. It was an astounding sight. I was going through the city towards the Meidan to view the wreckage caused by the explosions on the previous night and to learn the details of the capture of several thousands of prisoners by a handful of Australians. Ahead of me I heard a great deal of rifle shooting, and at first I imagined I was going to be in the thick of street fighting. In a few moments I saw the Arab entry. Hundreds of men covered with dust were following behind a British officer dressed as an Arab, holding their rifles at arm's

---

1. See Appendix D.

length and firing at the sky as rapidly as they could empty their magazines. Some were mounted on ponies, fiery, wiry, little beasts; others on camels, and they rushed forward without order and under no sort of road discipline excepting that they would not pass their leader. My driver drew up close to a building to let them pass. I was glad he did the right thing. As they came by me they saluted our khaki with a tremendous fusilade, and those of them who could make out a British uniform in the suffocating dust cloud which they raised, fired their salute into the road, an act kindly meant but distinctly dangerous to the person they intended to honour. Some of them bumped violently into the car, but laughed loudly and paid no heed to injuries thus caused to their animals. They were very excited, or perhaps I should say elated, and I was pleased when they had passed on and had left a clear if dusty road in front of me. The feeling uppermost in my mind at that time was one of profound admiration for the stout-hearted British officers, few in number, who had managed to get some sort of fighting discipline into those Arab irregulars. Their condition was such as to make any man trained in the British Army despair. Only tact, great courage and the stern necessity of aiding old England in the hour of need, could have made British officers secure such results. War makes strange companions, but the love of adventure is so strong in Britons that our officers were quite content with their job. I would not have had it for all the jewels in the East.

There was some discussion as to who were the first troops to get into the city of Damascus. I have indicated that, if possible, British troops were not to go into the city, but it was necessary that they should do so to make a complete capture of the Turks, and to settle the question whether Arabs or British took Damascus I give the report of Brigadier-General Wilson, of the 3rd Australian Light Horse Brigade, which is accepted as final, General Wilson says:

> Jemal Pasha, commander of the Turkish 4th Army, arranged to hold a meeting of the notables of Damascus at the Municipal Gardens at 4 p.m. on September 30, 1918, for the purpose of handing over the military governorship of the City to Shukri Pasha Ayoubi. The last-mentioned person was an Arab formerly in the Turkish Army and favourable to the Sherif of Mecca. There was in the City at this time a person of Algerian birth named Emir Said. This man for some time had been employed by the Turkish Government in raising a volunteer force of Arabs to fight against the Sherif. Emir Said's sympathies were really

202

in favour of the Sherif, but he disguised them and drew arms, ammunition, and money from the Turks. Some time prior to 2 p.m. on the 30th news was received in the city that the British cavalry were approaching. A report was also circulated that the Germans intended to burn the City before they left, and Shukri Pasha and Emir Said then went to Jemal Pasha and informed him that they would not allow the City to be burned. They advised Jemal Pasha to leave the City forthwith and said if he did not he would probably be attacked by the local Arabs. In Jemal Pasha's presence these people then produced a Sherif's flag and displayed it at the Town Hall and declared for the Sherif. Jemal Pasha left the City at 2 p.m. by the Beyrout road.

On the night of Sept. 30-Oct. 1 this brigade bivouacked in the hills overlooking the village of Dumar about four miles north-west of Damascus on the Beyrout road. The road was during the night covered by six machine guns, and heavy casualties were inflicted on the enemy trying to escape by that road, and the balance of them were turned back into the City. The Beyrout road was thus closed to the enemy from sunset on the 30th September. At 5 a.m. on October 1 the brigade descended to the main road at Dumar and marched along that road south-easterly into Damascus. The 10th Light Horse regiment formed the advanced guard, Major Olden being in charge of the vanguard. On entering the north-western suburbs a good deal of rifle shooting was indulged in by the inhabitants, some shooting or sniping at the column. In a few cases the snipers were observed and their fire was returned. To discourage the sniping Major Olden moved the vanguard at the gallop until he arrived in front of the Town Hall where he halted. The time was now between 6.30 and 7 o'clock. Major Olden then asked for the Civil Governor and was told he was upstairs. Major Olden dismounted and went into the Town Hall, where he found a large assembly of notables and people in uniforms as if arranged for some public function. Emir Said was sitting in the municipal chair, and when Major Olden asked for the Civil Governor, Emir Said rose and came forward as such and shook hands. Through an interpreter Emir Said said, "In the name of the civil population of Damascus I welcome the British Army." Major Olden said, "What is all this rifle shooting that is going on?" and Said replied, "That is the people welcoming you." Major Olden then said, "It must cease, as it may lead to misunderstanding." Said answered, "You may have no fear. I will answer in the name of the civil population that the City is quiet." Major Olden then said, "Who are all these armed men in uniform about the streets?" and Said replied, "They are the police. What would you have them do?" Major Olden said, "They can retain their arms for the present and assist in maintaining order and preventing looting. A large force of cavalry is following me up, and if my orders are not obeyed you will be held responsible." Said replied, "You need have no fear. We have been expecting the English for some days and have made preparations to receive them." Emir Said then made a speech of welcome, and stated what they would be prepared to do to assist us. He then asked Major Olden to have refreshments. This Major Olden declined, and asked for a guide to the north-east or Aleppo road. Emir Said detailed an officer called Saki Bey to act as such. This officer stopped with the brigade till the following morning. The advanced guard then moved on followed by the remainder of the brigade, passed through the City and moved to the north-east road, passing the English hospital en route. Touch was gained with the enemy rearguard at the wadi Maraba. Up to the time—about seven o'clock—that this brigade completed its passage through the City, thereby closing the only remaining available exit for the enemy, no member of the Sherif's Army was visible in any part of the City within the view of this brigade.

This report settles the question as to whether British troops or Arabs were first in Damascus. The Australians were in the city hours before the Arabs. So was an Indian cavalry regiment, the advanced guard of the 14th Cavalry Brigade, which was well ahead of the leading Arab troops.

CHAPTER 21

Street Fighting in the City

Damascus was a weird city on the night of its capture. Late in the afternoon I went through the city to Desert Mounted Corps' headquarters on the southern extremity and remained there for an hour or two. The sun had gone down a long time before I returned, and the citizens who were peaceably inclined had all gone home to bar their doors. There were looters abroad, and as, according to arrangements made, I believe, with our Arab allies, there were no British troops within the four corners of the city, very little protection was afforded to any one possessing property. The Turkish civil police who had been continued in charge of the streets did not quite know how they stood, although their duties had been clearly pointed out. The inhabitants knew them and did not like them, and the marauding Bedouins who held life cheap, were not to be stopped in their depredations by any man in Turkish uniform. So the Turkish policeman hid himself and was thankful to be out of the way, and in a two-mile drive through the city I did not see one man doing his duty. It was not a nice or comfortable ride. The night was dark and, excepting for an occasional rifle or revolver shot fired by a thief, Damascus might have been a city of the dead. We ran over the bodies of some dead Turks which nobody had troubled to remove from the streets, but the only living people we saw were looters. Some of them appeared shy and anxious to hide from the beams thrown out by our headlights. Others were bold and came towards the car as if to search it, ready to take every risk to obtain anything of value. Sometimes a kick, sometimes a collision with the car which did them no good, upset their calculations, and, though we left oaths in an unknown tongue and the discharge of firearms behind us, nothing happened. The stillness of the night was only broken by the looters, and their day of reckoning proved to be the morrow.

On the day before we entered Damascus the long high, trail of dust seen south-west of the city against the brown hills warned Jemal Pasha, who had been commander of the Turkish 4th Army, that Turkish hold on the city, which had lasted six centuries, was about to be released. Liman von Sanders had already left the sinking ship and was probably then in Aleppo. Jemal and the wali left the city and got over the Anti-Lebanons by the Beyrout road and then trekked north through Baalbek, Homs, and Hama to rejoin the Generalissimo of an army that no longer existed. They left behind them in Damascus and on the Hedjaz line, crawling painfully up to Damascus, about 22,000 troops, a number as large as Desert Mounted Corps had available for fighting at this period. But the Turks' moral was gone. Before we surrounded the place they had trouble among themselves. The Germans in Damascus were hated. The citizens detested them; the Turks and the Arabs fighting in Turkish battalions had been victims of their brutal, overbearing conduct.[1] They were outnumbered and it came to be their turn to feel fear. Germans could not show themselves in the streets without risking their lives. Citizens spat upon them, Turkish soldiers fought them. Some left their barracks and hid themselves in private houses, and on October 2 an Armenian came to me and asked what he should do with three Germans, one of them wounded, whom he was sheltering from the fury of the people. The Germans were between millstones, and they gladly sought safety by giving themselves up to British troops. They were completely humbled and cowed, and their experiences during the last few days in Damascus will ha them for the remainder of their lives.

The Turks, too, had cause to be uneasy. They were masters of the Germans now, but the Arabs with them revolted and refused to fight. When we were outside the city they declared themselves adherents of the King of the Hedjaz, and were ready to proclaim him in the city. Turks and Arabs took up separate quarters in the same barracks and, the Arabs becoming openly hostile, several Turks were killed. In the streets the citizens beat the Turkish soldiery and jeered at them when they saw that their wrongs were about to be righted by the British, and probably many of the dead Turks in Damascus were massacred by their former Arab comrades and by civilians. They were in a desperate plight, and doubtless thousands of them looked with relief at the arrival of a troop of Australians at the main barracks on the early morning of October 1. The Australian

---

1 See Appendix E.

GERMAN AMBULANCE SECTION LEAVING DAMASCUS FOR EGYPT

officer was in a predicament. Arabs were there as well as Turks, and neither were willing to give up their arms in view of the hostility between them. The officer was not going to march away thousands of armed men, and he sent back to his brigade for assistance. Young officers had some difficult situations to deal with in these days and they nearly always did the right thing. A regiment of Light Horse was ordered to collect these prisoners in the city, and made quick work of disarming the crowd and brought them in. Those who did not surrender in a body were in a hapless state. I witnessed many instances of the fear of Turkish soldiers. Small groups of them assembled in dark corners of the streets waiting for an opportunity to give themselves up. They were usually without arms, which had been taken from them by the civilian population, and their personal belongings had likewise gone. Any one in khaki was looked upon as a saviour, and as there were few British soldiers allowed in the city, those who did go in on duty had an awkward time in declining to take the surrender or to conduct the Turks to a place where they would be safe from the people's violence. I saw an Australian supply officer asked by about forty Turks to capture them. He said he did not want to be troubled with them, and that they must either go outside the town to a spot he indicated or they could go to the devil. But the spokesman for the Turks wanted him to take them, and said they would be proud of the honour of surrendering to a British officer. 'No, Johnny, I don't want that lot to-day,' the officer replied as he moved to go away, but the Turks went after him. He could not shake them off until he espied a padre, and then, assuring the party that the clergyman was a military policeman, he was left free to tackle his supply problems. I believe the padre got the whole party safely out of the city.

One of the first real delights of the Australians in Damascus was meeting with an Australian pilot who had been a prisoner for a fortnight. When he was over Amman he had engine trouble and was forced to descend. It was impossible to get away in daylight and the enemy captured him. From Amman he was sent north by train. At the best of times travelling is not luxurious in Turkish troop trains, and the pilot got little food or water, and had unpleasant companions, not all of whom could speak to him. He did not hear of the progress of the battle, but he had unwelcome proof of our activity, for when the train reached Deraa it was held up on the line while an awful mess was cleared away in front. His comrades of the Air Force had been busy with bombs, and another flight came over and wrecked his train just as it was going to pull through. Thereafter he had to walk, and he only reached Damascus a day or two before his brother Australians entered the city. We also released a yeoman who was taken prisoner at Katia, in the Sinai Peninsula, at Easter 1916. That poor fellow had had a bad time.

Nearly one hundred Italians were also found in Damascus. They had been taken prisoners on the Isonzo, and after working in labour battalions in Germany and Austria they were sent to exist under the Turks in Syria, and were employed in railway construction and repairs. Another man who was soon free under the British flag was Mr. Forder, a missionary who had worked among the Bedouins for years. He used to make Jerusalem his home, and was known to most of the wandering men in the Jordan valley and on the Moab plateau. The nomads had a great respect for Mr. Forder, and his influence over them was considerable. The German heard of him—probably a German subject, some person who described himself as a religious man, denounced him—and they ordered the Turks to arrest him as a spy. He was thrown into prison and kept with felons of the worst type for two years, but was then sent to Damascus on parole. He was very thin and obviously half-starved when I saw him outside the poor caravanserai near the city hall, but he was happy, and carried a small Union Jack which he had hidden during his imprisonment, and this was the only British flag shown in Damascus.

There are keen men of business in the bazaars. The Bank of England £5 note was well known to them and indeed throughout the East. Before the war it was held at high value, but after 1914 the Germans did all they could to depreciate it. Many of the notes found their way into Syria—I believe there were £2,000,000 of them in Aleppo alone—and their value among the traders fell considerably. The Damascus money market at the end of September was a sure indication of the trend of events. In the third week of that month English notes were worth 30 per cent, of their face value, but when the news was received that General Allenby had forced through in the coastal sector they rose to 42 per cent. On a distant glimpse of the advancing cavalry telling Damascus that the city was about to be taken, the notes at once became worth 80 per cent, of their face value, and, though they did not reach par when I was in the city, the tendency was always upward. Turkish paper money collapsed to 15 per cent, and it was not readily accepted at that. There were thousands of pounds of it lying in the Abana gorge where the Australians had wrecked a train, and the Australians had such small regard for it that a trooper who had left a ragged girl holding his horse outside an hotel while he tried to purchase some bread from the proprietor, gave her a Turkish £100 note as a gift. Somebody asked him if he knew what he was doing, and he replied: 'Oh yes. It may do the kid good. Anyway I don't want it. I picked up a bucketful.' The child ran away to spread the report that our Army was full of millionaires, and the traders certainly put an exorbitant price on anything a soldier wanted to purchase.

On the day the Turks surrendered in Damascus a number of the Christian inhabitants remained in the vicinity of the hotel. They knew that the British had won the city, but they had seen little of them. The Hedjaz flag was flying above the seat of government, men of the Hedjaz army were in the streets telling everybody that the King of the Hedjaz was King of Damascus, and that the city belonged henceforth to the kingdom of Arabia. The Christians could not disguise their concern. They had hoped and prayed for a British Protectorate if we did not annex Syria, and they spoke quite earnestly when they said that, bad as it was to be under Turkish extortion they infinitely preferred it to being governed by the Arabs. They thought their last state would be worse than the first, and their faces grew graver when they saw no parade of British strength except outside the luscious gardens which hold the city in a fragrant embrace. Few of them were old enough to remember the awful massacre of Christians in Damascus, but their fathers and mothers had told them of the frightful days when people were slaughtered because of their religion, and they trembled lest, under a new rule, there should be a repetition of the scenes when the Christian quarter was sacked and its inhabitants butchered. Nothing would reassure them but the promise that our troops would come in. This one could not tell them because there was an understanding that, as Damascus was to come under the Arab sphere of influence, our troops were not to enter Damascus unless it was imperative to do so to carry out operations. It was only because the 3rd Australian Light Horse Brigade could not get on to the Duma road by working round the north of the city that they advanced through the place.

The Christians went home that night full of misgivings. They barricaded their houses, but these precautions did not in every case secure their property, and what occurred on the morning of October 2 supported their fear that they were on the eve of a fresh massacre. In the brief description of my ride through Damascus on the previous evening I have indicated that there was no protection of property. As soon as we had got into the city, General Chauvel had told the official who was said to be the military governor what steps he must take to secure the preservation of order, and he offered to provide troops to assist him. With large numbers of marauders prowling about the city strong and energetic action was necessary on the part of the governor, who, however, took an Eastern view of things and allowed chaos to have its way. The Arabs had not the experience required to handle a delicate situation. They might be bold in attacking the Turk, but they had no experience of policing a city of the size or importance of Damascus, and they seemed to be content to leave till to-morrow what should have been settled to-day. When day broke some of the citizens were hard put to it defending their possessions. The Bedouins had become overbold, were searching houses for valuables, and even holding up people in the streets. There was fighting in every quarter, and as the morning wore on the position became very ugly. For a long time I watched events from the window of the hotel. I saw Bedouins carrying away bundles of loot on camels and horses, and when any one interfered with them there was shooting and somebody died. Some men of the Hedjaz army were sent to stop looting, but though their intentions were good they did not carry out their orders as British troops would have done, and I fear many a law-abiding citizen, going about his business, met with a sudden death. The Arabs could not discriminate, or thought they had not time to discriminate, between a Bedouin and a man pursuing his lawful trade. Any one who had a bundle was regarded as a thief, and expostulation was taken as an indication of resistance and the rifle was used. I do not think even the Bedouin was properly treated. I saw some of them under arrest being taken by Arabs to their headquarters, and they were made to carry the property they had stolen, or to leave behind the animals which the bundles were packed.

Several times these Bedouins while under arrest were attacked not merely by citizens but by Arab soldiers, and some of them were shot. An Arab soldier posted at the foot of the bridge below my hotel window had an automatic rifle. He had a good field of fire up the street which ends at the Hedjaz railway station, and if any Bedouin or other person carrying a parcel moved across the street faster than at walking pace, the automatic rifle sprayed bullets over the road; there were several dead lying there. Before the Turks surrendered to us many of the citizens had stolen their rifles and ammunition. That had added to the chaos. There were people carrying weapons who had never been trained to arms, and their haphazard way of using them against

Indian Cavalry passing through Damascus

anybody and anything, on no pretext whatever, was alarming to the authority installed to preserve the peace. Children were out with rifles. I saw a boy who could not have been more than twelve try to pull something from beneath a Druse's rough robe. The man cuffed the boy's ear, whereupon the child raised a rifle and fired into the man's stomach, and was knocked over by the recoil. It was a pitiable exhibition of an attempt to police the city.

The people might easily have got completely out of hand, but just when the situation appeared to be getting very alarming, Colonel Lawrence, who fortunately was in the hotel, borrowed a piece of paper from me and wrote a request that some British troops might be sent into the city. In a short time there was a squadron of Australian Light Horse at the Hedjaz railway station. They galloped in and, as if by the touch of a magician's wand, the trouble ceased. It was marvellous. Firing stopped—the Australians saw to that—people who had been carrying rifles stole home with them, the dead were picked up from the streets, and those who had anything to lose breathed freely. The Christians were right. They needed British soldiers to protect them.

Everything was as near as possible to normal during the afternoon, and it was sound policy that detachments from the three cavalry divisions which had made the rapid advance on Damascus should march through the city from the south to the north. The inhabitants had allowed their excitement to cool down considerably, and they were not so demonstrative in their welcome as on the previous day. General Chauvel and his Staff were well greeted, however, and there was a large crowd to witness the column pass the seat of government. The parade must have made a deep and abiding impression upon the populace. They saw British yeomen and Australian Light Horse, with detachments of superb regular Indian cavalry and the Imperial Service Cavalry raised by patriotic Indian princes. The splendid horses, which in less than a fortnight had carried the troops some two hundred miles, were in fine condition despite their hard work, and few of the sightseers had ever seen such complete equipment or such disciplined ranks. Their eyes had met only Turkish cavalry, whose slovenly men and ill-cared-for horses were a sorry sight in comparison. But the people were even more impressed by the batteries of horse artillery and their teams, and there is no doubt that when General Allenby reached Damascus next day he was regarded as the Commander-in-Chief of the finest force in the world. The traditions of the British Army were understood, and it is safe to say that after that parade British prestige never stood higher in the Near East. It was the topic of conversation in the bazaars, and from the bazaars of Damascus it would spread through the whole of Central Asia. The Army preserved its good name wherever it went, and the conduct of the troops in fighting, as well as the chivalry they showed to a defeated enemy and their generous treatment of the people in conquered territory, will be remembered to Britain's credit for generations.

Chapter 22

The Broken Turk

It will never be possible to give more than an estimate of the number of prisoners taken in and about Damascus. The Germans and Turks who passed through the A.P.M.'s branch were roughly 22,000 including the sick, but the prisoners who reached the cages at Ludd and were sent on to Egypt fell considerably below that number. A large proportion of them, comparatively speaking, died. Thousands of the enemy taken about Damascus had marched up from the Amman area. Others had escaped from the demoralised 7th and 8th Armies, and they had subsisted for a fortnight on what the country could give them. It was very little. Most of them were starving when they got to Damascus, and looked it. The prisoners presented one of the most terrible pictures of war. Dirty, with frames shrunken by privation, badly clothed and almost shoeless, columns of them trudged along in silence, too weary and spiritless to talk, careless of any one's sufferings but their own, paying no heed to a comrade who had fallen down never to rise again. There was not a trace of sympathy in any face. The hard brutal facts of war seemed to have penetrated every soul, and when a man in an escort gave a last drink of water to a dying prisoner, I have watched scores of men ready to rush forward to snatch the precious drink from a dying comrade's lips if the escort left him. No one would share a crust with his fellow, no one thought of holding out a helping hand. The cruelties of war had dried up every drop of the milk of human kindness, and it was not until a prisoner was *in extremis* that he asked for aid. There was more sympathy for the Turks in one of the small escorting parties than among the whole of the prisoners themselves. We had been told over and over again by people who thought they knew the Turk that he was a gentlemanly fellow. If he ever was a gentleman the gentle instincts had been worn off or roughened by the stern, barbaric life he had led during war. From what I saw of him as he came down from Damascus as prisoner I believe he was no better than primitive man. Perhaps I do him an injustice, for I saw him when his lot was hard and his condition deplorable But it is in those circumstances that the finer traits in man manifest themselves. The Turk was starving and we could do but little to help him We were a long way from our base. The Navy was helping by landing supplies at Haifa, but that was more than a hundred miles away and the motor lorries had to travel over some of the worst roads in the world. The drivers were grand fellows and their work will always be remembered with gratitude, but by labouring night and day they could only get to Damascus sufficient supplies to keep our own troops on shortened rations. Some lorries were allotted for the supply of prisoners, but they were not adequate to feed over twenty thousand starving stomachs, and we had to think of our own fighting men first. As it was, the short rations and the lowered vitality caused by summer work in the Jordan valley, made our men less capable of resisting the Damascus fever which scourged their ranks in the next week or two. There was a big death roll among the prisoners. Their daily marches were of short duration, and, though to hurry them down to where there was food the lorries returning from the front were packed with prisoners, some of them too exhausted to hope for recovery, many lay down to die. It was terrible, but it was quite unavoidable. The escorts were almost as hungry as the prisoners, for they gave half their rations away, and many stories could be told of the generosity of British and Indian soldiers, whose self-denial was what you would expect of those big-hearted men. If the prisoners had been kept in Damascus, a dangerous proceeding from a military as well as from a humanitarian point of view, their plight would have been as bad. Apart from the needs of the civil population there was no adequate reserve of grain on which we could draw to keep the prisoners for a week or two, and it was infinitely better policy to lose no time in getting them to a place where we could give them food and medical treatment. The losses on the road were due not so much to our inability to furnish the prisoners with full rations while they were being brought down through Syria, as to the Turks' failure to feed their troops during the retreat. The prisoners for the most part were starving when we took them. If they had been in good condition practically all of them would have got through. I am told that on some days as many as four hundred Turkish prisoners died of exhaustion, but I do not give these figures as authoritative, and I was never able to verify them. The condition of affairs in the Turkish hospitals in Damascus was shocking. Most of the doctors and

GERMAN PRISONERS TAKEN IN DAMASCUS

nurses had fled. Some of the men of the Turkish 4th Army arrived at the hospitals, footsore and weary with their long march of 120 miles in eight days in attempting to escape, and, going to the beds of patients not dangerously ill, turned them out and occupied the beds. There were no medical comforts to be dispensed, the sick were without food or necessaries, and, when we got to the city, some patients had been four days without food or attention and there was no one to renew dressings. In the hospitals the dead were lying alongside the sick, the sanitary arrangements were hopeless, and the wards had been used as latrines for days. The main hospital was a sickening, offensive sight, and dead bodies of patients were to be seen in the neighbourhood which had been thrown out of the building several days before. The Arabs did not appreciate the danger of this appalling state of things, and showed no willingness to find food for the sick, or to clear up the shocking mess at the hospitals. Englishmen appealed to the Arabs to make the local bakers work at night to bake bread for the patients, but they would do nothing until General Chauvel visited Emir Feisal to point out the awful responsibility if the patients were allowed to starve. Even then it was the Australians who did the work. The stoutest of them all was Colonel Farr, who was in charge of the supply branch of Desert Mounted Corps. He went into the streets of the city and collected labour to dig trenches in which to bury the dead. He took his labourers into the wards to clean them. He begged, borrowed, or stole (he will forgive me for saying this) medical comforts, and worked like a   Trojan to help remedy a state of things that was an everlasting disgrace to the Turks. He did more. He found a store of flour and grain, and, commandeering it as he was entitled to do, he carried sacks on his own broad shoulders to bakeries, and then watched the bakers all night, to see that they did not sleep at their work. If ever a soldier earned recognition it was Colonel Farr. I asked him how he was getting on with his troubles after he had spent a night at the bakeries, and he told me he had kept the bakers so busy that he had secured not only enough bread for the hospitals but a fair supply for prisoners. To the remark that other people were saying that he ought to get a ribbon for his work, he made a characteristically Australian reply: 'No, but I have got something else—an easy conscience.'

The captures of Desert Mounted Corps amounted to a very big total. I have not the official figures which showed the number of prisoners actually taken in Damascus, but, between the commencement of operations and the 22nd of October, the prisoners counted by the A.P.M. through the Corps' cages were 2417 officers and 46,409 other ranks, of whom 158 officers and 1703 other ranks were Germans, the percentage of German officers taken being very high. Of this number the Australian Mounted Division secured 25,000, excluding 3876 prisoners captured by the 5th Australian Light Horse Brigade while attached to the 21st Corps. The division also captured 31 field guns, 2 howitzers, 6 mountain guns, 256 machine guns, as well as 19 automatic rifles and 5914 rifles. The 5th Cavalry Division took 6 German officers and 266 German other ranks, and 252 Turkish officers and 9314 other ranks, a total of 9938 prisoners. They also captured 27 guns and a large number of machine guns. These figures do not include a big number of Turks evacuated direct to hospitals, and Desert Mounted Corps reported that there were many Turks still straggling about the country, the majority of whom, if they did not die of starvation, would be killed by Bedouins. During the hundred-miles pursuit from Deraa to Damascus the roads were strewn with the enemy who had died of exhaustion, and dead horses and vehicles were littered over the whole route. The battle casualties of the Corps were extremely light, and considering how easy it was for the enemy to hold up bodies of troops in a country which offered many favourable positions for defence the figures are most remarkable:

	Killed	Wounded	Missing
British officers	11	36	1
Indian officers	5	12	
British other ranks	51	200	15
Indian other ranks	58	117	27
Totals	125	365	43

The sick rate of Desert Mounted Corps had, however, become exceptionally high in the first two weeks of October. Nearly five thousand men of the Anzac Mounted Division were evacuated as sick from Es Salt after the Amman operations. The sickness was attributable to the men having spent a long time in the Jordan valley, which rendered them liable to contract malaria and other diseases when they got into the country the Turks had been occupying. On our side of the line the country was clean and as sweet as precautions could make it, but immediately the Anzac Mounted Division moved forward over the old Turkish positions they found the ground in a deplorably dirty condition. Flies and mosquitoes were a great pest, and in three or four days more harm was done to our troops than during their whole stay in the valley in the summer heat. Malaria and influenza contracted in Damascus also brought down many brave men. Our medical personnel were greatly overworked in attending the sick. Doctors stuck to their posts though ill themselves and several lost their lives, and it was only by their self-sacrifice and devotion that serious loss of life among British troops was prevented. The sickness grew at an alarming rate, and when a man fell ill every effort was made to get him out of the country as rapidly as possible, and if that could not be done he was sent to a district a long way from that in which he developed fever. Hospital ships came to Beyrout when we had captured the port, and they carried men down to the healthier air of Egypt where we had a splendid system of military hospitals; indeed there is no doubt that the rapidity with which men were given a change of scene and air saved a large number of lives. Other hospitals were arranged on the plain between the Lebanon and Anti-Lebanon, one of them, at Bar Elias, capable of giving rest and treatment to a large number of officers and men, and some patients were motored over the Lebanons to hospitals in Beyrout. There can be no question that the influenza epidemic which was killing hundreds of thousands of people throughout the world swept over General Allenby's Army, but a considerable proportion of the cases of sickness was due to malaria, which in September and the beginning of October is always bad in this country. A factor which must be taken into consideration was the work the men had been doing since the operations began. From the 19th September the Corps had marched a very long way, generally at night, and sometimes over very hard country. The 5th Cavalry Division (on their way to Aleppo in the middle of October) had travelled 332 miles, the 4th Cavalry Division 300 miles, and the Australian Mounted Division 173 miles, all, exclusive of manoeuvring and operations from standing camps, and men who had had such arduous marches, always on the alert for an enemy surprise, were not in good condition to resist an epidemic.

In his report to G.H.Q. on Desert Mounted Corps' share in the operations General Chauvel paid a high tribute to his men. It is the final paragraph plain narrative of the soldier:

> I cannot speak too highly of the gallantry and endurance of the troops under my command, and of the fine *esprit de corps* which has led to dash and initiative of a high order, nor of the Staff work throughout the Corps which resulted in the converging on the objective of three divisions on two widely-separated roads, over miles of country, at the right moment.

No description of the operations which ended Turkish rule in Damascus would be complete without reference to the part performed by the Arab army of the King of the Hedjaz. The story of the Arab army has not been written, and I doubt if any one could write it except Colonel Lawrence. Certainly no other British officer knows so much about it, and probably a great deal will remain secret, but if he would tell the world something of the Arab army's operations, and could be persuaded not to efface himself, we should have one of the most fascinating books on the war. I hope we shall see it. I can only tell a small part of the operations of the Arabs in the final phase. The information was given to me by Major Stirling, who had been a Staff Officer of the 52nd Division, those Lowland Scots who fought so valiantly in the Sinai Desert and in the first part of the Palestine campaign, and who left us to go to the Western Front and gain imperishable laurels. Major Stirling spoke Arabic fluently, and volunteered in 1918 to serve as one of the British officers in the Hedjaz army. I met him in Damascus soon after he rode into the city, and it was not easy to recognise him in his Arab dress and under the dirt of travel. He was just off to the Turkish bath, the only luxury Damascus could give one at this time, and he briefly sketched the story of the Arab co-operation thus:

The Arab column started from Akaba and covered 620 miles to reach Damascus in twenty-two days, having to zigzag right up the country for water. When the column set out from the Gulf of Akaba it consisted of 400 Hedjaz regulars, two armoured cars, four French guns carried on camels and mules, thirty Gurkhas as a demolition party escorted by thirty men of the Egyptian Camel Corps. The force gathered strength during the march. The Chief of the Ruwalla tribe, one of the most powerful in Arabia, brought in 3000 horsemen, the Haurani peasantry mounted on horses came in small bodies to join the Sherif's army, and by the time the column got to the neighbourhood of Deraa it was made up of 11,000 camelry and horsemen. Every day the strength increased, but the Druses did not come in until the 'show' was practically over. The column got to the south of Deraa on the night of September 16 and blew up a portion of the railway line.

In estimating the value of the Arab assistance it is important to remember that General Allenby's breakthrough in the coastal sector was on September 19, and that if the Turks had preserved their

AUSTRIAN 5.9 HOWITZER TOWED BY A.S.C. LORRY

railway communications they would have been able to get away a considerable quantity of material as well as many men. The Arabs unquestionably performed valuable services in raiding the railway, and they did far more than our aeroplanes could accomplish, effective as bombing from the air proved to be. On September 17 the Arabs worked round to the north of Deraa and destroyed six kilometres of railway, and on the night of September 17-18 went west of Deraa, burned the Tel esh Shebab bridge and the Mezerib station, destroyed all rolling stock in it and smashed six German motor lorries. On the following day the Arabs moved to the south of Deraa to await General Allenby's offensive, having completely stopped railway communication down the Hedjaz line and between the Turkish 7th and 8th Armies and Damascus. The Germans were continually bombing the Arabs throughout their operations. They had an aerodrome not more than ten minutes' flying distance away from the Arabs, and they made frequent trips to try and frighten off the raiders. Two of the aeroplanes were seen to come down through engine trouble. The two armoured cars with the Arabs at once set out after them, and on seeing them the pilots ran away, but the cars went up to the machines and riddled them with bullets, entirely disabling them. However, the bombing became so insistent that Colonel Lawrence sent a message to G.H.Q. for aerial protection, so two fighting planes went out from Ramleh, and Ross Smith's Handley-Page served them as a sort of depôt ship, going out with stores of petrol and oil. The two fighters quickly brought down five German planes, and thereafter the Germans decamped, and the Arabs were left free from attentions from the air. The Turks made strenuous efforts to repair their railway line. The main armies had been without communications for five days, and Amman had been isolated for eight days when the Turks imagined they were about to restore the railway. A trestle bridge which had been destroyed was reconstructed, but on the 23rd the Arabs again swooped down on it and made it useless. The Arabs then advanced to Sheikh Saad, north of Deraa, and awaited developments, but when General Barrow's division was moving from the valley of Jezreel they again went south to Deraa, and captured the town sixteen hours before the 4th Cavalry Division entered it.

The Hedjaz force left Deraa on September 29 to march on Damascus under the Emir Nasir, the next chief in importance to Emir Feisal, and helped to fight the Turkish 4th Army all the way up the Hedjaz line. In the last twenty-four hours the Arabs travelled seventy miles. They had their supply troubles. The column was 400 miles from the base at Akaba as the crow flies, and the men had to live on the country and make long searches for water. It was a trying time but their enthusiasm was wonderful. It was also a trying time for the British officers with them. They lived on as sparing a diet as the Arabs, but they had also to run the gauntlet of Arab suspicion. While they were with the Hedjaz regulars they were never in danger, and the King's soldiers had an admiration for Colonel Lawrence second only to their veneration for their Lord the Sherif. But the irregulars who swelled the column during the march did not know the British officers, and they were anxious about their identity as soon as they detected that they were not Arabs. Furthermore, when they were joined up with the 4th Cavalry Division they were suspected in their disguise by our own troops, and both Colonel Lawrence and Major Stirling were three times arrested by British soldiers, which speaks well for our vigilance.

CHAPTER 23

Infantry at Beyrout

The story completed of the capture of Damascus, we can now return to the work of the infantry. It was General Allenby's plan that, while employing the full weight of his cavalry to reach the northern city, he should operate with infantry on the coast and secure the ports of Syria. If the capture of Damascus would have a far-reaching effect on Mahomedan peoples, the taking of Beyrout and Tripoli would also be significant of the Turkish collapse in the eyes of Europe and America; and just as Haifa was necessary as a supply base when we gained the Nazareth-Tiberias line, so was Beyrout important when we got farther north. Some of us knew that our arrangements with France pledged us to give Syria to our Ally when we had conquered the Turk. The Syrians are a shrewd race and the news of our pact with France had reached them, and they expected, not unnaturally, that the first troops they would see would be the soldiers of France. But the advance up the coast was work entrusted to General Fane's 7th Indian Division. It is not possible to exaggerate the arduous nature of that advance. The Scottish and English regular battalions and the magnificent soldiers of India composing the division did not have much fighting to do after they left Messudieh, but they had heavy marches and had to make roads and fight nature for many miles. We are a people scrupulously careful to avoid treading on other people's toes. In order to keep our bargain with the French, who, having to govern Syria in the near future, were not anxious that there should be a big parade of Britain's strength, it was laid down in orders that our soldiers were not to go into any of the towns in large numbers. Tommy Atkins likes to write home a description of the sights he has witnessed, and there was a little heartburning in the 7th Division when, on arriving at Beyrout, only about two per cent, of the men were allowed into the city. They were encamped in low-lying ground

INDIAN PIONEERS MAKING LORRY ROAD FOR TRANSPORT
ROUND THE LADDER OF TYRE

and there were parts of Beyrout that were attractive, but the British who took the place had to stay outside. Tommy likes to have his 'grouse,' and there certainly seemed some ground for his complaint when, more than a week later, the French arrived along the road he had prepared for them and walked into Beyrout the occupiers, if not the captors, of the place. Nor was this feeling lessened by the fact that the population seemed more desirous of fraternising with the British than with the French. However, the order was given and the soldier had to accept the situation, if not with good grace.

The 7th Division began their march before the Commander-in-Chief held a conference at Jenin on September 26, when final instructions were given for an immediate advance to Damascus. It was then necessary to relieve speedily the regiments of the 5th Cavalry Division at Haifa and Acre so as to enable them to concentrate for their new forward movement, and accordingly one battalion of infantry was sent from the neighbourhood of Tulkeram to Haifa in motor lorries. It arrived, after a moderately good journey, on the night of the 25th. The remainder of the division proceeded on foot, and arrived with the Corps' cavalry regiment and No. 2 Light Armoured Car Battery on September 29. A battalion of the 28th Infantry Brigade was sent on to Acre, but no further advance was possible until the Royal Navy delivered stores by sea, and had made arrangements to cope with any submarine effort to prevent a continuous supply by ships. It was also necessary provide craft of the lighter type which could be towed under escort of motor launches to Tyre and Sidon, where supplies could be landed to replenish the supply columns moving with the infantry. There was another substantial reason why the division could not leave Haifa immediately. The hard sandy beach on the shores of the beautiful bay which holds Haifa and Acre at its two ends was good going for wheels, but north of Acre there was nothing worthy of being designated a road. Between Nakura and Abiad was a track six feet wide but impassable for wheeled transport, and the division had to send men ahead to make a road.

Farther on was the Ladder of Tyre, a series of steps cut into a rocky cliff. That bold promontory had been an impediment to movement up the coastline for countless centuries. Armies had avoided it and made a detour many miles inland. It was negotiable by men on foot by means of the rock steps hacked into its face, and natives had been accustomed to take lightly-laden camels and donkeys over the height, but their progress was slow, and nothing on wheels had ever been moved across the hill. In few moments the 7th Division's mind was made up. To make a road over the hill would mean a long and difficult undertaking. Time pressed and there was no opportunity to construct a zigzagging highway with easy gradients, miles long, such as might suggest itself to a road engineer in times of peace. The quickest and shortest route that could be made ready for heavy traffic was to cut a shelf out of the face of the cliff where it reared its rough, forbidding head above the Mediterranean. The shortest distance round the face of the Ladder of Tyre was one thousand yards, and there were other bluffs still presenting a barrier to the passage of guns. But the Ladder of Tyre was the biggest obstacle. An infantry battalion and the 7th Division's pioneers set to work with all sorts of tools and explosives. It was not enough to blast an enormous amount of rock in the cutting itself, but huge boulders overhead which threatened to fall and crush anything passing beneath had to be loosened. The Corps' cavalry regiment, leading their horses over the hill, estimated that it would be a month before the road could be fit for the heavy guns, but the pioneers had hewn into and blasted the rock to such good purpose that, in two days, when the 7th Division marched forward, they were able to take with them a field-artillery brigade and a 60-pounder battery. The surface was still very rough and the bends in the road were sharp, but the field guns were hauled by their own teams and the heavies were man-handled round the bluff in four hours. The work had been extremely hard and continuous night and day and, in General Bulfin's words, it was accomplished 'in an incredibly short space of time.' General Bulfin's car was the first motor to use the road and it had to be assisted by hand. When the 7th Division had passed northwards the 54th Division, with the assistance of three battalions of Indian pioneers and two companies of the Egyptian Labour Corps, took on the work of completing the road, and in a few days motor lorries were using it, and two anti-aircraft guns, each weighing ten tons, went over it under their own motor power. It was a fine feat of engineering, although the descent on the northern side was rather rapid, and a stout wall on the sea side of the road made it perfectly safe.

The 7th Division marched the hundred miles to Beyrout in seven days. They went forward in three columns. The first, which started from Acre on October 4 and reached Beyrout on October 8, was made up of the Corps' cavalry regiment, No. 2 Light Armoured Car Battery, and a company of the Leicesters. The 28th Infantry Brigade composed the second column, which followed close on the heels of the first, and the remainder of the division was in the third column. The 8th Mountain Artillery Brigade and the 15th Heavy Battery

R.G.A. were with them, and the whole division were concentrated at Beyrout by October 10. Never were there so many camels on the road. Accompanying the infantry were camel supply columns carrying five days' supplies and, the Navy's arrangements working perfectly, these were refilled at Tyre and Sidon, at each of which places three days' supplies were landed. From Tyre onwards we found an excellent road, quite the best highway in Syria, and superior to the road running from Beyrout over the Lebanons to Damascus. It had been kept in good repair, and only in one or two short patches had a car driver to pick his way. A speed of thirty miles an hour between Tyre and Sidon was easily within the compass of a lightly laden Ford.

General Bulfin reached Beyrout on October 8 and established his headquarters there. He was enthusiastically received by the populace, and the citizens flocked into the suburbs to welcome the troops. They had seen the British in the town on the previous day. An officer had been sent by Desert Mounted Corps from Damascus to make a road reconnaissance over the Lebanons. He travelled from Zahle in the plain between the Lebanon and Anti-Lebanon ranges and found the road in good condition all the way. It could have been destroyed in numerous places, but the enemy had abandoned all hope of delaying us and had left a free path for our advance. The inhabitants were most friendly and were reported to be very anxious for the advent of the British. They had formed local governments, but they feared looting by outlaws and asked for police protection. The patrol found a peculiar situation in Beyrout. It had been the deliberate and considered policy of G.H.Q.—doubtless it was ordered by the Foreign Office after consultation with our Allies—that no flags were to be hoisted when we captured a town. When the New Zealanders took Jaffa in November 1917, one of them hoisted the Union Jack over the headquarter buildings. There was trouble over that, and foreign representations were made to G.H.Q. on the subject. The Intelligence department told me 'there was no such happening'—I have it in writing—but they were mistaken, for I have seen a photograph of the ceremony of hoisting the flag, and it has been published in a weekly illustrated journal in London. But the Commander-in-Chief insisted that no British flag was to be flown, and when we took Jerusalem, and General Allenby made his historic entry into the Holy City, I think the only Allied flag which was not in the streets was our own. I did see one dirty Red Ensign flying from an Arab's dwelling, but where it came from no one knows. The French, Italian, and Greek flags were put up on some religious and private buildings, but General Allenby's orders were carried out to the letter. Indeed, the only British flag permissible on that day was the small Union Jack carried on the radiator of the Commander-in-Chief's car, but when he made his official entry General Allenby left his car beyond the suburbs of Jerusalem. One was proud to see how the British played the game.

When I went into Damascus on the 1st of October I heard the Arabs boast that the Hedjaz flag would be flying in Beyrout in a few hours. The significance of that information was obvious. The Arabs wished to obtain control of Syria and they wanted to get to Beyrout before us, not with an army, for that was not possible, but by means of an emissary. The Hedjaz flag was going to cause some difficulty. When the armoured-car patrol got to Beyrout the officer ascertained that the ex-President of the municipality, Omar Daouk, was acting as governor-general with a committee of the leading citizens to assist him, and he appointed his own *gendarmerie* and police until the arrival of Shukri Pasha Ayubi, the Hedjaz emissary, who reached the city at two o'clock on the 7th, having travelled on horseback from Saida (Sidon). Earlier in the day at Saida General Fane had had to tell the Hedjaz representative that he must not fly his flag in the town, and that the British had taken over the government and security of the place. Mr. Ford, the American missionary in Saida, had informed General Fane that the people would not accept the Hedjaz government and that the appearance of a Hedjaz representative would cause trouble. The inhabitants wished the British to take over the government, and General Allenby appointed a British governor temporarily, intending to replace him by a French officer when one arrived. Omar Daouk reported to the armoured-car patrol officer that he had received a communication from the Hedjaz authorities at midnight on September 30 that it was hoped to establish government at Beyrout, and on the Turkish governor, Ismail Haki Bey, being informed of this he sent a letter to Omar Daouk saying he could do as he liked, for he (Ismail) was going away. When Shukri arrived as Arab governor of Beyrout he demanded that everything should be delivered up to him. These matters were straightened out by General Bulfin's tactful diplomacy, and the Hedjaz flag, which it will be understood was a source of irritation to the crews of French destroyers in the port as well as to the whole of the Christian population of Beyrout, was hauled down quietly one night.

All Germans left Beyrout on September 30. They left behind them the trail of the Hun. The poor of Beyrout were enduring the agonies of starvation, yet the Germans threw all their ample stores of food into

230

NATIVES AT A WELL REPAIRED BY ROYAL ENGINEERS

the sea. They had no pity for the poor. A prominent Syrian resident told me that in the past two years 25,000 people had died of starvation in the city, and he was certain that at least 40 per cent, of the Lebanese died during the war. The Turks' incapacity in government was well illustrated by this terrible story. America has always shown an interest in Syria, and the Beyrout University, with a brilliant American scholar at its head, has done a wonderful work in educating Syrians. Americans told the Turks that large sums were available in the United States for providing food for destitute Syrians, and they promised that, if adequate facilities were given to allow the foodstuffs being distributed through reliable channels, no one should know where the gifts came from, and as far as the recipients were concerned they could be led to believe that the food came from the Turks themselves. The offer was made in such a way as not to wound the susceptibilities of the ruling race. The Turkish official who was approached asked that the gift should be sent in cash for distribution by him. There had been a plague of locusts in the Lebanons and all crops were ruined, and if all the money in the world had been brought to Beyrout it would not have purchased corn, for there was little, if any, available. Appeals to the official to change his mind were in vain. The Americans tried several times to get permission to bring in food, but the answer was always the same, that they could give money and the Turks would distribute it. With the failure of the negotiations nearly half of the Lebanese died, and some of the Christian villages in the hills lost practically their entire population. With the full knowledge of the facts, and with the daily evidence of thousands children in the streets crying for bread, well-fed Germans threw all their stores into the sea.

They must have had hearts of stone.

CHAPTER 24

The Final Stage

Immediately after the capture of Damascus the Commander-in-Chief decided to continue his advance northwards, not by a rapid cavalry raid on Aleppo, such as would have gratified the desires of the non-military gentlemen who took a part in the councils of the Allies, but by proceeding in stages. They were swiftly executed marches. Though the troops were feeling the effects of their exertions, fatigue wore off in a day or two, and the condition of the horses was remarkably good. But General Allenby had to look at his supply situation. Beyrout was absolutely essential as a base. The railway from Haifa, through Samakh to Deraa and on to Damascus, was being put in order and was available, but the rolling stock was extremely limited, and the motor-lorry columns remained the principal means of supply for Desert Mounted Corps. We had installed a local resources board at Damascus, and local purchases for the Army, which would not encroach upon the reserves needed for the civil population, were giving the troops some change from the hard field rations they had been living on for a fortnight. But when a further move northwards was started the supply difficulties increased with a bound. The lorries had to come from Haifa, a distance of much more than a hundred miles, and they had to victual not only Desert Mounted Corps, but 20,000 prisoners on the road, some of them on their way to Ludd, others who were strong enough, employed in putting the highway into better shape. Every ten miles added to the journey enormously increased the problem, and if when the cavalry were on the move there proved to be no opportunity of enabling horses to live on the country, the supply situation might become precarious. When the cavalry started the infantry were still three days from Beyrout. We did not know the position there, though it was clear we should be in the port and open it up as a base of supply very soon. The railway from Beyrout over the Lebanons to Damascus, a French undertaking, was destroyed in sections where the gradients were so steep that cogwheel engines had to be employed, and it had to be taken for granted that the enemy would see to the destruction of all locomotives that could be of service on that line. That railway, therefore, had to be ruled out of our calculations, and the single road, and nothing but that road, could be relied on. In deciding upon the route to be taken during the advance the supply situation was the determining factor. It put out of consideration by the General Staff a possible advance up the road running from the north-east of Damascus through Nebk to Homs, Hama, and Aleppo. We knew that road was passable and was fit for lorries in most parts, and the places which were bad could be improved with some little trouble. But the absolute necessity of obtaining supplies landed at Beyrout made it imperative that the cavalry should go over the Anti-Lebanon range and proceed up the plain to the west of it.

There was another reason why General Allenby never hesitated in his choice. The country in the hollow had to be cleared. The Germans had made a substantial centre of Rayak. It was an important railway junction. Trains from Beyrout to Damascus passed through it, and all supplies coming from Europe, from Constantinople and Asia Minor were brought down to Damascus and the old Turkish front through Rayak. Our command of the sea denied the enemy any other route. German technical troops had made that little settlement on the plain a central distributing depôt. There they established engine shops, repairing sheds for rolling stock and lorries, and workshops for various services. They had a large aerodrome there too, and though Damascus had fallen, some of the enemy held on to Rayak till we forced them out of it. In moving up the plain the troops could get supplies from Beyrout about as easily as if they were at Damascus with their base at Haifa, and when Homs was captured and the port of Tripoli opened by the advance of the 7th Indian Division, that base would enable them to be certain of supplies up to Aleppo, so long as the weather remained good. A set-off, however, were the enormous distances and the troubles of the motor-lorry drivers—destined to be difficult beyond conception. However, it had to be done, and when one reviews the position in the light of experience acquired after the final triumph was attained, it seems marvellous that the strategists sitting in conference at home should have suggested that General Allenby should embark on a cavalry raid on Aleppo immediately after he had broken through the Turkish trench system north of Jaffa. It may be that some distinguished generals would have fallen in with the suggestion, especially as the War Cabinet intimated that they would accept the risks involved. But General Allenby's scheme was the only practicable one.

The first part of the final stage, then, was Rayak. This was forty-five miles from Damascus, and a section of the road to it had been constructed for the purposes of the war. The road runs for a long distance through wild, mountainous country. For some thirty miles most of the cavalry had to travel by the main Beyrout road, a well-engineered highway, with sound bridges and culverts. Before the war it was in excellent condition, but it had been allowed to fall into disrepair, and at some places the winter rains had washed big holes in it and had weakened the walls. The bottom of the road, however, was still hard, and the lorry drivers, whose estimate of the quality of roads in this country was based on their experience of mud tracks, voted it good. There were some fair watering places by the way, and at Khan Meizelun, where the Germans had formed a dump, there was a glorious spring of fresh, cool water gushing out of a rock, and few travellers in that part of the world have passed this fair spot without refreshing themselves. The cavalry rested at the water, and did not invade the sick collecting station or the unsavoury Turkish shelters which the enemy had put up there. From Meizelun the road rises to the side of a hill 4125 feet above sea-level and then falls in a steep and winding course to the ravine of the wadi El Korn. After a descent of nearly a thousand feet the road follows the course of the wadi, a stony torrent bed, till it again reaches a height of over 4000 feet at Jedeide. Thence it passes over the watershed and falls rapidly to Mejel Aanjar, where it forks; one road leads to the plain and, crossing the Nahr el Litani, runs to Shtora and Beyrout, and turning to the right at Shtora, to Zahle; while the other goes to Rayak. One gets an idea of the troubles of the Turks from the fact that this latter road was built to economise fuel. All over the country trees had been cut down for the service the railway, and olive-trees, which do not yield a crop till they are twenty years old, were sacrificed by tens of thousands. Wood was so scarce that it was found more economical to transport supplies from Rayak to Damascus by road than by railway, and, to provide a shorter route than that from Rayak through Zahle and Moallaka, the Germans laid out a road twelve miles long on the edge of the hills to join up with the main highway at Aanjar. The distance from Damascus to Aleppo by the route up the plain between the Lebanon and Anti-Lebanon ranges was 244 miles.

OLD TEMPLE OUTSIDE BAALBEK

The advance was divided into three stages: (1) Damascus to Rayak and Zahle, 40 miles; (2) Rayak to Homs, 89 miles; (3) Homs to Aleppo, 115 miles. It was originally intended that the 5th Cavalry Division should be in front, supported by the 4th Cavalry Division, the Australian Mounted Division remaining for a time at Damascus till the conditions there were settled and until infantry could reach the neighbourhood, but the 4th Cavalry Division had been caught in the influenza epidemic and had to be isolated. The 5th Cavalry Division were ordered to commence the first stage of the advance on the 6th of October, so as to be within striking distance of Rayak by dawn of the 7th. On the 3rd of October the division were bivouacked at El Jedeide, a station on the Beyrout-Damascus railway eight miles west of Damascus, but the wheels of the division were behind at Katana, south-west of the city. It was hoped that the transport would be able to get over the hills by a rough path leading from Katana to Khan Dimez on the Beyrout road, but a reconnaissance found the track to be unfit for wheels, and the transport was moved to the outskirts of Damascus on the 4th and, escorted by the Sherwood Rangers, rejoined the division on the evening of the 5th when it got to Khan Meizelun. No. 12 Light Armoured Motor Battery and No. 7 Light Car Patrol joined the division at the same place. Reports came in that ammunition dumps and rolling stock were being destroyed at Rayak, and orders were given to the 14th Cavalry Brigade and the armoured cars to march that night on Rayak, twenty-four miles away, and seize the place at dawn on the following morning, the remainder of the division marching at dawn, the 13th Cavalry Brigade in support of the 14th, and the 15th Cavalry Brigade on Zahle. Later news told that the enemy had evacuated Rayak, and the move of the 14th Brigade was postponed till 6 a.m. on the 6th. Rayak was occupied by them at 2 o'clock on the afternoon of that day and Zahle one hour later, no opposition being met with at either place. Two guns, two Germans, and 175 Turkish officers and other ranks were captured.

If it would not be accurate to say that Rayak had been destroyed it was certainly covered with wreckage. The effects of a couple of raids by our airmen were seen all over the depôt and aerodrome. Direct hits had made a mess of the station buildings, and the aerodrome had suffered severely, so much so that the Germans had decided to evacuate the place, and when the cavalry got there they found that the enemy had burned thirty aeroplanes and their hangars. The burnt machines were five Pfalz, six D 5a Albatross, eighteen C 5 Rumplers, and one C 4 Rumpler. We found stores of wings, under-carriages, engines and

237

bombs. Our bombs had killed a number of Turks and had destroyed some ammunition depôts, and the Germans had done their best to blow up what remained. They had not completed their work when the report that the cavalry were almost upon them sent the last of them off in trains and lorries. Some 500 to 600 cavalry and about 1000 officers and men of the 146th (German) regiment, with eight heavy guns, had passed through Rayak for the north in the first two days of October, and the Germans in Rayak had, on the 25th September, seen how the tide of battle was flowing against them, when Liman von Sanders arrived from Damascus and left for Aleppo after a few hours' stay. But, amid all the damaged property, our engineers were gratified to find a considerable quantity of engineers' stores, some railway engines, and, in the railway yards, many broad and narrow gauge trucks. The value of the rolling stock and the use to which we could put it was well understood by the enemy, who in the next day or two sent aeroplanes from Homs to try to finish a job their engineers had had to leave. We lost several men as the result of their bombing, but the material damage was small, and, as soon as the enemy found that our Air Force were using his old aerodrome as an advanced landing-ground, their pilots did not venture over Rayak again. The cavalry were no sooner in Rayak than the engineers made a hurried inspection of the railway, and on the following day they ran their first train from Zahle through Rayak to the break in the Rayak-Damascus line. Except that the traffic was run and controlled by men in khaki, the scene in Zahle railway station was such as one would imagine it in times of peace. Natives sat about and gossiped, and took a calm interest in a railway management that put some life into its work. Local parties were enrolled for railway purposes, and men who had had some experience, and there were many of them, were formed into breakdown gangs to repair the damage to the line. The headmen of Zahle and the other villages in the vicinity were called before General MacAndrew, and were instructed by him to elect and form local governments, and promise was given of assistance in maintaining law and order.

The 4th Cavalry Division had not yet felt the full effects of the influenza epidemic, and were marching from the south-west of Damascus to El Hame on the 6th of October, and two brigades proceeded along a track by the side of the Rayak-Damascus railway to Zebdani, where they arrived on the 8th after travelling over a long distance of exceedingly bad ground on the barren hills. The 12th Cavalry Brigade took the Beyrout road and bivouacked at Bar Elias. The Australian Mounted Division, which remained in the neighbourhood of Damascus, made a long reconnaissance up the road running to Aleppo from the north-east of the city, and found it clear of the enemy as far as Khan Arus, thirty miles from the city. There were heavy thunderstorms and rains in the plain on October 8. All the watercourses were filled, the roads became troublesome for the transport drivers, and large fatigue parties had to be detailed to clear culverts and repair them for the heavy traffic they would be required to carry. The natives stood by and watched with surprised interest the energy the troops threw into their jobs. There was a washout in the village of Moallaka. The water swept across the road in a torrent and inundated the native hovels built on the lower level of the village, but instead of helping to clear a channel, the occupants of the flooded houses maintained an unconcerned attitude while the British and Indian soldiers diverted the flood water which was eating away the road. Perhaps the natives were wise enough to understand that British troops could remedy matters much better than they could themselves.

The 5th Cavalry Division remained in the Zahle-Rayak area until the 10th, and they then pushed out patrols in the country which falls away towards Baalbek, as far as Hosh el Ghanin and Rumeide, across the road and plain north of Rayak. An armoured-car patrol had visited Baalbek on the 10th and reported the place unoccupied and quiet. The day before we entered Baalbek General MacAndrew and some officers of his staff went into the ancient town, and the inhabitants gave many signs of their pleasure at the General's visit. Baalbek possessed the equivalent of a town band. The instruments were old and required cleaning, and apparently there was a vacancy for a conductor, but the band did its best with 'God save the King,' and many wrong notes were atoned for by the bandsmen's zeal. They got through their part of the official ceremony as well as the girl who was called forward to sing a song of welcome. Anyhow the music was a sign of the people's good intentions, and the headman of the town proved that these were genuine by producing five hundred prisoners who had been collected by the inhabitants. He was anxious that these should be taken over by us at once, as they were hungry men and the stock of provisions in Baalbek was not large enough to keep the people free from anxiety during the coming months of winter. General MacAndrew reassured him, and asked to be conducted over the wonderful ruins of temples and palaces which are an enduring monument to Roman genius for architecture.

Orders were received by General Chauvel on October 9 that the Commander-in-Chief intended to advance to the Homs-Tripoli line as soon as possible. Desert Mounted Corps were to leave one division at Damascus, and push forward to Homs as rapidly as they could in view of the difficulties of supply, and the 7th Indian Division would co-operate by moving up the coast from Beyrout to Tripoli. In accordance with this plan the 5th Cavalry Division were ordered to move one brigade forward to Baalbek and two brigades to Tel esh Sherif, ten miles south-west of Baalbek, on the 10th of October, by which date the Sherifian force was under orders to proceed to Nebk to get into line with Desert Mounted Corps. The Commander-in-Chief had authorised the Arab army to move up this road, and to operate in conjunction with Desert Mounted Corps between Homs and Hama against the Turkish communications. The 13th Cavalry Brigade were in Baalbek on the 11th, and the whole division were ready to march from that town on the 13th. The advance was in two columns, Column A, consisting of the armoured cars, the 15th Cavalry Brigade and divisional headquarters, proceeding one day ahead of Column B, the 13th and 14th Cavalry Brigades and the divisional train. Four days were allotted for the march, the da stages being to Lebwe (29 miles), El Kaa (16 miles), Khusseir (13 miles), and Homs (18 miles).

The route taken by the cavalry had been very little used before the war. The country was wild, and in many places there was an entire absence of cultivation. Around some small villages the natives raised light crops, but their methods were primitive and rarely did one see a serious effort to husband water running to waste. The land was poor until we approached Homs, where, by an old but useful system of irrigation, the land was made productive. Between Baalbek and Lebwe the natives grazed flocks of sheep and herds of goats. They were a wild lot of people and some of them gave us trouble. As I was trekking up country in rear of the 5th Cavalry Division, I was warned at Baalbek to look out for snipers. The transport drivers had been shot at, some thought by Turkish stragglers who had not been captured, but others had Bedouins fire at them. The Bedouins were out to kill so as to obtain whatever property a soldier might have on him, and then foot it to the hills where they would be safe from arrest. We were shot at several times, and I believe after my car had run up to Homs some patrols of the 4th Cavalry Division had to go up the road to stop the pests. A few examples were made and there was some improvement, but the lawless life the natives had led made them think light of murder, and the road was always unsafe for any traffic not moving under escort. To Bedouin marauders all men are foes. Probably they cared as little for the Turks as for the British, but they detested the Germans. The rovers on the plain had got information that the Turkish army was defeated, and they were out for any loot they could find. A prisoner of war, belonging to the 3rd battalion of the German 146th regiment, told us that he was one of an escort for baggage belonging to his regiment which left Damascus on September 30, when it was obvious to the Germans that the city was about to fall into our hands. The escort of sixty men was moving on Rayak by the road near the railway, but, when they were about to get out of the hills on to the plain, the Bedouins fell on them, and our prisoner believed he was the only man to, escape with his life.

As a result of an air fight on the 19th October we got another illustration of the attitude of Bedouins towards any one wearing German uniform. Captain Ross Smith, finding nothing to do with his Handley-Page, had again taken his seat in a fighting plane. The Australian Flying Squadron were operating with the 5th Cavalry Division, and Ross Smith had gone out to look at the road towards Aleppo. When fifteen miles to the south of the town he met an enemy two-seater and at once engaged it. The enemy plane was hit and came down, and the pilot and observer, who made some signs of their willingness to surrender, moved off a little distance towards the hills. Ross Smith came down too, but the ground was soft, and if his little machine had been cumbered with the weight of two passengers he would have been unable to rise. He therefore set fire to the enemy plane, and did not take the Germans prisoners. After he had returned to his advanced landing-place, at Homs some Bedouins came out and demanded that the Germans should give up their uniforms. The pilot showed fight and was severely wounded in the arm, and when the airmen surrendered to the cavalry later on, stripped practically of all their clothing, the injured man's arm was in such a bad state that its had to be amputated.

The Bedouins had seen all sorts and conditions of troops come and go along this road. The war in fact had made this a new highway of communication with the outer world. Prior to the war there was scarcely a traveller on the road in a month, but the Germans, seeing that the Turks had no means of getting supplies by sea, had brought vast quantities of men and stores down it from Aleppo to relieve congestion on the railway. There were depôts and halting places at regular intervals, and where stone was not available in the vicinity of the road the highway was engineered in a rough-and-ready fashion, but nowhere could it be described as good.

The topographical reports we had received through agents were not always reliable. They had seen the ramshackle Turkish carts rumbling and tumbling over the road and they described the track as fit for wheels. Well, perhaps it was in a military sense, for army drivers seem to get their vehicles, whether they are lorries or general service waggons, over all conditions of rough places, but the worst farm accommodation road I have seen in the British Isles compared very favourably with stretches of the Homs road. From Baalbek, the highest point on the route, the road descended through the valley of the Orontes, here nothing more than a meagre stream, and crossed a number of small mountain torrent beds which were usually dry. At Lebwe and El Kaa we found some enemy establishments, supply depôts, field bakeries, and casualty clearing stations, but it need hardly be said they were far below our standard, and where they had not been destroyed we left them severely alone.

Khusseir was a healthier-looking spot and its inhabitants, half Moslems and half Greek Christians, seemed to have tried to learn something of the benefits of cleanliness, though there was room for a fuller application of water for personal use. They took more pains to till the soil than their neighbours farther south, and doubtless the country about their village looked prettier when crops were growing than in the fall of the year when we passed through it.

From Khusseir to Homs the road traversed a cultivated plain, and the population appeared to be making full use of the waters of the Orontes for irrigating their land. The cavalry took a line close to the railway. There was another and better road shown on our map, but this proved to be entirely inaccurate. Our map-makers, who had done work of remarkable accuracy throughout the campaign, had lacked the services of the photographers in the Air Force during the rapid advance, and were forced to rely on old maps and captured German maps for their provisional series of the country north of Damascus. They rectified all errors soon after the cavalry had penetrated the land. The cavalry described the highway on the whole as a 'fair-weather lorry road,' but pointed out exceptions. The first three miles north of Lebwe were very rough, with loose stones and lumps of rock. There was a wide inundation area south of Khusseir, and where the road crossed the wadi Harun, about seven miles from Homs Lake, it was loose and rough and could not be used for lorry traffic without substantial improvement.

Homs, looking at it from a distance, appeared be a large, clean, whitewashed town. On entering one preferred the distant view. There is no enchantment in Homs. Dirt and squalor and the haphazard sani-

RUINS AT BAALBEK

tary arrangements were appalling, and it is remarkable that there are not annual outbreaks of epidemic disease to reduce the population. There is room for a town-planner in Homs. The main street as you enter from the south is passable, but the exit from the place is as bad as could be imagined. When I got into the town there was a military traffic-controller. Some movement in the streets threatened to hold me up and, having no desire to dally in that unsavoury spot, I sought the assistance of the policeman. He showed me a way I could never have found for myself. The main road passed beneath a rude arch into a bazaar roofed in with mats and loose timbers which made it as dark as night. The shopkeepers had their wares displayed in front of their shops, and the roadway was only wide enough to take a Ford car comfortably. The stone-flagged pavement was strewn with vegetable refuse which lay rotting in pools of stagnant water, and this, combined with the smell of the cooking of weird dishes in the eating-houses and the smoke from hundreds of lamps, was revolting. The people slipped away from the front of the skidding car and took refuge, laughing at their escapes, in the shops. One was heartily glad to be out in the sunlight again and to be comparatively free from the noisome smells. You could not be entirely out of range of them until you were right away from the town. The armoured cars got into Homs on the 15th of October. Our aviators had preceded them and had dropped bombs on the Turks to indicate that we were on their track, and the enemy had fled before the cavalry were within twenty miles of the town.

The 5th Cavalry Division occupied the district on the 16th. An Arab governor had already been appointed when General Mac Andrew arrived, and the Sherif's quartered flag was prominently shown. The governor was preserving order very well, and he assisted us in requisitioning supplies. At our request he issued a proclamation warning the people that they must not on any account touch the cable lines laid by the British, but the Bedouins cut the wire and stole lengths of it in many places, and it was not until severe measures had been taken with the culprits that our telegraphic communications were allowed to remain intact. Small parties of enemy cavalry were reported to be in the vicinity of Rastam, a dozen miles or so north of Homs, but the 5th Cavalry Division did not move after them immediately. A reconnaissance had to be made to ascertain the condition of the Homs-Tripoli road, in order to see whether it was fit for lorry traffic. A great deal depended on this road because, while the cavalry could be supplied at Homs, and some considerable distance north of it, from Beyrout—where the 7th Division had arrived and the Navy were landing stores in the harbour for the Army—scores of miles could be saved if Tripoli could be used as a base. The road, like all thoroughfares in a land ruled by the Turks, had been permitted to fall into a bad state in parts, but fortunately the armoured cars could get over it, and where armoured cars could travel the lorry driver was willing to take risks. The road was generally from 24 to 30 feet wide. It passed through a sparsely populated area, and it was, with the exception of that between Beyrout and Damascus, the only route through the Ansarie mountains and Lebanons. For the first thirteen miles from Tripoli it followed close to the sea on the narrow coastal plain, and it then turned north-east and ran across cultivated country for ten miles, when it got into the barren, stony hills where it was almost impossible to move off the road. There was a steady ascent to within seven miles of Homs, at which point the road was 1800 feet above sea-level. The Turks had had a broad-gauge railway from Tripoli to Homs and the line followed the same route as the road, but the enemy had removed the rails during the war. The whole of the 5th Division was concentrated north-west of Homs by midday on the 17th, and here most of the men and horses had a welcome rest for two days beside a beautiful supply of water coming from the Orontes and a number of irrigation channels and springs.

CHAPTER 25

Aleppo

The division began its march to Aleppo (115 miles) on the 19th, soon after news was brought in that the leading brigade of the 7th Indian Division were in Tripoli. Squadrons of the Duke of Lancaster's and Herts Yeomanry had arrived in the port a few days earlier. Enemy cavalry had been reported at Tel Bise, a station on the railway eight miles north of Homs, and at Rastam, a village on a hill overlooking the road five miles farther on, but these retired before we advanced. At Rastam there is a stone bridge over the Orontes at a place just north of the village. The banks are very steep here, and the river bed is some forty feet below the level of the road. The enemy had ample time to destroy all the ten arches of the bridge, but he did not make a good job of it and only blew up three. Before the division got on the march the staff had heard of the damage, and the 5th Field Squadron Royal Engineers was sent forward with the 15th Cavalry Brigade to repair the bridge, a supply of materials being carried with them in lorries. The cavalry were able to ford the river, but motor transport could not be got across until the bridge was made sound. The engineers, working under many disadvantages, renewed the broken arches and strengthened weak parts of the bridge, and had it opened for all classes of traffic by the next evening. General MacAndrew received reinforcements in the shape of motor batteries for his leading column, which now consisted of the 15th Cavalry Brigade, and Nos. 2, 11, and 12 Light Armoured Motor Batteries and No. 1 (Australian), No. 2 and No. 7 Light Car Patrols. Column A left Rastam early on the 21st, and in the evening were three miles north of Hama. The Australian Flying Corps had previously made a bombing attack on Hama and dropped seven hundred pounds of bombs on the aerodrome there, on the railway station, and on troops in the neighbourhood, and on the following day an aerial reconnaissance reported that the enemy had evacuated the town.

General Allenby had decided that he would try to reach Aleppo on the 26th, and there was a prospect that the French, operating from the sea, would try to effect a landing at Alexandretta about the same date. The French were anxious to get a footing at Alexandretta, and instructions had been issued from Paris to Admiral Varney, commanding the French Syrian naval division, to occupy the port. The admiral very properly informed General Allenby of his instructions when the Commander-in-Chief was in Beyrout on the 15th October, and General Allenby directed him to submit his plans. It was obvious that such a proposal came within the direction of the campaign, and in order to prevent difficulties and to arrange for the closest co-operation in all naval and military operations, the War Office suggested that the French Government should first communicate their wishes to London, and the Chief of the Imperial General Staff would then issue instructions to General Allenby. Of course there could not be operations in Syria by the French detachment except under General Allenby's command, and the French Government agreed. Indeed the French naval authorities would be dependent on British ships for the transport of their troops. While the French Government laid great stress on the importance to them of Alexandretta being occupied by a French and Armenian detachment, the plan was too vague, and with the troops and facilities available the undertaking did not promise a successful issue. The suggestion was that two companies of infantry should be landed north of the port, but before the proposal took definite shape the situation at Alexandretta grew worse. The Turks received reinforcements, mines were laid, and Admiral Varney's ships were fired upon and bombed. The proposal to land a party was thereupon abandoned for the present, but in his desire to further the wishes of the French Government, General Allenby continued to give anxious consideration to the occupation of Alexandretta.

With this end in view the Commander-in-Chief ordered another division besides the 5th Cavalry Division, to march on Aleppo to hold the city after it had been captured, while the 5th Division proceeded to Alexandretta to co-operate with the French acting from the sea. In ordinary circumstances the 4th Cavalry Division would have followed the 5th, but the sickness from which all ranks were suffering made the division incapable of marching. The wastage from malaria was so great that there were not enough men to look after the horses. Influenza of a virulent form ran through every regiment and there were few men fit for duty. The field hospitals were full, and the medical authorities held that the only prospect of reducing the abnormal sick rate was to give the division complete rest for a few days. General Headquarters entirely agreed and cancelled the move of the 4th Cavalry Division. In their place the Australian Mounted Division were warned to be prepared to march from Damascus on Aleppo at six hours' notice, and to be in Homs on the sixth day after leaving Damascus. The 5th Cavalry Division expected to leave Aleppo on the same day as the Australians arrived at Homs. This meant that the 5th Cavalry Division would be operating 115 miles ahead of any kind of supports, but it was advisable to get to Aleppo before the garrison there could be reinforced and while the enemy in front of us were thoroughly demoralised.

General MacAndrew had to make a decision as to which of two routes he would take. The maps showed that the route taken by the railway promised the better supply of water, but the reports of agents and people in Hama influenced him in selecting the old diligence route, a part of the pilgrim way to Mecca. This decision proved absolutely sound, and the cavalry moved up the ancient Darb el Haj, which had been the main line of communication between Palestine and northern Syria for centuries. Caravans which had maintained trade for many hundreds, if not thousands, of years had used this one long trail, and over it had passed the armies of martial kings with the lust of conquest. But none of their hosts had poured over the land at the same pace as our cavalry and motor batteries. From Hama, a cleaner and much better organised town than Homs, and a far better centre of trade, the road ran over undulating country intersected by a few wadis until it got on to a partly cultivated plain. The highway was not metalled anywhere, but the traffic from time immemorial had hardened it, and it was fair going with no obstacle to military movement. Some of the villages passed, such as Khan Shaikun, twenty miles from Hama, and Maarit en Naaman, fifteen miles farther north, appeared in the distance like large standing camps. The villages were surrounded by mud walls and the houses, built in a conical shape, were white-washed, and in the bright sunlight looked like a mass of bell tents. They must have puzzled the Air Force during their early flights over the district. The Sherifian force under the Emir Nasir was instructed to march on Aleppo along the railway, and to keep in touch with the 5th Cavalry Division, and it was hoped that the Arabs, who by the time they reached Hama were 1500 strong, would raise a large body of horsemen on the way north. The Arabs certainly gave us admirable support about Aleppo.

On the morning of October 22 the armoured cars preceded General MacAndrew's Column A from Hama, and tried to get into touch with the enemy. The column reached Maarit en Naaman early in the afternoon, and during a halt contact aeroplanes brought in news that a small force of Turks with motor transport was about Khan Sebil, some ten miles ahead. A few Arabs in a motor car came down the road from Aleppo and confirmed this report, and armoured cars were sent out to attack the enemy. The cars on reaching Sebil found that the Turks had observed their approach and had withdrawn in six lorries, under cover of the fire of one large armoured car and of machine guns in the lorries themselves. Armoured cars and light-car patrols went in pursuit. There was a very bad patch in the road. For about a mile and a half the road goes over a hill of rock, and cars could not move at much more than walking pace. The German armoured car, a big lumbering vehicle with a high clearance, made better speed over this stretch than the Rolls-Royce and Ford cars, though its wheels had iron tyres, but whenever there was a slight improvement in the surface the Rolls armoured batteries drew closer and engaged the Germans. There was a hot running fight for a mile or two, but the German car had to give in. When I saw it derelict on the road its thick armour plating was covered with the marks of bullets, some of which had penetrated the turret. The engine was, however, intact, but if the car had got on to the plain it would have been quickly overtaken by its pursuers. Almost immediately afterwards our armoured-car crews were witnesses of a big mistake by enemy aviators. Two hostile aeroplanes came flying from the north-west, and on seeing the Turkish lorries moving towards Aleppo took them to be a part of our column. The planes dived and machine-gunned their friends, and paid no attention to our batteries. A Ford car got ahead of the batteries, and came up with the last of the six lorries abreast of the village of Maardibse. It brought the lorry to a standstill, and killed or wounded twenty-five of the occupants and captured five others. A few Turks managed to get away to the hills on the east and west of the road. Our cars went on for another fifteen miles and kept up a heavy fire on the lorries, but the iron-tyred wheels were better suited to the rough surface than pneumatic tyres, and this advantage prevented the capture of the entire convoy. The column bivouacked for the night about three miles north of Serakin after a long and trying march.

The cars and cavalry were on the move again early next morning, and when they had advanced a dozen miles to Banis they overtook a lorry, which they captured with the German driver and four Turks and its equipment. The last sector of the road from Sheikh Ahmed to Aleppo (twenty-one miles) was the worst part of the journey excepting the rocky patch already described. The ground falls away to the valley of the Kuwaik, the river which runs through Aleppo. This river crossed the road north of Banis, and there was then a rise over stony ground for about three miles, when the road descended rapidly to the valley and again passed the Kuwaik at Khan Tuman, ten miles from Aleppo. The road about Tuman was rather soft, and it looked as if there would have to be a deviation made for motor transport, but it was soon improved by the troops. Beyond Khan Tuman there were some stiff ups and downs over rocky hills, and then came a rough muddy road to the bridge over the river, a mile and a half from Aleppo. The cavalry and cars operated on this twenty miles of road for three days, and the appearance of this small force must have led the enemy to believe either that it was extremely bold or that it was supported by a large body moving up from Hama. A reconnaissance pushed through the hilly country north of Khan Tuman on the afternoon of the 23rd and got into the plain south of Aleppo to within five miles of the city, and they reported, as did the Royal Air Force, that the enemy held short lengths of trenches astride the Hama–Aleppo road about three miles south of the town, as well as the ridges running south-west from Aleppo. The enemy force was variously estimated at from 2000 to 3000 rifles, with artillery and machine guns, and another 6000 or 7000 Turks were reported to be available in Aleppo.

On the 23rd General MacAndrew gave the Turkish commander in Aleppo an opportunity of surrendering the city. Captain Macintyre, M.C., of the 7th Light Car Patrol, left our lines at ten o'clock in a Ford car and under a white flag, and entered the city with a letter demanding its surrender. As Captain Macintyre passed through the enemy's outposts he was blindfolded, and he and his driver were conducted to the suburbs of Aleppo to a Turkish divisional headquarters, where he explained his mission. After much show of courtesy and an offer of lunch, a communication was made over the telephone to headquarters, to which building—the former Austrian Consulate, I think—Captain Macintyre was invited. He presented General MacAndrew's letter. The Turks were in no hurry to reply, or they displayed no anxiety about the matter, though there was much talking over the telephone, and it may be communication was opened with Constantinople. They were very amiable and insisted on Captain Macintyre eating a rather elaborate meal prepared in his honour. During the afternoon he was given the following reply to General Mac Andrew:

The Commander of the Turkish garrison of Aleppo does not find it necessary to answer your note.
(Signed) *Mahomed Hazati*, C.G.S.
Aleppo

While waiting for the return of Captain Macintyre our cavalry at Khan Tuman saw a Turkish cavalry patrol approach the village from the south-west, and allowed it to get within five hundred yards. The patrol then recognised that they were opposed by British troops and turned off into the hills at the gallop. They were fired on, and the Australian Light Car Patrol dashed after them and, before they reached a district that was impassable for cars, rounded up four of the eight men. At a quarter past five, when the communication refusing to surrender Aleppo was in General MacAndrew's hands, the division withdrew to the plain south of Aleppo, where they bivouacked for the night in a position which would give the armoured cars freedom of manoeuvre should the enemy attack. General MacAndrew decided to hold on here until the remainder of the division arrived on the 25th, and to attack on the 26th. At seven o'clock on the morning of the 24th the column again moved forward to Khan Tuman, sending reconnaissances towards Aleppo and Termanin, a village in the hilly country about fifteen miles to the west of the city, the object of the latter being to find a road by which the armoured cars could attack the town from the north-west and threaten the enemy's retreat along the Alexandretta road. The patrols which advanced towards Aleppo found the enemy in the same positions as on the previous day, with cavalry patrols pushed out to the hills north of Khan Tuman, while the cars which tried to reach Termanin reported that there was no track in that direction which would take them. It was therefore decided to withdraw for the moment to the village of Zoibe, five miles south-west of Khan Tuman.

The next day the cars again made a reconnaissance of the Aleppo road, but were met by a considerable fire from light field guns and machine guns astride the road. The 15th Cavalry Brigade had outposts all along this line in the afternoon. The Turkish commander in Aleppo had decided to retire in consequence of an aeroplane report that infantry were coming up in lorries behind the cavalry. As a matter of fact the lorries were carrying supplies from Tripoli for the division.

The Arabs had been coming steadily up the railway, driving small bodies of Turks in front of them. On the 25th they moved across the 5th Cavalry Division's road east of Aleppo, ready to attack that flank in co-operation with our cavalry on October 26. They sent their emissaries into the town to get into touch with the Anneze Arabs, who were in and about the town waiting for a signal to rise, and a part of Emir Nasir's force penetrated into Aleppo on the night of October 25–26. They and their friends inside the town fought the Turks with vigour, and the Arabs' action undoubtedly had an effect on the situation, a Turkish battalion as rearguard having to fight its way out in square formation, and suffering heavily in killed.

At six o'clock on the morning of October 26 the armoured-car column, the 15th Cavalry Brigade, and Divisional Headquarters were at Khan Tuman and the remainder of the division was passing through Seraikin, due to arrive at Khan Tuman at noon. At seven o'clock the 15th Brigade went over the hills to clear the enemy from the neighbourhood of the Hama-Aleppo road, and to get astride the Alexandretta road. The armoured-car batteries and light-car patrols left Tuman soon afterwards, General MacAndrew and his staff accompanying them, and drove into Aleppo at ten o'clock. Many enemy were still about, but the cars ran at a fast pace and there was no incident beyond an occasional rifle shot at the column. The inhabitants gave the General a great welcome. Aleppo has a population of 200,000, and except the bazaar quarter which, like the trading quarter in all Oriental towns, is cramped and very overcrowded, with narrow streets and dark alleys, there are substantial buildings built of stone, and in the suburbs there are some handsome residences. We found Aleppo far less fanatical than Damascus, and the inhabitants seemed quite genuinely to appreciate our arrival.

During their advance west of Aleppo the 15th Cavalry Brigade at ten o'clock came near a considerable force of Turks covering the Alexandretta road, about a thousand yards from a little place called Haritan, four miles north-west of Aleppo. The only definite information received by the brigade at this time was that 300 cavalry were on the road eight miles from the town, but a quarter of an hour later Brigadier-General C, R. Harbord, commanding the Imperial Service Cavalry Brigade, had a verbal message that about a thousand scallywags of all descriptions with two small guns had left Aleppo that morning and were retiring in a northerly direction. At eleven o'clock an advanced guard of two squadrons of the Jodhpur Lancers and a sub-section of the machine-gun squadron topped the ridge overlooking Haritan from the south-east, and were received with heavy rifle fire from the direction of the village. They at once took up a dismounted position on the ridge. In view of his information as to enemy strength General Harbord decided to attack at once, and he issued orders to the Mysore Lancers to move round the east of the ridge on which the advanced guard was established and charge the enemy from the east, the Jodhpur Lancers to move in support as a 'mopping-up' party. At the same time the remaining four guns of the machine-gun squadron were sent to reinforce the advanced guard, who were to cover the mounted attack. At half-past eleven No. 12 Light Armoured Motor Battery was ordered along the main road to cooperate. The battery came into action, but something went wrong with the battery leader's car which had to return, and owing to a misunderstanding the other three cars also came back. The Mysore and Jodhpur Lancers advanced, but Major Lambert of the Mysore Lancers, finding that the Turkish position extended farther to the east, decided to move in that direction to gain the enemy's left flank. At a favourable opportunity Major Lambert gave the order to charge. This charge was driven well home, fifty of the enemy being killed and twenty prisoners taken. The enemy, however, were found in far greater strength than was supposed, and, as the further movement eastwards had taken the Mysore Lancers beyond supporting distance of the machine guns, and as for want of weight they were unable to penetrate the enemy's main position, they were forced to rally to the, rear and take up a dismounted position, the Jodhpur Lancers prolonging their line to the left. This action obliged the enemy to reveal his full strength, which was estimated at 3000 infantry and 400 cavalry, with eight to twelve guns of various calibres and from thirty to forty machine guns. With this force they advanced as if to attack the position we were holding, but when within eight hundred yards they halted and began to dig themselves in, fearing a further attack from us. Desultory firing was kept up till nine o'clock, when the enemy began to retire, and he had withdrawn at midnight. Our casualties were twenty-one killed, including four British and one Indian officer, and forty-two wounded. The 14th Cavalry Brigade relieved the Imperial Service Cavalry Brigade, and armoured cars which followed the Turks found that a road bridge two miles north of Haritan had been destroyed, but the cars managed to pass round the bridge and to keep the Turks under observation. They eventually withdrew to a position about Khan Narista and Nebbul. Touch was maintained, and on the 28th it was reported that a further retirement had been effected to a position commanding the main Alexandretta road, 1000 yards west of Beir el Jemal. That day the Arab force occupied Muslimie Junction and found that the station, permanent way, and points had been destroyed, and the engines and rolling stock damaged. The 14th Cavalry Brigade took over the defence of Muslimie Junction from the Sherifian army, and this was the situation when, at ten o'clock on the 31st of October, a message was received by wireless from G.H.Q. to the effect that an Armistice had been concluded and that hostilities would cease between the Turkish Government and the Allies at noon that day.

The water supply of Aleppo had not been mined or damaged. All hospitals and government stores in the city were taken over by Emir Nasir's force, and guards placed over them. In Aleppo we captured 821 prisoners, eighteen guns, and a large amount of rolling stock and railway material. The 5th Cavalry Division had now completed a march that will be numbered as one of the finest in the annals of war. From the 19th of September to the 26th of October they had marched and fought over five hundred miles of country, and during this period they had captured fifty-two guns, six German officers, 273 German other ranks, 371 Turkish officers, 11,191 Turkish other ranks, and 151 Bedouins. The towns the division occupied included Nazareth, Haifa, Acre, Zahle, Moallaka, Homs, Hama, and Aleppo, and all this had been accomplished at the cost of thirty-nine killed, 160 wounded and nine missing, a truly wonderful record. It was a magnificent division, its officers and men endowed with the cavalry spirit from their gallant and dashing leader downwards. A misfortune befell the division when the triumph was complete. Months after fighting was over General MacAndrew met with an accident in Aleppo and was badly burned. His wounds were serious, but they were yielding to treatment when his heart gave out, and the division mourned for a leader they loved, whilst the British Army lost an officer who would have gone far in the service. He was not well when I saw him in Aleppo after the Armistice, and he was upset by the sickness reports which showed that his division had not escaped the malaria and influenza which was incapacitating a large proportion of General Allenby's army in the hour of final victory. But General MacAndrew intended to carry on, and his indomitable energy, perseverance and pluck kept him at his post. His name was carried back to India by the warriors who served in his command, and it will be remembered with the gallant captains who have won martial fame throughout the Indian Empire. The record of the division's work would not be complete without a table showing the casualties to animals. Every cavalryman will appreciate these figures, which show how in marching and fighting for thirty-seven days, during which the division averaged almost a hundred miles per week, the lessons taught in times of peace on the care of animals were well learned. When General Allenby saw these figures he remarked that the division were as good horse masters as fighters. Here is the illuminating table:

	Riding	Draught	Pack	Total
Killed	152		5	157
Died	265	57	5	327
Destroyed	179	44	14	237
Wounded and evacuated	63			63
Evacuated	735	129	38	902
Missing	169	57	8	234
				1920
Establishment				8971
Percentage of wastage				21.41

In accordance with the arrangement that when Aleppo was taken the 5th Cavalry Division should be relieved there by the Australian Mounted Division and prepare to advance to Alexandretta, the Australians left Damascus during the last week of October for the north. The division proceeded up the old pilgrim road through Duma and Nebk, that is, east of the Anti-Lebanon range, and when the news was received that hostilities had come to an end it was approaching Homs.

The total casualties for Desert Mounted Corps, including General Chaytor's force, for the month of October were 116:

	Killed	Wounded	Missing
Officers	6	11	3
Other ranks	25	68	3

The prisoners passing through the Corps' compounds during October were:

	Officers	Other Ranks
German and Austrian	4	273
Turkish	1061	15375
Chaytor's force	557	9432
In hospital		2934
Total	1622	28014

The story of sickness which spread through the Corps during the operations is best told in this simple table:

Admissions to hospital	9117
Evacuations	7136

As I have pointed out, most of the sickness arose because our troops had to move through areas which the enemy had occupied, and probably the precautions we had taken in our own lines would have prevented an outbreak of fever in the British Army if there had been no advance. The Germans suffered very heavily. At the end of July, 30 per cent, of the men of the 703rd regiment were in hospitals with paratyphoid, and the numbers going sick were increasing rapidly. A few days before the attack 85 per cent, of the men of the German 146th regiment stationed about Shunet Nimrin were suffering from malaria. At this time our force in the Jordan valley was free from fever, though they were in country which would have been worse than Nimrin if great care had not been taken to kill disease at the source

CHAPTER 26
From Tekrit to Tripoli

The 7th Indian Division, the division that battled and won from Tekrit to Tripoli, did not have much time for rest in Beyrout. It was necessary that the port of Tripoli should be opened as a supply base, and that the landing of stores from the little coasting steamers, which the Quartermaster-General's branch pressed into service for the carriage of supplies from the big establishment formed in the Suez Canal, should proceed as quickly as possible. Reports had been received that the Turks were not numerous in Tripoli, and little or no opposition was anticipated, but there was a rough march in front of the infantry. The Corps' cavalry and No. 2 Light Armoured Motor Battery preceded the infantry. Both the cavalry and the 7th Division started from Beyrout on the morning of October 12. The cavalry and cars completed the fifty-eight miles' journey on the evening of the 13th, and there was no mistake about the jubilation of the people in Tripoli when they entered the town. The people in the Lebanons were even more friendly. I reached Tripoli the day before the leading infantry brigade got into the town and, not appreciating the close attentions of numerous evil-smelling insects in the hotel, I took my car into an olive grove a mile outside and slept in cleaner surroundings.

Early next morning a party of between thirty and forty Lebanese riding on the road on wiry little ponies, stopped to talk to me while I was shaving, and seemed surprised that any one should get his face clean before the sun was high in the heavens. Some of the men spoke quite good English. Several had been to the United States, but one, who had remained in the country all Syrians love so passionately, showed the good influence of the American college at Beyrout. If he had been educated in England he could not have spoken our tongue more fluently. The men were anxious to know when they could expect to see English troops. I told them there were British cav-

257

THE INDIAN DIVISIONAL TRAIN ENTERING TRIPOLI

alry in Tripoli already. They had heard this and wanted to know if the mounted men intended to stay on, or if they were merely spying out the land. They were pleased to hear that, so far from there being any intention to allow the Turks to reoccupy Tripoli, British infantry were on the road and would be in the town in a few hours. To those who did not understand me this news was at once communicated, and it was delightful to see the pleasure it afforded them all. A few who had been interested in my driver's preparations for breakfast came round me lest they should miss anything I could tell them. They wanted to know how the war was progressing and when it would end, and if there was really any doubt that England would win. It was England always, not the Allies. I assured them England would triumph and, after a slight pause, their chief spokesman said, 'It must be so Justice always wins.' Some compliments were passed and then the men spoke of the bad conditions under which they had lived during the war, but though they laid stress upon the sufferings of their people from starvation and persecution, they said their lot was probably better than that of the soldiers who were winning freedom for them. They became very serious when they asked the question, 'Was England going to remain in Syria?' I did not know, but they could be certain that the troops would not leave the country until the Turk was driven out.

That did not satisfy them. Would the people have the right to say what government they wished to live under, and under whose protection they could work out their destiny? Was their future to; decided by the Allies in conference without consideration for the desires of the people themselves, and would England allow another Power to come into the country? These awkward questions were rained on me, and the only answer I could give was unsatisfactory—I did not know. Even this was more agreeable than the expression of my belief that we should leave the country when the war was over. The men were very strong in their declarations that's they wanted England and no other country to rule them. I broke off the conversation by saying I must have my breakfast and get on, and the Lebanese were again very polite and left after giving cheers for England, 'the land of the free.' This talk had confirmed everything I had heard in Syria. I know practically nothing of the reasons which prevailed upon the Allies sitting in conference over the peace terms to give Syria to France. There was an old agreement that France should have Syria north of a line drawn from Acre to Tiberias, and for all I know to the contrary it may prove a very excellent arrangement for the Syrians themselves. But unless they changed their minds after October or the beginning of November the

British trawlers off Tripoli

Syrians did not want it, and scores of them, men with a stake in the country, declared that they wanted England's protection, and wished for no other country to enter the land.

The 19th Brigade led the 7th Division in the march from Beyrout to Tripoli. The route was divided into stages of about ten miles a day, but for the second half-of the journey the column was very long owing to the few areas in which troops could camp, and in the last part of the march water was not plentiful. For about fifteen miles from Beyrout the infantry had to keep to the high road which passed through a district full of gardens. There were some pretty townships and villages frequented in the summer by Beirutians. Perennial streams were traversed by stone bridges, and close by the place where the troops crossed the Nahr el Kelb, they were interested in an ancient bridge whose delicately fashioned arches and piers had withstood the pressure of torrents for centuries. But it would not carry heavy loads and our transport forbore testing it. Junie, where Napier landed troops in 1840, seemed a thriving little town of 4000 inhabitants, and the nice villas on the shore road told of its favour as a summer resort. It will become more prosperous now the Turk is out of the way. Beyond Mameltein the infantry marched along a cliff road to Tabarja, where the hardy seafarers off this rocky coast seek shelter during storms. Jebeil, twenty-five miles from Beyrout, is the terminus of the light railway running from the latter port—the line was not in running order just then—and there were signs that under stable government its population of 3000 would increase. Jebeil was a much nicer place than Batrun, a dozen miles away. From the latter town the troops moved around the promontory of Ras esh Shekka (Cape Madonna), where the mountains come right down to the sea. The road around this huge bluff is an excellent piece of engineering. It is admirably graded and the road has been cut in the rock. In two places the mountain has been tunnelled and windows have been cut on the sea side of the rock to give light. During the rainy season a considerable amount of rock falls on the road, and, if the Turks had retired this way, a few shells fired from destroyers at the face of the mountain could have brought down enough rock to close the road.

From this point the highway proceeds several miles inland to avoid the other bold promontory of Ras en Netur, and it winds over hills in a number of well-graded zigzags to a district where the people have brought the land into a good state of cultivation For ten miles before Tripoli is reached from the south the tillers of the soil, a hard-working, thrifty lot, raise good crops of corn, olives, and fruit. Over this route the 19th Brigade brought the division, and they got into Tripoli on the 18th, two days before the French detachment entered Beyrout. The division encamped north of Tripoli and were preparing to advance on Ladikiya when the Armistice was concluded. There was an amusing illustration of the imperturbability of the Turkish official when the Corps' cavalry and armoured cars came into Tripoli. The officers attached to Signals at once made for the Turkish post-office. The hour for closing was past and the officers had to force an entrance. They tested the wires, and collected and put into a place of safe keeping all the books and stamps. Next morning the Turks came down to open the office at the appointed hour and were amazed to find the British installed there. The excitement caused in the town by the arrival of the cavalry had not awakened them. The postal officials were quite ready to carry on under us. They knew that their salaries would be paid without deduction and went to work as if nothing had happened. The Signals officers continued in their service the men who had been employed as linesmen and got much useful information from them. The wires were soon opened, and the day after our occupation Tripoli was getting all the important news from the outside world for the first time since war began. And the people marvelled.

CHAPTER 27

The Airmen's Part

The autumn campaign in Palestine will furnish military historians with striking examples of the importance of air mastery in warfare, and of the urgent necessity, not merely for the provision of a full supply of the best aeroplanes for all purposes, namely fighting, reconnaissance, and bombing, but of an absolute superiority in the quality of the personnel. The flying men in General Allenby's Army rose to the occasion. They always did. They knew great things had to be done, that success to be full and complete must be spread over a long period, and that, if the victory was to be absolutely decisive, the Air Force must work at high pressure throughout the operations. The Air Staff, pilots and observers, mechanics, one and all in the force, gave of their best, and, though in the rush and tear of present-day battles the flying fighters will never rest satisfied with new records and achievements, the Palestine Brigade of the Royal Air Force can rely upon military critics of all time judging their efforts as a distinct stage in the advance of aviation.

I have already referred to the steady, consistent progress which gave us the mastery of the air in Palestine. From the day of Beersheba onwards our aerial supremacy was unquestionable. The German knew it, and whenever he came over us he floated in the higher altitudes where observation was uncertain and photographic records were of doubtful value. But even did he choose the rarefied atmosphere of 18,000 or 20,000 feet, he risked meeting a patrol, and the air fighting of August had been so disastrous to him that his visits over our lines became few. The activities of the permanent patrol blinded the aerial eyes of the enemy. Three extracts from captured diaries of enemy flying corps officers are illuminating proofs of our mastery of the air:

25th to 31st August 1918—In consequence of lively hostile flying activity no reconnaissances could be carried out.

1st to 14th September—No flights over enemy country.

25th to 31st August—The loss of two more machines compelled the suspension of all flying of reconnaissance machines on front of 8th Army. Attempts will be made to continue flights occasionally on the rest of the front. This last is from the diary of enemy Flying Corps headquarters.

A letter found on a German taken prisoner gives an idea of what the enemy thought of their own airmen:

> A second theatre of war such as this one is not to be found anywhere. We have been starved and have suffered from thirst. Everything was saved up but only for the "gentlemanly" officers, so that they could sell it and procure money. Then, when it came to the real thing, there was no officer to be seen. And where were our airmen? They rolled in luxury and strutted around in their white uniform, but when it came to the Day not one of them was to be seen anywhere. I have lost all respect for them.

Prisoners were unanimous about the important share bombing took in their overwhelming defeat. They described it as horrible and horrifying, and one or two of our men who were captured and afterwards rescued by us spoke of it from first-hand knowledge. A Royal Air Force officer taken east of the Jordan saw a bombed train burning at Mafrak, with thirty-five dead removed from it and others still in the train. During the advance it was exceedingly difficult to keep supplies up to the aeroplanes operating with the cavalry. The airmen had to change their forward positions repeatedly, and the roads were so indifferent and the distances so great that road transport could not be relied upon to provide the stores required. Petrol and oil were carried in spare aeroplanes for distances of over 100 miles; but indomitable energy, foresight, enthusiasm and whole-hearted co-operation between all sections of the force overcame every obstacle. The airmen even found time to help other branches of the Army. They carried letters to the front, and, when the cavalry were in urgent need of horse shoes and nails, the farriers received their supplies by an aeroplane service. When the Arabs at work near Deraa were getting agitated over enemy bombing, and two of our fighting planes went over to stop the trouble, our Handley-Page, travelling as a sort of lorry bus, carried pilot, observer, two mechanics, 216 gallons of petrol, some 20-lb. bombs, and other stores. Its arrival aroused extraordinary interest among the Arabs, who, seeing man after man alight from it, and the discharging of its large cargo of petrol and bombs, ran their hands over every part of the machine they could touch, exclaiming in high glee: 'Now we have seen the biggest war-bird in the world.' The Arabs like to touch everything that is new to them. They will feel the buttons, war ribbons, and badges of rank on an officer's uniform, though they seldom betray their surprise at anything. Sometimes, however, they cannot conceal their astonishment. When one of our planes landed in Arabia, the Arabs crowded around it to satisfy themselves, by touching every part, that their eyes did not deceive them. Their usual stolid demeanour was maintained till the pilot took from the machine a packet of sandwiches, when they cried in amazement, 'Look, it eats!'

It is not out of place to say a word or two here of the position Egypt occupied in regard to the Air Force in the closing year of the war. There was a time when the Egyptian Expeditionary Force was starved of aeroplanes, and the men who went out on old buses, of a type quite obsolete on the Western Front, were outclassed by the enemy in everything except courage. In those days a few pilots only were trained in Egypt. They learned the art of flying under considerable difficulties. The machines available were Maurice Farman long-horn and short-horn type, and Caudrons of early manufacture. After ten o'clock in the morning there are many bumps in the air in Egypt, and at home the desert was looked upon as dangerous for flying. General W. G. Salmond, General Groves, Colonel Primrose, Captain Grace (brother of one of the pioneers of flying who lost his life in the Channel when aviation was in its infancy) insisted that Egypt was an ideal school for the education of pilots. In England they said 'No,' and they were only convinced with much trouble. General Salmond went home and put the case before the Air Command, and it was largely due to his persistence and the clarity of his facts, that the scheme was sanctioned for making Egypt one of the biggest training centres of the Empire. The scheme was not in full operation when hostilities ceased, but, if the war had lasted through the winter, Egypt would have supplied at least a thousand pilots during the winter months. In the early autumn there were several thousand cadets undergoing training in Egypt, and a great many of them would have been turned out as pilots and observers at a time when, owing to weather conditions at home, there could have been little flying. There could be no more advantage in training in Germany than in England, and Egypt would have given us an immense preponderance of airmen. I think there were a dozen flying schools in operation in Egypt when Germany asked for an armistice. Those at Heliopolis and Aboukir were enormous institutions, training over a thousand cadets between them, while in the desert between Cairo and the Canal there were large aerodromes exclusively given up to instructional purposes. In six months the instructional hours' flying in the air increased from 3375 to 12,127 hours, and the training given was as strict as the scheme drawn up at home. Egypt established an aircraft factory and had engine repair shops in which Egyptians were employed. Under expert supervision they became good craftsmen, and in the state of our man-power at the time they were of considerable assistance. There was a large expenditure on establishments, but much of it will be useful in the future, for Egypt has proved already that it will be the half-way house in aerial travel between West and East.

CHAPTER 28
Miracles of Supply

The axiom that an army marches on its belly is as sound to-day as it was in Napoleon's time. Once a force is out of touch with supplies its power declines and the depth of an advance must depend upon the radius of action of the supply columns. This self-evident proposition enables one to estimate the value of the 'Q.' work in General Allenby's Army, and to give to the Quartermaster-General's branch the praise its efficiency deserved. The front was long; the base was far behind, and the problem of transport always loomed large. The original sources of supply were so far overseas that 'Q.' had to think Imperially; but even with all their calculations in thousands of miles of ocean transport and submarine hazards, the officers of the supply and transport branch never had so much anxiety as when they were completing and carrying out their plans for General Allenby's tremendous thrust through Northern Palestine deep into Syria. The nature and extent of the advance considered, it must be conceded that 'Q.' had a prodigious task. Of how well it came through the ordeal, the cavalry, gunners, and infantry in the front line were the best judges. There was always food for men and horses and ammunition for guns, and that is the real test.

Here are a few facts which will bring home to our people what stupendous work was successfully accomplished in the first three weeks of the advance,and these three weeks were the crucial period.

We had then got to Damascus, some 190 miles from the original advanced supply base which had been opened at Rantieh on the morning operations began, and one cavalry division was fifty miles farther to the north. For the greater part of this time supplies were carried entirely by motor lorries, captured Turkish railway lines not being in good enough order to give much assistance. In these three weeks the aggregate mileage of lorries in supply columns was 720,000 miles. Nearly three-quarters of a million miles! Daily they carried 700 tons of rations on the 'mobile' scale for man and horse, besides hospital supplies and disinfectants, brought from the Suez Canal, more than two hundred miles away, by the military railway across the desert.

In the first few days, when the cavalry had to exert all their powers of mobility to bar the exits from the country they were enclosing, the difficulties of supply were as great as ever faced an army commander. There was practically no food or fodder to be requisitioned in the occupied area, and the possibility of the country yielding anything for man or beast could not be taken into account. The cavalry's effort was long and well-sustained—one division covered nearly eighty miles in less than twenty-four hours—but the lorry columns kept up with them, and so well did they support the cavalry that, at the end of the first two days, the divisions still possessed the two days' emergency rations and the iron ration with which they started. The cavalry had outdistanced the divisional trains; the lorries bridged the gap. For eight days the supplies for cavalry stretched out on a wide front a hundred miles or more north of Rantieh, were drawn from that base. Then the Navy eased the situation by opening the port of Haifa and landing supplies there. By hard work the Turkish railway was got into order, and the captured rolling stock was made fit for the haulage of a heavy weight of supplies. This line was of great military value, yet so swiftly had the cavalry ridden northwards that the enemy had had little time to damage it. Beyond Samakh, on the southern edge of the Sea of Galilee, where the line runs through the Yarmuk valley to Deraa, our Arab allies had hit the retreating Turk very hard by destroying bridges. Directly the railway from Haifa was opened the lorry columns forsook Rantieh as their supply base and operated from Samakh, proceeding up the western. shores of the Sea of Galilee to the Yakub bridge over the Jordan, and thence through Kuneitra to Damascus. How splendidly they maintained the service may be gauged from the fact that, the day after Damascus fell to our arms, I saw lorries parked outside the city, the drivers snatching brief sleep after delivering supplies, before picking up loads of prisoners for the return journey. Supplies were drawn from Samakh until the Navy put stores ashore at Beyrout. What a picture of sea power that furnished the Beirutians! The port had been deserted for four years, save for the occasional appearance of a couple of German submarines to revictual themselves. Soon all was bustle and orderly activity, and the lorries abandoned Samakh and toiled over the heavy gradients of the mountains of Lebanon to Beyrout to refill for the cavalry, which, in their irresistible sweep, were continuing the advance towards Aleppo through Baalbek and Homs. At this time the troops about Damascus were being fed by rail from Haifa, the supplies being carried on camels from Samakh for five miles, to a point where the railway was in good order, put on rail again and hauled to Deraa and up the Hedjaz line to Damascus. Then Tripoli, sixty miles north of Beyrout, was occupied, and once more some of the lorries changed their route, running their loads from Tripoli to Homs. The 7th Indian Infantry Division, which marched up the coast from Haifa to Tripoli, had a lively appreciation of the Navy's assistance, for its supplies were landed from specially constructed lighters at Tyre, Sidon, Junie Bay and other places, and the train of 7200 camels which transported the stores from beach to brigades, was one of the most impressive spectacles of war or peace that the inhabitants had ever seen.

The supplying of the Anzac Mounted Division which captured Es Salt and Amman was another noteworthy example of 'Q.' efficiency. Before the battle began twenty-one days' supplies were assembled at Jericho, and, fed from this dump, the lorries went out to Amman, forty-eight miles away over the Jordan, climbing the shockingly bad hill road to Es Salt and crossing the rough surface of the plateau to what remains of the ancient Roman city of Philadelphia. A column was lucky to get through in fifteen hours, but backwards and forwards the lorries went, one day on the outward journey and the next spent in returning, the drivers getting what little rest mosquitoes, flies, and heat permitted. Their efforts contributed to the amassing of the mighty aggregate of three-quarters of a million lorry miles in three weeks, and, if their average mileage was not equal to that of some companies, they did all that could be asked of them, and to keep up a run of forty-eight miles a day in such country was about the limit of human endurance. The average mileage per lorry in all the columns was certainly not less than seventy miles per day, and the vehicles were in motion fully eleven hours each day. To appraise this record one must consider the country traversed. Roads, as we judge roads at home, were few and widely separated. Excepting where our Army had made them behind our old line there was nothing better than a second-class road, and between the best of Turkish metalled roads and the torn-up tracks through which lorries had to plough a way, there was as wide a difference as between the surface of Whitehall and a farm road after traffic in wet weather.

Drivers, of course, were strange to the conditions. They had to learn where it was best to avoid the unrolled stones and to grind down a track alongside the road. There were numerous pitfalls, culverts incapable of bearing a loaded lorry's weight, weak bridges and so forth, and the first lorries working up the line had as many difficulties as might befall them in absolutely virgin country. The only substantial check during operations was on the road east of the Jordan, from the Yakub bridge to which I have already referred. So rough was this track that new tyres were completely destroyed after three trips from Samakh to Damascus, 570 miles in all. It speaks well for the soundness of their manufacture that they were able to stand even one journey.

I have several times spoken in admiration of these lorry drivers. They were stout fellows. They were willing men, too, and the pride they took in their vehicles and their care of them, materially contributed to the smooth and efficient running of the convoys. One lorry, which had been on the road two nights and a day, reached its base, and before the engine had time to cool it was necessary to send it out on a journey of fifty miles. Rather than allow another man to steer the machine the driver and his mate volunteered to undertake the trip, and only got three hours' sleep at the end of it. These men were just an average sample of the service. They were not only upholding the good name of the M.T. columns, but assisting in the Army's victory in which they were anxious to have a full share. The ambulance drivers were of precisely the same class, and their high standard of work during these strenuous times had been marked by similar loyal devotion to the cause, regardless of toil and trouble. Their reward is the knowledge that they took a big part in a historic victory for the Empire, and had an important share in the triumph won by 'Q.'

How many travellers proceeding through the Suez Canal, the connecting link between East and West, understand the part the Egyptian Expeditionary Force played in the world war? They can leave Port Said and sleep throughout the journey to Suez if they will only keep their eyes open at Kantara and see how the Imperial Chain was kept intact. Kantara tells the tale eloquently. Those of us who know the full story have recollections of Ismailia, of Serapeum, and of other posts on the way to Suez, and a grave or two on the canal banks and derelict camping grounds and improvements fashioned by soldier hands still remain as monuments of Britain's work to stem the tide of German aggression. It would be well if some persons owing allegiance to allied nations, who have little knowledge of what occurred in the war beyond what happened at their doors, were given personally conducted tours in the Near East, to convince them of what we had done not only for ourselves but for them, in that theatre of war. Kantara would open their eyes. We built there a massive base which had for its superstructure the security of Palestine and Syria. Thence starts the long railway artery which feeds the country. There, where only a mosque, a rest house and. a customs station had been, miles of wharves came into being for the unloading of ships sailing the seven seas, and in the camps and buildings which at one time housed 120,000 men on military work, the problems of supply were partly solved. Around Kantara there were dumps of grain as large as the smaller Pyramids, the depôts of cases of tinned foods were almost as big, and the parks of R.E. stores and the reserves of ammunition, stores of clothing and hospital supplies, helped to build up Kantara as a vast distributing centre for the provisioning of the army in the field. At Port Said there was an enormous cold-storage building which will be useful in times of peace, but most of the other establishments were put up for the services of war, and the cost, which must have run into millions, was exclusively borne by us. They were necessary for the campaign, and they were ready when they were wanted. The Quartermaster-General pursued a vigorous policy, and it was due to his far-sightedness that Kantara became an important military town. Major-General Sir Walter Campbell adopted a broad outlook in his purchases for the Army. He saved the Empire enormous sums, and the majority of his orders for material were placed before those fictitious values had been reached which marked the close of the war.

CHAPTER 29

How Signals Worked

Hard work well and truly done demands that tribute should be paid to the Signals branch of the Royal Engineers. The area covered by the force and the character of the operations created problems of telegraphic and telephonic communication entirely different from those met with on the Western Front. In the Palestine theatre we had to deal with vast distances. Signals operated from Solium and Siwa far away in the Libyan desert, through Alexandria and Cairo to towns on the Suez Canal, across the sandy wastes of Sinai to every important point in Palestine, on to Damascus and Aleppo and along the coast as far north as Tripoli, in addition to a number of places across the Jordan. I have had a conversation over a military trunk line to Cairo more than 400 miles long, and the talking was as easily and distinctly heard as any I have experienced between London and Manchester, less than half the distance. The military in Beyrout could call up Alexandria over more than 600 miles of line, and there were wireless stations in the Red Sea which were in frequent touch with G.H.Q. I will merely narrate a few facts which tell of the devoted work of the signal service during the September advance, of men who shared to the full the hazards of war with the cavalry, artillery and infantry, whose labours were certainly not less than those of any other branch, and who, when called upon for a greater effort than most people believed possible, responded with   redoubled energy, and achieved a result which will shine on the records of His Majesty's Corps of Royal Engineers for all time. It is hard for people at home to realise the rapidity of the cavalry's movements. The 5th Cavalry Division covered nearly eighty miles on the glorious 19th of September. Note that and it will be easy to appreciate the energy of Signals, for there was hardly a period of five minutes on that or any other day during the operations, that General Headquarters was out of signal touch with cavalry headquarters, or headquarters with divisions, except when these were actually moving. Tearing along with the cavalry were wireless sets, whilst despatch riders swerved and jolted over rough country and through thigh-deep weeds at a pace which threatened broken necks as well as smashed motor cycles; ground wires were laid immediately behind the advance, and airline sections installed wires and poles in an incredibly short space of time.

When the cavalry got into Nazareth they found a map, in Liman von Sanders' headquarters, showing the whole of the system of wires throughout Asiatic Turkey, including recent installations. That map was marked 'To be distributed on Sept. 27, 1918.' It is typical of the enterprise of Signals that the map was reprinted by them and a copy was in the hands of all concerned by the date on which the Turks intended to distribute it. We made good use of its information.

Counting only what the Army had taken in the first four weeks of the advance, Signals were then making use of 1520 miles of Turkish telegraph route, embracing about 40,000 telegraph poles and 5000 miles of telegraph wire. Colossal as are these figures they do not include the full month's extension of the area in which Signals operated, for they built new and better routes of their own, and supplemented the available Turkish resources by running additional lines on old enemy routes. The advance up to Damascus was so rapid that the Turks had no time to destroy their lines completely. Poles were invariably left standing, and when some were down the cause was usually attributable to the fact that retreating Turks had hacked at them for fuel. Repair parties were organised to run all over the country and put lines in order. At Nazareth they found that a lot of excellent instruments, used for communication with Constantinople, had been smashed with a heavy crowbar, but they collected much material, such as telephones, in quite serviceable condition. Generally most repairs were required about the towns. These were effected with commendable speed, and it may be said generally that the permanent line kept up with the advance. At least once it was abreast of the cavalry. When a brigade left Nazareth to occupy Acre, and two brigades set out from Afuleh to take Haifa, Signals worked along an existing telegraph route diagonal to the advance, and actually got it in order and operating by the time cavalry were outside Haifa. With Damascus 195 miles away from the spot where we concentrated for attack, it was not unreasonable for any one outside the signal service to believe it would take a long time to install a permanent line to that wonderful city of the East. The cavalry won that famous goal on the twelfth day from the kick-off ; Signals

AFTER THE LONG PATROL

had a wire working into the city the same evening. Except on the first day very little ground cable was used; it was much quicker and more satisfactory to repair the permanent line. On the first day, when wheeled transport and guns were likely to damage cables, test points were established five miles apart, and if a line was broken between them the points became terminals, and messages were passed between them by means of gallopers.

Of course visual signalling between brigades and divisions was maintained, and wireless was always in use, but every endeavour was made to get the wires talking. The only time when Desert Mounted Corps had no other means than wireless to keep contact with a division was when the 4th Cavalry Division moved round the south of the Sea of Galilee on to Deraa, and thence north to Damascus. For three or four days they were only in wireless touch with Corps, though aeroplanes carried messages. Indeed all through the operations the Royal Air Force assisted the Staff greatly, particularly by dropping messages stating precisely where the front line had reached. There was one little party enjoying the title of a 'mobile section'—all branches of Signals seemed to me to be very mobile—consisting of an officer and three men, who must have covered more ground than any other soldiers in the force. They travelled in a Ford van, and all roads and tracks were passable, in their judgment, so long as there was something to discover in an old Turkish telegraph route. They were the only soldiers who went along a certain track from Damascus to Homs, and they alone could tell of the enthusiasm of the natives of this isolated area at the appearance of British troops. The mobile section added to Signals' knowledge of routes and material available for the service, and their days and nights spent in outlandish parts, when snipers were active and other Arabs inquisitive, were most useful.

We must not forget the despatch riders. These gallant fellows were the admiration of every man in the field. In the rough country they risked a fall with every revolution of their engines. They ran long stages and travelled at high speeds. They stood the racket well, but it was doubtful if human endurance and the wear and tear of machines would have allowed them to carry on the big journeys indefinitely, and Signals were glad when an aeroplane mail service relieved them of a portion of their arduous duties. Carrier pigeons were used to some extent, but the pigeoneers bemoaned the fact that the advance was too rapid and too prolonged to allow of their birds being used as much as was hoped. It was interesting that all the pigeoneers were Yorkshire or Lancashire miners who were fanciers at home. The pride they took in their birds was very creditable to them, and they were so careful that their birds should not find their way into another loft that they wrote the names *'Lively,' 'Robin,'* *'Smoky,'* and so on, in indelible ink on the wings. The pigeon corporal intended that there should be no mistake about the credit due to his loft. At one time it was necessary to get some carrier pigeons into Arabia. Six were packed into a basket at Ramleh and put into an aeroplane. It must have been a strange journey for them. The basket was attached to a parachute, and was dropped by the pilot above an Intelligence officer's tent at Azrak, 100 miles east of the Jordan, where the birds were kept for a few days. On their release five of the six pigeons returned to their loft in good time, in spite, as the pigeon officer said, of the rough journey they had experienced.

This is a brief and wholly incomplete statement of what the signal units of the Royal Engineers accomplished during the operations. General Manifold had reason to be proud of his branch of the Army. Efficiency and the foresight which prepares for any emergency made success possible, but, without the loyal cooperation of all ranks in Signals, the men in the wide-stretched front line could not have been served so well. And the General Post Office may take to itself a share of Signals' triumph, for many of the expert operators and linesmen with General Allenby's Army learned the business in the service of the G.P.O.

Appendices

Appendix A

G<small>ENERAL</small> A<small>LLENBY</small>'s Force employed in the last phase of the campaign was constituted as follows :

DESERT MOUNTED CORPS

4<small>TH</small> C<small>AVALRY</small> D<small>IVISION</small> (Maj.-Gen. C. de S. Barrow, C.B.).

10th Cavalry Bde. (Brig.-Gen. Howard-Vyse).	*11th Cavalry Bde.* (Brig.-Gen. Gregory).	*12th Cavalry Bde.* (Brig.-Gen. Wigan).
1/1 Dorset Yeo.	1/1 Co. of London Yeo.	1/1 Staffordshire Yeo.
2nd Lancers.	29th Lancers.	6th Cavalry.
38th Cen. Ind. Horse.	36th Jacob's Horse.	19th Lancers.

5<small>TH</small> C<small>AVALRY</small> D<small>IVISION</small> (Maj.-Gen. H.J.M. MacAndrew, C.B., D.S.O.).

14th Cavalry Bde. (Brig.-Gen. Clarke).	*15th (I.S.) Cavalry Bde.* (Brig.-Gen. Harbord).	*13th Cavalry Bde.* (Brig.-Gen. Kelly).
1/1 Sherwood Rngrs.	Jodhpur I.S. Lancers.	1/1 Gloucester Yeo.
20th Deccan Horse.	Mysore I.S. Lancers.	9th Hodson's Horse.
34th Poonah Horse.	1st Hyderabad I.S. Lancers.	18th Lancers.

A<small>USTRALIAN</small> M<small>OUNTED</small> D<small>IVISION</small> (Maj.-Gen. H. W. Hodgson, C.B.).

3rd A.L.H. Brigade (Brig.-Gen. Wilson).	*4th A.L.H. Brigade* (Brig.-Gen. Grant).	*5th A.L.H. Brigade* (Brig.-Gen. C. Macarthur Onslow).
8th Regt. A.L.H.	4th Regt. A.L.H.	14th Regt. A.L.H.
9th ,,	11th ,,	15th ,,
10th ,,	12th ,,	16th ,,
	French Chasseurs d'Afrique.	

A<small>NZAC</small> M<small>OUNTED</small> D<small>IVISION</small> (Maj.-Gen. Sir E. W. C. Chaytor).

1st A.L.H. Brigade (Brig.-Gen. C. Cox, D.S.O.)	*2nd A.L.H. Brigade* (Brig.-Gen. Granville Ryrie).	*N.Z. Mtd. Rifles Bde.* (Brig.-Gen. Meldrum).
1st Regt. A.L.H.	5th Regt. A.L.H.	Auckland Mtd. Rifles.
2nd ,,	6th ,,	Canterbury Mtd. Rifles.
3rd ,,	7th ,,	Wellington Mtd. Rifles.

Attached to Anzac Mounted Division.

38th Royal Fus. (Jewish batt.). 1st British West India Regiment.
39th Royal Fus. (Jewish batt.). 2nd British West India Regiment.
20th Indian Infantry (Imperial Service) Brigade.

XXth CORPS

10th Division (Maj.-Gen. J. R. Longley, K.C.M.G., C.B.).

29th Infantry Bde. (Brig.-Gen. C. L. Smith, V.C., M.C.	30th Infantry Bde. (Brig.-Gen. F. A. Greer, C.M.G., D.S.O.).	31st Infantry Bde. (Brig.-Gen. E. M. Morris, C.M.G.).
1st Leinsters.	1st Royal Irish Regt.	2nd Royal Irish Fus.
1/101st Grenadiers.	1st Kashmir I.S. Rfls.	2/101st Grenadiers.
1/54th Sikhs.	38th Dogras.	74th Punjabis.
2/151st Infantry.	46th Punjabis.	2/42nd Deolis.

53rd Division (Maj.-Gen. S. F. Mott, C.B.).

158th Infantry Bde. (Brig.-Gen. H. A. Vernon, D.S.O.).	159th Infantry Bde. (Brig.-Gen. N. Money, D.S.O.).	160th Infantry Bde. (Brig.-Gen. V. L. N. Pearson).
5/6th R. Welsh Fus.	4/5th Welsh Regt.	1/7th R. Welsh Fus.
4/11th Gurkhas.	3/152nd Indian Inf.	1/17th Indian Inf.
3/153rd Indian Inf.	1/153rd Indian Inf.	1/21st Punjabis.
3/154th Indian Inf.	2/153rd Indian Inf.	1st Cape Corps.

XXIst CORPS

3rd Lahore Division (Maj.-Gen. A. R. Hoskins, C.M.G., D.S.O.).

7th Infantry Brigade (Brig.-Gen. S. R. Davidson, C.M.G.).	8th Infantry Brigade (Brig.-Gen. S. M. Edwardes, C.B., C.M.G., D.S.O.).	9th Infantry Brigade (Brig.-Gen. C. C. Luard, C.M.G.).
1st Connaught Rngrs.	1st Manchester Regt.	2nd Dorsets.
2/7th Gurkha Rifles.	47th Sikhs.	1/1st Gurhka Rifles.
27th Punjabis.	59th Scinde Rifles.	93rd Infantry.
91st Punjabis.	2/124th Baluchistan Infantry.	105th Mahratta Light Infantry.

7th Meerut Division (Maj.-Gen. Sir V. B. Fane, K.C.I.E., C.B.).

19th Infantry Bde. (Brig.-Gen. G. A. Weir, D.S.O.).	21st Infantry Bde. (Brig.-Gen. A. G. Kemball).	28th Infantry Bde. (Brig.-Gen. C. H. Davies, C.M.G., D.S.O.).
1st Seaforth Highrs.	2nd Black Watch.	2nd Leicesters.
28th Punjabis.	1st Guides Infantry.	51st Sikhs.
92nd Punjabis.	20th Punjabis.	53rd Sikhs.
125th Napier's Rifles.	1/8th Gurkha Rifles.	56th Punjabi Rifles.

280

54TH DIVISION (Maj.-Gen. S. W. Hare, C.B.).

161st Brigade	162nd Brigade	163rd Brigade
(Brig.-Gen. A. B. Orpen Palmer, D.S.O.).	(Brig.-Gen. A. Mudge, C.M.G.).	(Brig.-Gen. A. J. Mac-Neill, D.S.O.).
1/4th Essex.	1/5th Bedford.	1/4th Norfolk.
1/5th ,,	1/4th Northampton.	1/5th Norfolk.
1/6th ,,	1/10th London.	1/5th Suffolk.
1/7th ,,	1/11th London.	1/8th Hampshire.

60TH DIVISION (Maj.-Gen. Sir J. S. M. Shea, C.B., C.M.G., D.S.O.).

179th Brigade	180th Brigade	181st Brigade
(Brig.-Gen. E. T. Humphreys, D.S.O.).	(Brig.-Gen. C. F. Watson, D.S.O.).	(Brig.-Gen. E. C. da Costa, C.M.G.,D.S.O.).
2/13th London.	2/19th London.	2/22nd London.
3/151st Infantry.	2nd Guides.	130th Baluchis.
2/19th Punjabis.	2/30th Punjabis.	2/97th Deccan Inf.
2/137th Baluchis.	1/50th Kumoan Rfls.	2/152nd Infantry.

75TH DIVISION (Maj.-Gen. P. C. Palin, C.B., C.M.G.).

232nd Brigade	233rd Brigade	234th Brigade
(Brig.-Gen. H. J. Huddleston, C.M.G., D.S.O., M.C.).	(Brig.-Gen. the Hon. E. M. Colston, C.M.G., D.S.O.).	(Brig.-Gen. C. A. H. Maclean, D.S.O.).
1/4th Wilts.	1/5th Somerset Light Infantry.	1/4th D.C.L.I.
72nd Punjabis.	29th Punjabis.	123rd Outram Rifles.
2/3rd Gurkhas.	3/3rd Gurkhas.	58th Vaughan's Rifles.
3rd Kashmir I.S. Infantry.	2/154th Infantry.	1/152nd Infantry.

Appendix B

The Turkish War Office was either blind to obvious facts or had been misled as to our strength in artillery. Yilderim General Headquarters had requested that the Turkish Minister for War should provide twenty- five extra heavy batteries, but the Turkish War Office replied that the German High Command had refused all demands for 15-cm. guns and 21-cm. mortars, and—this was written in July—

'in view of the situation on the Western Front it is not intended to press the demand.' The War Office stated that it was intended to send eight batteries, but refused more as they considered that 'the Yilderim Army had a numerical superiority over the British in heavy artillery, that the extra supply of ammunition involved would create difficulty in the conveyance of other supplies, and that the lack of roads and. water on the Palestine front would make the increase of artillery a questionable policy.'

Appendix C

Some captured documents suggest that the enemy believed an attack was imminent. There is no doubt the Staff were apprehensive of an offensive, but in all the Turkish papers secured by us during the advance there was nothing to indicate that the enemy knew the form the attack would take, or where or when it would fall. A letter written by a German Staff officer in Nazareth on September 18 is very instructive, for it shows that on the day before the offensive began nothing was known of General Allenby's intentions. Probably within six hours of the time the letter was written disaster had overtaken the Yilderim army. The officer said:

As you are aware, the military situation has not improved, the supply of men and materials becomes more difficult day by day, and the number and material preponderance of the British ever greater. Various signs point to the fact that we shall soon be face to face with serious events. The British attack will not be delayed much longer. I welcomed your peace suggestions warmly, but would they bring us nearer to the longed-for object? By the time that you receive this letter the decision will already have taken place. It is really time an end were reached.

The suggestion that the British would take the offensive a few days before the Kurban Bairam, which began on September 16, must not be taken as indicating any knowledge gained through spies. There were always rumours of attacks at the approach of feast, and natives on both sides were busy with stories of preparations. This extract is from a 'personal' letter written by Lieut.-Colonel Muhammed Khairi, O.C. 26th Division, to O.C. 26th F.A. Regt., dated 23rd August 1918:

It has been reported that the British will take the offensive on a very large scale a few days before the Kurban Feast. By endless instigation and devilish sedition they have been trying to induce our men to desert, and further to weaken our army by various means, such as purchasing arms and animals from men employed in our supply and transport service. It has been proved that some men of the 53rd V Division who came to visit their comrades in the 76th Regt. told the N.C.O.'s of the regiment that the men of their division were going to desert on the day of Bairam; the N.C.O.'s in their turn went about spreading the news and inviting men to do likewise.

The culprits were arrested, and handed to be court-martialled and severely punished as a warning to others. It is therefore necessary that all officers should be exceedingly watchful and exercise the utmost rigour and severity in dealing with their men and in no way tolerate the spreading of such sedition in their area. They should strictly prohibit communication between their men and those of the neighbouring divisions, and even between the regiments of their own division. No one should be allowed to visit back areas unless provided with a permit. Men coming from neighbouring divisions should at once be arrested and returned to their units without being allowed to communicate with our men. When necessary, for the purpose of intercommunication, officers or reliable N.C.O's should be employed.

This order has been communicated in writing to the Commanders of Infantry Regiments 59, 76, 78, 82, and Artillery Regt. 26, Divisional Attack Coy. and Engineer Coy. It must not be communicated to clerks and rank and file.'

Appendix D

The report of Colonel Lawrence written in Damascus for the General Staff is interesting. It is a very brief, modest document and is worthy of a man who during the long years of war remained in the desert to keep the Arabs true to our cause:

The Arab force left Deraa on September 29 under Sherif Nasir and Nuri Bey Said, following up the 4th Cavalry Division on the right flank. We marched by the Hedjaz railway, and in the morning of September 30 came in contact with an enemy column of 2000 men and four guns retiring from Deraa. Our mounted men kept up a running fight with these till 4 p.m., when Sherif Nasir galloped ahead of them with thirty horses and threw himself into Khiara Chiftlike, south of Kiswe, to delay the enemy, as General Gregory's brigade was just marching into Khan Denun. The Turks showed some fight, but were shelled effectively by the British while the Arabs hung on to their tail. The Arabs took about 600 prisoners, fourteen machine guns, and three guns. From Kiswe the Sherif sent a mounted force forward to get contact with his followers in the gardens east of Damascus to find that his local committee had hoisted the Arab flag and proclaimed the Emirate of Hussein of Mecca at 2.30 p.m. Sherif Nasir with Major Stirling and myself moved into Damascus at 9 a.m. on October 1 amid scenes of extraordinary enthusiasm on the part of the local people. The streets were nearly impassable with the crowds, who yelled themselves hoarse and danced, cut themselves with swords and daggers, and fired volleys into the air. Nasir, Nuri Shaalan, Audi abu Tayi, and myself were cheered by name, covered with flowers, kissed indefinitely, and splashed with attar of roses from the housetops.

On arrival at the Serai Shukri Pasha el Ayoubi was appointed Arab military governor, as all former civil employees had left with Jemal Pasha the previous day. Martial law was proclaimed, police organised, and the town picketed. The Rualla are behaving very well, but the Druses are troublesome. I have no orders as to what political arrangements should be made in Damascus, but will carry on as before till I hear further from you. If Arab military assistance is not required in further operations of Desert Corps I should like to return to Palestine, as I feel that if I remain here longer it will be very difficult for my successor.

T. E. Lawrence

G.O.C. Desert Mounted Corps has seen above and agrees with my remaining with the town administration until further instructions. *T. E. L.*

The Arab army since September 26 have taken 8000 prisoners and 120 machine guns.

Appendix E

There was trouble in the Turkish army not merely, between the German and Turkish rank and file, who frequently came to blows, but between German and Turkish officers in high command. Among the documents captured by us were many showing that acute feeling existed between Liman von Sanders and his staff and Turkish generals, and Jemal Pasha, the G.O.C. of the Turkish 4th Army, did not hesitate to hit back. These commanders set a bad example. Von Falkenhayn had no confidence in Jemal, as the following illuminating telegram shows. It was sent by Von Falkenhayn at Aleppo to Col. von Dommes (his C.G.S.) at Constantinople, on 21st September 1917:

Before I reply definitely to the C.G.S. I should like to be informed on the following points:

How can you and Lossow recommend acceptance, when you have before your eyes —

The continually false information furnished by the 4th Army H.Q. on the military situation, on conditions of supply, and upon its communications to the rear.

The way in which the 4th Army H.Q. misuses the railway for its private ends and thereby cripples it for military purposes. This is a question of a vital artery for us.

That to accept Jemal's proposals means handing over to him supervision of the whole of the German cash supplies with no means of control; and yet we know well enough what he will do with such a supply of cash.

That to accept, since the proposals are to bring even Yilderim L. of C. inspectorate under his influence, would also place the decision as to the Irak Expedition in his hands.

That the 4th Army Commander has in no way kept his promises about Aleppo.

That to accept would throw all responsibility upon Germany for whatever may happen here and leave the German Commander with no possibility of organising for victory.'

LEONAUR

ALSO FROM LEONAUR
AVAILABLE IN SOFTCOVER OR HARDCOVER WITH DUST JACKET

DOING OUR 'BIT' *by Ian Hay*—Two Classic Accounts of the Men of Kitchener's 'New Army' During the Great War including *The First 100,000 & All In It.*

AN EYE IN THE STORM by *Arthur Ruhl*—An American War Correspondent's Experiences of the First World War from the Western Front to Gallipoli and Beyond.

STAND & FALL by *Joe Cassells*—A Soldier's Recollections of the 'Contemptible Little Army' and the Retreat from Mons to the Marne, 1914.

RIFLEMAN MACGILL'S WAR by *Patrick MacGill*—A Soldier of the London Irish During the Great War in Europe including *The Amateur Army, The Red Horizon & The Great Push.*

WITH THE GUNS *by C. A. Rose & Hugh Dalton*—Two First Hand Accounts of British Gunners at War in Europe During World War 1- Three Years in France with the Guns and With the British Guns in Italy.

EAGLES OVER THE TRENCHES *by James R. McConnell & William B. Perry*—Two First Hand Accounts of the American Escadrille at War in the Air During World War 1-Flying For France: With the American Escadrille at Verdun and Our Pilots in the Air.

THE BUSH WAR DOCTOR by *Robert V. Dolbey*—The Experiences of a British Army Doctor During the East African Campaign of the First World War.

THE 9TH—THE KING'S (LIVERPOOL REGIMENT) IN THE GREAT WAR 1914 - 1918 by *Enos H. G. Roberts*—Like many large cities, Liverpool raised a number of battalions in the Great War. Notable among them were the Pals, the Liverpool Irish and Scottish, but this book concerns the wartime history of the 9th Battalion – The Kings.

THE GAMBARDIER by *Mark Severn*—The experiences of a battery of Heavy artillery on the Western Front during the First World War.

FROM MESSINES TO THIRD YPRES by *Thomas Floyd*—A personal account of the First World War on the Western front by a 2/5th Lancashire Fusilier.

THE IRISH GUARDS IN THE GREAT WAR - VOLUME 1 by *Rudyard Kipling*—Edited and Compiled from Their Diaries and Papers Volume 1 The First Battalion.

THE IRISH GUARDS IN THE GREAT WAR - VOLUME 2 by *Rudyard Kipling*—Edited and Compiled from Their Diaries and Papers Volume 2 The Second Battalion.

LEONAUR

ALSO FROM LEONAUR

AVAILABLE IN SOFTCOVER OR HARDCOVER WITH DUST JACKET

ARMOURED CARS IN EDEN by *K. Roosevelt*—An American President's son serving in Rolls Royce armoured cars with the British in Mesopatamia & with the American Artillery in France during the First World War.

CHASSEUR OF 1914 by *Marcel Dupont*—Experiences of the twilight of the French Light Cavalry by a young officer during the early battles of the great war in Europe.

TROOP HORSE & TRENCH by *R.A. Lloyd*—The experiences of a British Life-guardsman of the household cavalry fighting on the western front during the First World War 1914-18.

THE LONG PATROL by *George Berrie*—A Novel of Light Horsemen from Gallipoli to the Palestine campaign of the First World War.

THE EAST AFRICAN MOUNTED RIFLES *by C.J. Wilson*—Experiences of the campaign in the East African bush during the First World War

THE FIGHTING CAMELIERS *by Frank Reid*—The exploits of the Imperial Camel Corps in the desert and Palestine campaigns of the First World War.

WITH THE IMPERIAL CAMEL CORPS IN THE GREAT WAR by *Geoffrey Inchbald*—The story of a serving officer with the British 2nd battalion against the Senussi and during the Palestine campaign.

STEEL CHARIOTS IN THE DESERT by *S.C.Rolls*—The first world war experiences of a Rolls Royce armoured car driver with the Duke of Westminster in Libya and in Arabia with T.E. Lawrence.

INFANTRY BRIGADE: 1914 by *Edward Gleichen*—The Diary of a Commander of the 15th Infantry Brigade, 5th Division, British Army, During the Retreat from Mons

HEARTS & DRAGONS by *Charles R. M. F. Crutwell*—The 4th Royal Berkshire Regiment in France and Italy During the Great War, 1914-1918.

TIGERS ALONG THE TIGRIS by *E. J. Thompson*—The Leicestershire Regiment in Mesopotamia During the First World War.

DESPATCH RIDER by *W. H. L. Watson*—The Experiences of a British Army Motorcycle Despatch Rider During the Opening Battles of the Great War in Europe.